THE

Social History in Perspective
General Editor: Jeremy Black

Social History in Perspective is a series of in-depth studies of the many topics in social, cultural and religious history.

PUBLISHED

John Belchem *Popular Radicalism in Nineteenth-Century Britain*
Sue Bruley *Women in Britain Since 1990*
Anthony Brundage *The English Poor Laws, 1700–1930*
Simon Dentith *Society and Cultural Forms in Nineteenth-Century England*
Joyce M. Ellis *The Georgian Town, 1680–1840*
Peter Fleming *Family and Household in Medieval England*
Kathryn Gleadle *British Women in the Nineteenth Century*
Harry Goulbourne *Race Relations in Britain since 1945*
Anne Hardy *Health and Medicine in Britain since 1860*
Tim Hitchcock *English Sexualities, 1700–1780*
Sybil M. Jack *Towns in Tudor and Stuart Britain*
Helen M. Jewell *Education in Early Modern England*
Alan Kidd *State, Society and the Poor in Nineteenth-Century England*
Arthur J. McIvor *A History of Work in Britain, 1880–1950*
Hugh McLeod *Religion and Society in England, 1850–1914*
Donald M. MacRaild *Irish Migrants in Modern Britain, 1750–1922,*
Donald M. MacRaild and David E. Martin *Labour in Britain, 1830–1914*
Christopher March *Popular Religion in the Sixteenth Century*
Michael A. Mullett *Catholics in Britain and Ireland, 1558–1829*
Richard Rex *The Lollards*
George Robb *British Culture and the First World War*
R.Malcolm Smuts *Culture and Power in England, 1585–1685*
John Spurr *English Puritanism, 1603–1689*
W.B. Stephens *Education in Britain, 1750–1914*
Heather Swanson *Medieval British Towns*
David Taylor *Crime, Policing and Punishment in England, 1750–1914*
N.L. Tranter *British Population in the Twentieth Century*
Ian D. Whyte *Migration and Society in Britain, 1550–1830*
Ian D. Whyte *Scotland's Society and Economy in Transition, c.1500–c.1760*
Andy Wood *Riot, Rebellion and Popular Politics in Early Modern England*

Please note that a sister series, *British History in Perspective*, is available, covering key topics in British political history.

Social History in Perspective
Series Standing Order
ISBN 0–333–71694–9 hardcover
ISBN 0–333–69336–1 paper back
(*outside North America only*)

You can receive future titles in this series as they are published by placing a standing order. Please contact your bookseller or, in case of difficulty, write to us at the address below with your name and address, the title of the series and the ISBN quoted above.

Customer Services Department, Palgrave Distribution Ltd
Houndmills, Basingstoke, Hampshire RG21 6XS, England

THE LOLLARDS

Richard Rex

palgrave

First published 2002 by
PALGRAVE
Houndmills, Basingstoke, Hampshire RG21 6XS and
175 Fifth Avenue, New York, N.Y. 10010
Companies and representatives throughout the world

PALGRAVE is the new global academic imprint of
St. Martin's Press LLC Scholarly and Reference Division and
Palgrave Publishers Ltd (formerly Macmillan Press Ltd).

ISBN 0–333–59751–6 hardcover
ISBN 0–333–59752–4 paperback

This book is printed on paper suitable for recycling and
made from fully managed and sustained forest sources.

A catalogue record for this book is available
from the British Library.

Library of Congress Cataloging-in-Publication Data
Rex, Richard.
    The Lollards / Richard Rex.
        p.   cm.—(Social history in perspective)
    Includes bibliographical references (p.) and index.
    ISBN 0–333–59751–6 (cloth)—ISBN 0–333–59752–4 (pbk.)
    1. Lollards.   I. Title.   II. Social history in perspective (Palgrave (Firm))
    BX4901.3 .R49 2002
    284′.3—dc21
                                                              2001059200

10   9   8   7   6   5   4   3   2   1
11   10   09   08   07   06   05   04   03   02

Printed and bound in China

To my mother, Christina Rex, another Yorkshire dissident

CONTENTS

Acknowledgements   ix
Introduction   xi

1 The Church of England in the Later Middle Ages   1

2 John Wyclif and His Theology   25
   Wyclif's Philosophy   32
   The Bible   34
   Lordship in Grace   35
   Predestination and Necessity   38
   The Church   39
   The Papacy   41
   Faith and Salvation   41
   The Eucharist   42
   Sacraments and Signs   45
   Christian Life   48
   Royalty and Reform   50
   The Peasants' Revolt and the Condemnation
     of Wyclif   52

3 The Early Diffusion of Lollardy   54
   Lollard Preachers   55
   The Lollard Message   59
   Lollardy and Patronage   61
   Geography of Early Lollardy   64
   Social Distribution of Early Lollardy   71
   Lollard Texts   74
   Lollardy and Lay Piety   78
   Lollardy as a Movement   81
   Lollardy and Politics   82
   The Oldcastle Rising   84

4   Survival and Revival   88
       Geography of Later Lollardy   89
       Social Distribution of Later Lollardy   101
       Gender Distribution of Lollardy   104
       The Dynamics of Lollard Communities   108
       A Tudor Revival of Lollardy?   112

5   From Lollardy to Protestantism   115
       Comparative Geography of Lollardy and
       Protestantism   119
       The Moral Contrast between Lollardy and
       Protestantism   131
       The Social Contrast between Lollards and
       the English Reformers   133
       Lollardy and Calvinism   139
       The Fate of Lollardy   140

6   Conclusion   143

Notes   151
Bibliography   174
Index   186

ACKNOWLEDGEMENTS

The scholarly debts accumulated in writing a book of this kind are enormous, but, as they have mostly been incurred through the impersonal medium of print, I hope that they have been adequately acknowledged in the notes and references. Those notes, however, do not reveal which libraries enabled me to pile up my debts. As ever, Cambridge University Library has been the mainstay of my work, and I am particularly grateful to the Syndics for permission to reproduce on the cover a hand-coloured woodcut from one of their copies of Foxe's *Acts and Monuments*. The library of St John's College, Cambridge, has allowed me almost unrestricted use of its set of the Wyclif Society's edition of *Wyclif's Latin Works*. I am therefore particularly grateful to the Master and Fellows for their continued generosity to a former research fellow, as well as to the successive librarians, Ms Amanda Saville and Dr Mark Nicholls, and their staff. I should like to thank all those who have helped or encouraged me in a project which has lasted far longer than it should have done – and has outlasted not only a succession of commissioning editors at Macmillan Press, but also Macmillan Press itself! James Carley has, as ever, given me the benefit of his deep learning in medieval manuscript culture. Tom Freeman has generously shared with me the fruits of his incomparable knowledge of John Foxe and his great book. I am particularly grateful to Dr Charles Kightly for permission to draw upon his masterly, and sadly unpublished, doctoral dissertation (University of York, 1975) on the early Lollards, which remains of fundamental importance for anyone working in this field. Brad Gregory and Carl Watkins have read and commented upon various chapters. Margaret Spufford's comments on an earlier version of the fifth chapter (aired at a meeting of the Queens' College History Society) were helpful, perceptive, and stimulating. I should also like to thank the anonymous medievalist who read the whole text for Palgrave. He or she showed a fine eye for detail, a fine ear for style, and a fine nose for a fishy argument, saving me from a sackful of blunders, inelegancies, and inconsistencies. Those that remain are, of course, my fault, my own fault, and nothing but my fault. Many colleagues in the Cambridge Divinity Faculty and at Queens' College have tolerated alternating moods of elation and irritation as this project has made its fitful progress towards completion.

One tribute I can pay in a book about dissidents is to disagree with people, which I have done freely throughout. Perhaps here I could take the opportunity of assuring those with whom I have taken issue that no disrespect is intended thereby. The other tribute is in the dedication. Finally, my apologies to all those at whom, over the last few years, I have scowled or rolled my eyes despairingly upwards upon hearing the polite enquiry 'How are the Lollards?'

Faculty of Divinity
Queens' College
Cambridge

INTRODUCTION

K. B. McFarlane had such a far-reaching influence upon the study of late medieval history in late twentieth-century England that it is surprising to recall that the only book he himself published was *John Wycliffe and the Beginnings of English Nonconformity*, originally written for A. L. Rowse's series Teach Yourself History, and later reissued by Penguin Books.[1] To write a work which aspires to replace McFarlane's only published book is necessarily an act of hubris. For a Tudor historian trespassing outside his own field to attempt that task is to invite nemesis at the hands of those scholars who work 'after McFarlane'. Not that this effort seeks to justify itself by carping at its predecessor. The best tribute that can be paid to McFarlane's survey is precisely that for fifty years nobody tried to replace it. If a new survey is needed, it is simply because, thanks often to his pupils and even to theirs, a great deal more has been discovered in the last half-century about both Wyclif and his followers, the Lollards, as well as about the political and social context within which they lived.

Since McFarlane's time, by far the greatest contributions to extending our knowledge of Lollardy have been made by Margaret Aston, J. A. F. Thomson, and Anne Hudson.[2] It was Margaret Aston who, in a series of seminal articles, finally detached the study of Lollardy from the dead hand of confessional polemics and set research into the subject on a wholly new basis. Thomson's account of the Lollards after 1414 took up the story where McFarlane had left off, telling it on the basis of exhaustive enquiries into ecclesiastical archives. Most recently, Hudson's magisterial study, *The Premature Reformation*, has brought an unparalleled knowledge of Lollard texts to bear upon the social history of the movement to produce what will remain the standard monograph for the foreseeable future. If at times in this study I venture to dispute some of the conclusions of these three scholars (and they do not always agree among themselves), then I must emphasise all the more that I endorse others, and that without their fundamental achievements, efforts such as this would be impossible.

'Lollardy' is a strange, archaic word. The debate about its etymology is not one in which I claim special expertise. Catholic scholars in late medieval England fancifully traced it to the Latin 'lolium', meaning 'tare' – in Christ's parable the weed sown among the wheat, interpreted by medieval exegetes as false teaching disseminated among the true. The *Oxford English Dictionary* more soberly traces its origins to Dutch words for mumbling. In terms of its original connotations, its links to 'lolling' the tongue, with its associations of stupidity and incapacity, and the onomatopoeic overtones of what is still obviously, if somewhat obscurely, a pejorative tell us all we need to know at this level.

More important, especially given that the word has been taken for the title of this book, is the fact that in late medieval England, 'lollard' was not a proper noun but a general one. It meant 'heretic', and 'lollardy' meant 'heresy'. In itself, it carried no sense of a particular sect or school of the kind conveyed by such terms as 'Arian' or (later) 'Lutheran' (derived from specific individuals), or 'anabaptist' or 'unitarian' (denoting specific theological positions). Authors writing in Latin would sometimes use the term 'Wyclifista' to describe a follower of Wyclif, but there was no such noun in the vernacular.

Thus anyone in late medieval England whose religious beliefs or practices deviated noticeably from the norm was liable to be described as a 'lollard' or 'loller'. Like many pejoratives before and since, 'lollard' was further extended to become a general term of abuse. None the less, because the noun was current only in that particular period of English history (after the Reformation of the sixteenth century it soon became an archaism), it now serves us conveniently as a proper noun for the distinct, if still somewhat broad, band of dissident beliefs and practices which flourished in England at that time, and which owed its inspiration to Wyclif, at times invoking his memory in establishing or expressing its own identity (as in one of its more widely circulated pamphlets, *Wycklyffes Wycket*).

So the Lollards of this book are indeed a particular group of people, even though those who originally spoke and wrote of 'lollards' did not limit the term's connotations in such a specific way. Another book might be written on the usage of 'lollard' and 'lollardy' in late medieval England. It would cover a wider range – not simply Wycliffite heretics, but sceptics, anticlericals, rioters, rebels, felons, eccentrics, lunatics, and outsiders of all kinds. But it would not be this book. Here, 'lollard' is restricted to that more coherent group of people who gave the term its central meaning and its general currency. These 'lollards' knew who they were and knew one another. Their preferred self-description was 'known men', and, as R. G. Davies has observed, their movement was not so much a matter of what they knew as of whom they knew.[3]

The Lollards is divided into five main chapters. The first, on the late medieval English Church, makes no pretence to originality. It is a synthesis based on what is in itself an enormous body of historical writing, and it is inevitably patchy and selective. As it simply is not possible to do justice in a brief chapter to a subject which has attracted sustained scholarly attention from Pantin's *The English Church in the Fourteenth Century* to Duffy's *Stripping of the Altars* and beyond, the principle of organisation and selection has been to concentrate on setting out the relevant background against which the dissent of Wyclif and his followers emerged.

The second chapter, on Wyclif, sets out a new understanding of the public career and theological development of this difficult man. Evidence about his life is fragmentary and has been subjected to excessively heavy interpretation over a very long time, while his writings are typical of their age in the technical complexity of their content and the recondite Latin of their style. This chapter offers a significant revision to a widely accepted account of Wyclif's political role in the 1370s before going on to present a full yet succinct account of his mature theology. Although my debts to the many scholars who have worked in this field (most notably Anthony Kenny) are made clear, the analysis of his theological development is ultimately my own, and endeavours to show how the critical events of the later 1370s (notably Wyclif's excommunication by the pope and the subsequent outbreak of the Great Schism between rival popes at Rome and Avignon) stimulated Wyclif into taking his philosophical principles forward into radically new theological territory. I hope that he would have recognised his thought in the reflection I give of it here.

The third and fourth chapters consider the history of the Lollards themselves, broadly dividing their history into two phases – before and after the riotous assembly just outside the walls of the City of London in January 1414 which came to be known as the Oldcastle Rising. The brief early phase saw the growth and diffusion of Lollardy; the long latter phase can best be characterised as one of stagnation and survival. Neither of these chapters claims to add anything to the corpus of factual knowledge of Lollardy. It is unlikely that there is any new data to be found in the ecclesiastical records of the fourteenth and fifteenth centuries, which have been combed so often. The recent researches of, among others, Edward Powell and Maureen Jurkowski have shown that there is still something to be gleaned from the surviving records of the king's courts, as the association of heresy with sedition and the cooperation of the secular arm with the spiritual authorities in the policing of orthodoxy brought heresy, considered under certain aspects, within the purview of those courts.[4] But the future yields are likely to be low, and are unlikely to necessitate major alterations to the picture we can already put together.

Where these central chapters of the book claim to make their distinctive contribution is in their interpretation of the material. With regard to early Lollardy, it is maintained that the movement was simply never as popular or as powerful as many nervous contemporaries feared and some recent historians have hoped. While even the limited success which the movement achieved would make it absurd to argue that the medieval English Church was neither vulnerable to doctrinal and social challenge nor concerned about it, it also shows that what really needs explaining is why the wounds inflicted were so superficial. The answer is found partly in the nature of Wyclif's doctrines, which (unlike the more moderate teachings of Jan Hus) were just too radical to appeal widely, and partly in the particular failure of his doctrines to gain ground among key sections of society, notably the gentry and the friars.

The main question to be addressed with regard to later Lollardy is whether it was showing signs of revival and growth in the late fifteenth and early sixteenth centuries. While it is undeniable that growing numbers of Lollards were being prosecuted in this period, the case argued here is that it is not possible to account with complete certainty for this rise. Although the evidence is compatible with a revival in the movement's fortunes, it is equally compatible with an increase in reportage and an intensification of repression. The fact that later Lollardy displays none of the other hallmarks of a movement on the ascendant makes the latter explanation more probable. Among other things, however, the fourth chapter also contests a thesis which has gained in popularity in recent years, namely that Lollardy exercised a disproportionate appeal among women.

The last substantive chapter considers the relationship of Lollardy to the English Reformation in the sixteenth century, a question which has been the subject of intense historiographical debate for about a century. Again, little in the way of new information is offered about either late Lollardy or the early Reformation. But the chapter makes several new contributions to the debate, chiefly by bringing information from diverse sources and fields to bear upon it. The argument is simple: that Lollardy is of virtually no importance for the success of the English Reformation. This must ultimately be a question of interpretation, and I cannot therefore expect my judgement to be taken as final. But I hope that the chapter will at least make it much more difficult for the opposing case to be maintained in future.

The short epilogue to the book addresses the question why, if the Lollards were neither numerically significant in their own time nor of great importance for the course of English history, they have attracted so much scholarly attention. The answer offered is still less flattering, and still more problematic. For I suggest that this attention is disproportionate to their actual importance, and arises partly from an accidental and partly from an extraneous cause: the accidental, the disproportionate survival of Lollard texts; the extraneous, the romantic appeal of the Lollards as a criminalised minority. The problem this raises in its turn is why we should bother with the Lollards at all – a curious problem to raise at the end (and now at the beginning) of a book about them. But for the answer to that you can either wait or turn at once to the closing pages.

1

THE CHURCH OF ENGLAND
IN THE LATER MIDDLE AGES

Two models leap to most people's minds when considering the
Middle Ages: feudal anarchy and the age of faith. Even historians
sometimes find it difficult to escape the imaginative constraints
which these twin constructs impose. The fourteenth-century English Church conformed to neither of them. It was, for its time, a
well-ordered body, staffed at its higher levels by decent and com-
petent clergymen who saw that the ecclesiastical machinery ticked
over in broad accordance with canon law. This hierarchy, if it did
not preside over some pre-Raphaelite idyll of devout landowners,
leaseholders, and labourers, nevertheless knew of no principled
challenge to its teachings, and of little active dissatisfaction with its
pastoral provision. The educational attainments of the parochial
and unbeneficed clergy were – and were admitted to be – far from
ideal. The few graduates were concentrated in the upper echelons
of the clergy, and were often occupying benefices without cure of
souls which supported them in what they would have seen as their
more important bureaucratic employment in Church or State.
Most priests were at least functionally literate, as it is difficult to
see how they could otherwise have fulfilled their basic liturgical
duties to the satisfaction of their hierarchical superiors and their
parishioners. And while mediocrity doubtless prevailed, there
were many signs of better things. The legislation of diocesan synods,
which were still regular features of English Church life at this time,
testifies to the interest of those superiors in maintaining and
monitoring standards of pastoral provision, while the proliferation

1

of religious confraternities shows an increased appetite for things spiritual among the laity. If enthusiasm for the monastic life in general was ebbing, the more demanding life of the hermit was proving attractive to many people. And this 'eremitical' milieu produced a flowering of spiritual literature which circulated widely at the time and remains the most enduring monument of fourteenth-century English Christianity.

The Church held a privileged position in English society: one that was defined and upheld by the first article of Magna Carta, which protected the English Church from complete royal control until the constitutional revolution of the 1530s, when, in a moment of acute dynastic crisis, the monarchy skilfully exploited its own rising powers and new religious doctrines to deprive the Church of its twin props, baronial support at home and papal patronage abroad. But in Plantagenet times that dénouement lay far ahead, and the legislative and jurisdictional autonomy of the Church seemed an immutable and integral element of the English constitution. Like all privileges, those of the medieval Church at times aroused envy or evoked resentment, especially when they were insensitively exploited in periods of economic hardship or tactlessly insisted upon at moments of political crisis. The word 'anticlericalism' is at best a misleading description of this resentment, redolent as it is of the profoundly secularist aspirations of certain social groups in Europe since the Enlightenment. But it remains the only word we have, and will therefore have to do, provided that it is used with suitable reservations, chiefly that medieval anticlericalism did not usually offer a fundamental challenge to the sacred powers or even the secular privileges of the priesthood.

Anticlericalism is often said to be endemic in Christian, and especially Catholic, societies. It is better described as sporadic. Outbursts such as the sack of the abbey of Bury St Edmund's by an angry mob of townsfolk in 1327 or the assault on the Blackfriars of Boston in 1379 were responses to specific circumstances rather than expressions of some underlying (and therefore conveniently indetectible) groundswell of discontent.[1] In medieval Lincolnshire, for example, there were periods of anticlerical activity, but far longer periods in which there was little or none.[2] At the everyday level, for example, the clergy's right to the tithe (a right conferred and enforced entirely under canon law) was not disputed in principle, but disagreements over the method of assessment or payment were well able to spark off anything from a bloody affray to a protracted lawsuit. And while the Peasants' Revolt of 1381 witnessed some of the most violent anticlericalism of the century – including the sack of St Alban's Abbey and the lynching of the Archbishop of Canterbury – the danger of applying the concept of 'anticlericalism' to the revolt in too simplistic a fashion is amply illustrated by the fact that one of its figureheads, John Ball, was himself a priest, albeit one who had frequently been in trouble with the ecclesiastical authorities and who, being unbeneficed, was therefore untainted with the ambition and avarice often ascribed to his superiors.

The pretensions and priorities of the State – or to be precise, in the medieval context, of the Crown – were always more of a threat to the liberties of the Church than any number of riots or lynchings. Tension between Church and State runs through the history of the Middle Ages, an inevitable consequence of the social, economic, and political power which accrued to the clergy thanks to their monopoly of spiritual and their disproportionate share of worldly goods. The Crown could hardly allow something between a quarter and a third of the landed wealth of the country to lie permanently outside the scope of feudal and fiscal obligations, and for its own security needed to be sure that the considerable financial and political resources of the major bishoprics and abbeys did not fall into potentially hostile hands. There was plenty of scope for conflict here, but it was compromise rather than conflict that characterised Church–State relations in the later Middle Ages. Indeed, in Pantin's words: 'It was an over-readiness to compromise rather than intransigence that was the besetting fault of the late medieval Church.'[3] The Crown's legitimate interest in appointments to major benefices and the obvious need to tax clerical wealth for public purposes made some kind of compromise with the Church's theoretical immunities and liberties inevitable.

The situation was further complicated by the papacy's equally legitimate interest in clerical appointments and taxation. The English hierarchy often found itself attempting to play off its rival masters against each other, or else embroiled in confusing, three-cornered disputes with them. In the fourteenth century, the kings emerged as winners from this complex game. The high tide of ecclesiastical privilege had been reached in the thirteenth century, when the weakness of the Crown had seen barons, bishops, and popes variously dictate their terms. But when strong kings united the realm behind adventurous, successful, and above all remunerative foreign policies, the English Church swung into line with the rest of the nation. Edward I won the principle of taxing the clergy for royal purposes, and Edward III managed to tax it more effectively than any previous ruler.[4] The papacy for its own ends connived in the Crown's moves to tax ecclesiastical wealth, and the two parties in effect struck a mutually acceptable bargain over the provision of candidates to major church benefices – to the detriment of the traditional and canonical freedom of election in cathedral and monastic chapters for which the English Church itself had fought so hard over the preceding two centuries.

This resurgence of royal power within the Church (which was to continue through the fifteenth century) had important effects on the recruitment of the hierarchy. Scholar bishops in the tradition of Anselm and Robert Grosseteste were gradually edged out, and the few that remained were no longer found in the great sees like Canterbury and York, but were consigned to relatively poor and marginal sees such as Rochester and Chichester.[5] In their place came two groups, royal administrators and noblemen, reflecting the Crown's tendency to exploit ecclesiastical preferment as a means of rewarding servants. The tightening grip of the Crown on the Church reduced the ability of the hierarchy to impose restraints on royal policy. It was the barons rather than the bishops who brought down Richard II, and such bishops as did oppose the king henceforth (as Scrope of York under Henry IV or Nevile of York in the War of the Roses) were themselves of noble birth, and were usually acting from dynastic rather than ecclesiastical motives.

The aristocrats and administrators were not necessarily negligent of their pastoral obligations, although a figure such as Cardinal Henry Beaufort inevitably viewed his bishopric not only as a virtual birthright, but also as a platform for his chosen career as politician and financier. But it did mean that many bishops were unable to give their dioceses their undivided attention. Moreover, the practice of translating bishops from one see to another, either as part of a *cursus honorum* for favoured servants, or else in order to marginalise those out of favour, inevitably undermined episcopal effectiveness by reducing continuity. Another result was that among bishops with intellectual pretensions, lawyers tended to outnumber theologians.[6] Law rather than theology was the path to success in a clerical career. This professional reality was institutionalised in King's Hall at Cambridge, the college founded there (on the site now occupied by Trinity College) by Edward III as a seedbed for royal servants in Church and State – with civil law as its main academic discipline.[7]

The papacy, already obliged for various reasons to wink at the expansion of royal power, found its position with respect to the English Crown weakened still further by the papal schism which broke out in 1378 and lasted 40 years, to be resolved only at the Council of Constance (1414–18). With rival popes fulminating against each other from the two papal capitals of Rome and Avignon, England remained loyal throughout to the Roman succession, perhaps because the Avignon obedience was seen as subservient to French control. But the implicit threat of defection to the opposing camp gave the English Crown immense bargaining power in dealings with the popes, who therefore made numerous concessions in order to retain the allegiance of one of their most important supporters. The last attempt by a pope to tax the English Church directly for his own purposes was made in the 1370s, although of course incidental revenues such as Peter's Pence, first fruits, annates, and fees for dispensations ensured that England remained one of Rome's best sources of income. Papal provision to English benefices tailed off as the Crown rather than the papacy came to be seen as the power that really mattered in such affairs. The fate of Reginald Pecock, a mid-fifteenth-century bishop whose refutations of heresy led to his own conviction for the same crime, shows us where real power lay. After his abjuration and absolution, Pecock not unreasonably sought papal confirmation of his position as Bishop of Chichester. But Henry VI's government received this very coldly, put pressure on him to resign, committed him in effect to life imprisonment in a monastery, and replaced him.[8] The popes were in no position to aid or inspire resistance to the royal stranglehold on the hierarchy.

Jurisdictional rivalries between ecclesiastical and royal courts provided another bone of contention. This was hardly a major issue in terms of mass attitudes. Lawyers were second only to clergymen as figures of hate and fun in the literatures of complaint and inversion,[9] and the fact that many clergymen were also lawyers merely increased the ignominy to which both professions were liable. The legal privileges of sanctuary and benefit of clergy which were contingent upon the sacred status of the Church's property and personnel were a perpetual source of friction. On the whole, the Church fought its corner well against unfavourable odds. Indeed, during the Yorkist period the Church even managed to regain some lost ground. But the growing tendency was for the common-law courts to exploit the statutes of provisors and *praemunire* in order to frustrate or hijack proceedings in ecclesiastical courts. These statutes had originally been passed in the fourteenth century in order to exert pressure on the papacy during sensitive negotiations between England and either Avignon or Rome. Their avowed purpose was to reduce the impact of papal provision upon English clerical preferment, and once the Crown and the papacy had reached an understanding over this issue, they lapsed more or less into oblivion.

However, the statute of *praemunire* was revived in the fifteenth century during the power struggle between Cardinal Beaufort and the Duke of Gloucester, and its scope was enlarged first by the misreading and later the miscopying of the text in such a way as to extend the scope of the act to any papal bull brought into England.[10] This established itself in the common-law tradition and subsequently became the common lawyers' preferred weapon in disputes with church courts, before being taken up first by Henry VII as a means of mulcting the Church, and then by Henry VIII as a means of intimidating it. This development, though of enormous import for the future, was of little direct relevance to the history of heresy and dissent, as both canon and common lawyers were equally hostile to anything which threatened to subvert the established order of Church and State. Common lawyers might argue with their clerical counterparts over the boundaries between the temporal and the spiritual, but they never for a moment doubted that boundaries there were. Magna Carta was as dear to them as to the clergy – who once a year reminded their flocks of the charter's contents, which were binding under pain of excommunication – and the common law was crystal clear on the inability of temporal persons to exercise spiritual jurisdiction.

Professional rivalries among lawyers were matched by similar rivalries between different branches of the clergy, problems which often arose, ironically, out of attempts at reform. Since at least the twelfth century, medieval reformers had scented corruption in the Church's vast landed wealth, which, in itself and in its effect upon clerical lifestyles, struck them as starkly contrasted with the poverty and simplicity of Christ and his apostles recorded in the Gospels. By a further irony, Gregory VII's invocation of the 'law' of scripture and the Church against the mere 'custom' by which secular rulers, as he saw it, infringed the liberties of the Church, did much to inspire the use of scripture as a yardstick against which to measure the behaviour of the clergy. The doctrine of 'evangelical poverty', which developed in both 'orthodox' and 'heretical' directions, combined an emphasis upon the scriptures with a moral reaction against the nascent commercialisation of society. This combination was to be evident in the theology of Wyclif, which explains why the title of 'Doctor evangelicus' (the Gospel Doctor) was accorded to him in theological circles before his condemnation.

The most 'orthodox' expression of this evangelical impulse was in the orders of mendicant friars, which in the fourteenth century were still relatively recent innovations. The Dominicans had reached England in 1221, followed by the Franciscans in 1224, the Carmelites in 1241, and the Augustinians in 1249. New houses were still being founded in the early 1300s and, if a degree of institutionalisation and conventionality was now more than apparent in the mendicant orders, there was still ample evidence of intellectual and pastoral vigour. Numbers of friars had peaked at nearly 5000 around 1320, and would remain at that high level for some time to come.[11] After some fierce initial struggles, the friars had attained a dominant position in the theology faculties of the two universities of Oxford and Cambridge by about 1300, and various orders maintained flourishing *studia* in provincial centres such as York and Norwich, as well as in the capital, London. By the early sixteenth century, the intellectual life of the friars was largely confined to Oxford, Cambridge, and London, numbers were falling, and discipline was relaxed. The need for the movements of strict observance was by then manifest. But the fourteenth-century friars were still a force to be reckoned with, as would be shown by their prominence in the campaign against Wyclif and Lollardy. The orders were well able to meet the huge demand for friars as preachers and confessors.[12] And their talents in these capacities won them enormous influence among the nobility, the gentry, and the urban elites. Gentry wills in the later Middle Ages abound in donations to the friars,[13] and the fascinating description of the funeral monuments in the London Greyfriars compiled in the early sixteenth century paints a picture of a building paved, lined, and glazed with memorials to the great and the good.[14]

The very success of the friars, however, excited the jealousy of both the secular (i.e. diocesan and parochial) and the monastic clergy, not to mention of each other. At bottom, this jealousy was something of a turf war. The prowess of the friars as preachers and confessors won them large congregations, which in turn ensured a regular stream of fees, offerings, legacies, and pensions: all of it amounting in the eyes of the secular clergy to money and goods which ought by rights to have been theirs. In addition, the theoretical poverty of the friars (to some degree, though by no means wholly, a legal fiction) together with the jurisdictional autonomy of their orders, meant that they were not covered by the grants of taxation made by the Convocation to king or pope. At a higher level, that of bishops and diocesan administrators, the autonomy of the mendicant orders created further problems, as the bishops might well resent the activity in their dioceses of large cadres of well-trained clergy who owed them neither obedience nor support, and were answerable only to their own provincial authorities or ultimately to the pope. There was therefore considerable rivalry between the secular and the mendicant clergy, and it inevitably took on a theological dimension. The friars maintained that their way of life was inherently more perfect than that of the secular priesthood, while the secular theologians took their stand on the theological principle of episcopacy, and argued that the friars contravened the moral law in tempting Christians away from the spiritual provision of their parish church. In Ireland, Richard Fitzralph, Archbishop of Armagh, took up the debate in the mid-fourteenth century, and, preaching against the mendicants at Paul's Cross (the great pulpit outside London's cathedral) on a visit to England in 1356–57, he rekindled a controversy which blazed on at Oxford in particular for years after his death in 1360.[15]

The quarrels between the friars and the monks were not only financial, but also theological and vocational. Monks and seculars had long coexisted peacefully. Indeed, monasteries had first appeared long before parishes, even if monasticism had developed in many new directions during the Middle Ages. Because monasteries were financed largely by their endowments, and did not as such exercise a cure of souls among the laity, there was not too much conflict between monks and parish priests at the grass roots.

While monasteries tended to acquire rectories and then hive off the spiritual functions to vicars or curates while retaining the bulk of the tithe revenues, this did not differentiate them from other individual or corporate patrons or rectors. The tendency of abbeys and priories to seek papal exemptions from episcopal jurisdiction could lead to quarrels with bishops and archdeacons, but these were limited in scope and importance. The friars, though, were a serious threat to the monks for two reasons. First, they competed for recruits; and second, they competed for lay support, relying on a continuous stream of small donations rather than massive single endowments. The competition for recruits was probably most serious. Not only did the friars offer a more attractive lifestyle, with greater mobility and integration in the busy life of the towns, but they also had the cheek to argue that their combination of the active and contemplative life was a more perfect and evangelical state than the monks' contemplative withdrawal from the world. And, as if their secular and monastic opponents were not enough, the various orders kept up a similar squabble among themselves over the question of which particular order was best! At Cambridge, in 1374, a Dominican challenged a Carmelite to defend his order's peculiar claim to trace its roots back to the prophet Elijah. It is a worrying commentary on the historical sophistication of the later scholastics that the University judged the Carmelite the winner of the ensuing disputation.

Although no new religious order reached England in the fourteenth century, the accelerated growth of the Carthusians in this period gave them virtually the impact of a new order. The Carthusians were, in fact, of greater antiquity than the friars, having been founded in the late eleventh century. However, they had spread more slowly as their lifestyle, which combined the austerity of the hermit with some of the security of communal life, was of far more limited appeal. A Carthusian priory, or 'Charterhouse', had certain communal buildings, notably the chapel, but was divided mostly into what can best be described as little individual terraced cottages built around a courtyard. The finest example in Europe is the great Charterhouse near Pavia, and traces of the distinctive architecture can be seen quite clearly at Mount Grace in Yorkshire. The fathers spent most of their lives in silence in their individual dwellings, sustained by a vegetarian diet, and dedicating themselves to prayer and meditation. But the austerity of their way proved highly attractive in fourteenth-century England, especially to the nobility who furnished so many of their patrons and so many of their recruits. To the two existing Charterhouses (Witham, founded around 1170; and Hinton, founded around 1230), a third was added at Beauvale in 1343, followed by several more, culminating in the ninth at Sheen in 1415. This, the greatest and the last Charterhouse in England, was founded by none other than Henry V.[16] The Carthusians maintained their high standards of moral rigour and liturgical observance throughout the later Middle Ages, played a leading part in the devotional milieu and literature of that period, and were, among all the English religious orders, that which offered most opposition to the Reformation of Henry VIII in the 1530s. Although they were only a small number of men (there were no female houses, although the last new nunnery to be founded in England, Syon Priory, a house of the new order of Bridgettines, was founded by Henry V as a sort of sister house for his Charterhouse at Sheen, and was associated with the same spiritual milieu), the Carthusians were a key element in the late medieval Church of England.

It is a commonplace of medieval history that the emergence of the mendicant orders was conditioned by the birth of urban society. The parish structure which had developed over the preceding 500 years was imperfectly adapted to the urban environment, and the friars helped fill the gaps, supplementing spiritual provision in crowded and socially fluid centres, and offering a style of Christianity better suited to the aspirations and needs of a more articulate laity who were no longer necessarily distinguished from the clergy by illiteracy.[17] The emergence of the universities was similarly conditioned by urbanisation, and the training of a more educated clergy was an aim which the universities shared with the friars. These developments fed, and were fed by, the increasing lay interest in the spiritual life. The proliferation of lay confraternities and of vernacular religious treatises is evidence enough for this. But this increasing lay involvement carried a hidden risk: the temptation to heresy. If heresy was going to spread among the laity, it would inevitably do so among the devout and the involved rather than among the detached and the apathetic. When Wycliffite doctrines started to trickle down to the laity, it was precisely among the more literate and articulate groups – the gentry, the merchants, and the urban craftsmen, the groups who were more actively engaged in orthodox religious doctrine and practice – that it found an audience. It is not so much that Lollardy fastened on to latent discontents and dissensions as that it battened upon the very strengths of that to which it was opposed.

Nevertheless, this argument must not be taken too far. Before Wycliffite doctrines began to be put before the people, there is no indication that any other heresy had made any significant impact in England. One or two Albigensians were detected in England in the thirteenth century, and perhaps one or two hints of the heresy of the Free Spirit in the fourteenth. But there is no sign that the heretical tendencies (Beguines, Beghards, etc.) that found a following in the more densely urbanised Netherlands had flowed along the crowded trade routes to England. Fourteenth-century England was devoid not only of the special inquisitors commissioned to combat heresy on the Continent (for example, zealous Dominicans active in the Netherlands, Germany, southern France, and northern Italy), but even of inquisitors' manuals such as that of Bernard Gui. The tendency of such inquisitors, a sort of occupational hazard, to construe uncommon piety or mere eccentricity as deviance and unorthodoxy, which can be seen so clearly in late medieval Germany, was not evident in England until after Wyclif's time.[18] Much of the historical importance of Lollardy consists in the fact that it was the first time that the English ecclesiastical authorities had to grapple with the problem of heresy as anything other than the inconsequential aberration of an eccentric academic or the coarse scepticism of a thoughtful layman.

The burgeoning lay interest in religious matters is most obvious to the modern historian in the survival of vernacular texts produced for this new and rapidly growing market.[19] Previously, vernacular religious texts had been mostly written in French for an aristocratic or monastic audience. But in the fourteenth century, the composition of texts in English was a response to the Church's new sense of the need to ensure the adequate instruction of the laity in the basic truths and obligations of the Catholic faith. This need had been given formal expression in the legislation of the Fourth Lateran Council back in 1215. This had been endorsed and adapted by Archbishop John Pecham of Canterbury in 1281 in a statute which bore fruit in the fourteenth century. These laws laid down that the laity should be given instruction in their own tongue four times a year in the articles of the Creed, the Ten

Commandments, the six commandments of the Church, the seven sacraments, and the paternoster. Most of the catechetical texts which have survived are clearly based on this model, although they cover the material in varying degrees of detail, and often include other materials as well (the Ave Maria, the Beatitudes, the seven corporal works of mercy, the seven gifts of the Holy Spirit, etc).[20] Besides such basic texts, there were also lives of the saints, collections of miracles, and the chronicles which indiscriminately mixed temporal and spiritual materials. The texts are directed to two audiences: the priests whose task it was to convey instruction, and also the literate layfolk interested in finding out more for themselves.

Devotional reading of a far more sophisticated nature was also becoming available, for the later fourteenth century saw a flowering of a theological literature at once original, profound, and accessible. The seminal figure in this movement was Richard Rolle, author of a number of writings on contemplative prayer and the spiritual life which made him the most widely read author in late medieval England. But other writings almost as influential included the *Ladder of Perfection* (a remarkable study in the devout life by Walter Hilton), the *Cloud of Unknowing* (which some modern scholars have been tempted to ascribe to Hilton but was almost certainly by an unknown hand), and the *Revelations of Divine Love* by a female hermit, Julian of Norwich. The heart of this devotional movement lay in the solitary or eremitical religious life which constituted the great appeal of the Carthusians, but was by no means limited to that order. Richard Rolle himself led the life of a hermit, as did Julian of Norwich. One of Walter Hilton's friends joined the Carthusians at Hilton's instigation. And Margery Kempe's respect for the eremitical life was evident. Her apologia for her religious life, though dictated rather than written, was a late contribution to the genre, more personal and less sophisticated than its predecessors, yet manifestly in the same line of development. In a rather different vein, Langland's great poem *Piers Plowman* was second in popularity only to Chaucer's *Canterbury Tales* among what we usually regard as works of literature. In its own context it was clearly read as a work of moral and spiritual instruction.

Geographically, the two regions which dominated this efflorescence of spiritual literature were East Anglia and Yorkshire (which were also the main areas for religious drama[21]). It is no coincidence that Wyclif himself was a Yorkshireman, as in certain crucial respects Lollardy itself was a part of this broader movement of lay and vernacular piety. The links between the two regions in this matter of devotional literature can be illustrated in various ways. Walter Hilton studied for many years at Cambridge, then served nearby in the Bishop of Ely's diocesan administration before retiring to pursue the monastic life at the house of Austin Friars at Thurgarton in Nottinghamshire. Margery Kempe, herself from King's Lynn (Norfolk), was acquainted with the devotional writings of Walter Hilton and once met Julian of Norwich, and the only surviving manuscript of her book belonged at the time of the Reformation to the northernmost Carthusian house, Mount Grace. The quantity of surviving manuscripts shows that this literature circulated in an extensive devout milieu, and the frequency with which these classics of devotional writing occur in catalogues and booklists associated with Carthusian houses illustrates the central role of those houses in the movement.

Popular though it was, relatively speaking, the literature of contemplative prayer and the 'way of perfection' was not for everybody. Piety was far less sophisticated for the most part, even when literate in expression. The most widely owned religious books were, in fact, liturgical texts. Despite the systematic attempt to destroy Catholic liturgical books in the reign of Edward VI – a period which probably saw book burning on a larger scale than any other in English history – they still survive in impressive quantities. More than 700 manuscript Books of Hours produced for the English market are still extant today. But Books of Hours, missals, and the like were Latin texts, which few lay owners (and perhaps few priests) could read with understanding. The 'otherness' of the language of worship, however, was a symbol in itself of the separation of the sacred from the profane, and thus, despite the problem of incomprehension, probably strengthened rather than weakened adherence to the holy as defined by the clergy.

Reading a clutch of late medieval wills swiftly reveals that prayer beads were even more widely owned than devotional texts, although they survive even less frequently. This reminds us that lay participation in the medieval liturgy could take many forms, and that one way was the recitation of prayer with beads. Although historians inevitably look primarily to written sources, late medieval religion was more a ritual than a written culture, a fact succinctly recalled in the cant definition of images as layfolk's books. Reconstructing the material culture of late medieval lay religion is altogether more difficult than getting a sense of its literate culture, as books in general have had a far higher survival value than the often ephemeral, even gimcrack, and of course heavily used artefacts of public and private worship. However, the archaeological retrieval of pilgrims' badges, the stray copies or tattered fragments of indulgences and letters of confraternity (documents indeed, but valued more in being owned than in being read), not to mention the architectural survivals – pulpits, tombs, funeral monuments, bells, rood-screens, fonts, windows, and above all the churches themselves – give a deep insight into the nature of medieval Christianity. And the evidence of wills shows that the laity were quite happy to dedicate to church use napkins, cloths, embroideries, candles and wax, and other household stuffs serviceable for the decoration of altars and statues or for the enrichment of liturgical performance.

What we are learning to call 'traditional religion' was undeniably popular in later Plantagenet England. This term has been criticised on the grounds that religious practices changed in certain significant respects in late medieval England, but this criticism is entirely beside the point. Traditions change, and 'traditional religion' remains vastly preferable to the more common term 'popular religion'. 'Popular' religion, defined in contrast to 'elite' or 'official' religion, assumes a Marxist analysis of class-conflict which may be appropriate to the modern situation, but, as Eamon Duffy has shown, has no bearing on the Middle Ages.[22] The religious life of mainstream English Christianity continued to flourish and develop along traditional lines. This is especially apparent in the cult of the saints. The practice of pilgrimage, both within the kingdom and beyond, retained its popularity throughout this period.[23] The tomb of St Thomas at Canterbury, though about 200 years old by Wyclif's time, remained England's premier shrine. The shrine of Our Lady at Walsingham was growing in popularity, and many long-venerated saints stayed in fashion. At the same time, new devotions and cults were constantly arriving to supplement or displace the old. Many of these were native to England, and we should not be deceived by the fact that only a few resulted in formal canonisations. St Thomas Cantilupe (1320), St John of

Bridlington (1401), and St Osmund of Salisbury (1457) were the only English saints canonised between 1300 and 1500, but moves were made to canonise Richard Rolle and Henry VI, while local cults sprang up around such varied figures as John Shorne, John Dalderby, Bishop Grosseteste, and Archbishop Scrope. Richard II even tried to foster devotion to his murdered great-grandfather Edward II, while one of Richard's victims, the Earl of Arundel, himself became the focus of some popular veneration.[24] Other cults made their way here from abroad. One of the most popular was that of St Bridget of Sweden, whose rise was of course associated with Henry V's foundation of a house of Bridgettine nuns at Syon in Middlesex.[25]

The greatest devotional innovation in fourteenth-century England was probably the promulgation of the feast of Corpus Christi in 1318. This feast had been sanctioned in 1264 by Urban IV in order to confirm the people in their sense of the divine presence in the sacrament of the eucharist, and indeed partly in order to counter heretical doubts about the doctrine which emerged in the Netherlands and among the Albigensians and Waldensians of southern France and northern Italy and Spain. The new feast centred on the worship of the consecrated host which, according to the Catholic doctrine of transubstantiation, is, by virtue of the proper priestly utterance of Christ's words, the real body of Christ concealed beneath the physical appearances and qualities of what is no longer really bread. The act of consecration, which had received heavy emphasis with the introduction of the elevation of the consecrated elements around the eleventh century, was now undoubtedly the high point of the mass, especially as it was rare at this time for the laity to take communion. The mere sight of the host (known in common parlance as 'seeing one's maker') was believed to be rich in material and spiritual benefits. The well-known tale of the Lollard evangelist William Thorpe testifies to the magnetic attraction of the consecration. Preaching once in St Chad's, Shrewsbury, he saw his entire audience scuttle away to a distant side-altar at the tinkling of the sacring bell (and preaching was itself a considerable attraction in late medieval England).

Corpus Christi was a huge success in England, and many of the religious confraternities founded at this time were dedicated to the body of Christ, notably the great Corpus Christi guild of York (about 9 per cent of the English guilds recorded in a survey of

1388–89 shared this dedication).[26] The townsfolk of Cambridge
went so far as to found a college with this dedication in the university. The emergence of Corpus Christi is simply the most dramatic
evidence of the massive importance of the mass, and of the consecrated host which lay at its heart, in late medieval England. This
importance was reflected not only in the proliferation of 'private'
masses endowed or subscribed by laity and clergy alike, and in the
consequent explosion in recruitment to the secular priesthood,
but in the official and semi-official literature and art of the Church
(Corpus Christi plays and processions, Easter sepulchres for the
rite of burying the host, priestly funeral monuments, ornate chalices
and monstrances) and the widely held beliefs or superstitions
about the blessings to be derived from the consecrated host.[27]
Corpus Christi was the first of a genre of devotional concepts and
practices which focused on the person of Jesus, and was followed
in the fifteenth century by such devotions as the Holy Name of
Jesus, and the Five Wounds.[28] The appeal of Corpus Christi accounts
for the popularity of one of late medieval England's most popular
relics, the phial of Christ's blood presented to the Abbey of Hailes
(Gloucestershire) in the thirteenth century by Richard, Earl of
Cornwall. It was on the itinerary of that indefatigable pilgrim,
Margery Kempe, in the early fifteenth century, and it was already
so firmly established as to attract the especial ire of the Lollards,
who dismissed it contemptuously as the blood of a duck or drake.

The intended symbolism of the body of Christ was undeniably
socially integrative. The ancient myth of society as body had been
appropriated by St Paul as a description of the Church, and was
crucially reshaped by him through identification not with some
abstract Platonic idea, but with the real body of a particular man.
In his theology, the sacrament of the Lord's Supper became the
paramount symbol of the unity of this body, and that symbolism
developed over the centuries into the twin doctrines of the mystical body of Christ and the real presence of Christ in the eucharist.
By the later Middle Ages, the unitive function of communion,
albeit now restricted to an occasional event, was almost universally
appreciated even among the unschooled laity, and Easter communion was predicated on ceremonies of public and communal as
well as individual and private reconciliation, to such an extent
that a lack of charity between neighbours constituted a barrier to
participation in the sacrament.[29]

This is neither to romanticise the Middle Ages nor to deny the experience of conflict in society.[30] Indeed, the everyday experience of conflict and hatred was no doubt what made the symbolism of the eucharist so appealing. Medieval priests and labourers and wives were quite as aware as modern psychiatrists and literary theorists of the place of disorder and dysfunction in their society, even if they accounted for it in the categories of sin and lack of charity rather than alienation or repression. The symbol of the body of Christ was important to them precisely because charity and order were so precarious in their world. Unity is only ever a concern to those who experience, or at least fear, its opposite (though that probably includes almost everybody). The complete priestly domination of this quintessential symbol of unity guaranteed the place of the priest in medieval society whatever the personal or even collective defects of, or grievances against, the clergy as a professional caste. It is no accident that when dissent from the official Church emerged, it focused on the sacrament of the eucharist. The nexus of doctrines, rituals, and superstitions associated with this sacrament lay as close as anything to the heart of late medieval Catholicism not only as theology, but also as social practice. To contest this was to contest everything that was distinctive about late medieval Catholicism.

The 'reification' of the sacrament of the eucharist, by which its cult became ever more akin to that of relics, has been amply documented by G. J. C. Snoek, and explains much in the development of late medieval eucharistic piety. His further contention that this process, which reached its peak in the fourteenth and fifteenth centuries, was at the cost of the sacramental or communal conception of the eucharist (a cost measured in the decline in the frequency with which the laity took communion) is less convincing. The thesis itself is familiar enough from humanist and Protestant (and even some recent Roman Catholic) critiques of popular piety, but it rests more on assertion and evaluation than argument.[31] The infrequency of communion does not in itself establish its unimportance. Familiarity may breed contempt. The rarity of communion seems to have accentuated its unique sacramental significance. All the evidence we have suggests that communion was very important to Christians in this period, even if it was only once or twice a year. For an English parishioner, to be deprived of his (or her) 'rights' at Easter (through some quarrel with the priest) was

not only a social stigma, but a spiritual loss.[32] Part of the problem
for a woman who, like Margery Kempe, sought to receive communion more frequently than was conventional was that her
action could be seen not merely as blurring the distinction between
laity and priesthood, but also as raising herself above or setting
herself apart from the community, which was content to take communion together on prescribed occasions.

Priestly power in late medieval England (as elsewhere) rested
ultimately on the power of consecration vested literally in their
hands. If the laity set great store by seeing their maker, the priestly
office was described, in even more untheological terms (which
would have made Thomas Aquinas turn in his grave) as 'making
God'. Sir Roger Burley, an Irish priest serving in the diocese of St
David's in the 1480s, boasted of his ability to make Christ really
present for some communicants, but not for others – an indication
of the way in which official doctrine could actually be understood
by those unrestrained by a formal training in scholastic theology.[33]
Equally, the popular usages of 'seeing' and 'making' God demon-
strate that the apparently remote and inaccessible doctrine of the
real presence had entrenched itself firmly in vernacular culture.
Thus we should not be surprised to find William Colyn, a labourer
in a small corner of rural Norfolk, familiar enough with the implications of the doctrine to be able to tell his parish priest that it
would be better to do his penance in front of the sacrament rather
than before an image of Our Lady.[34]

The heightened awareness of the sacred power of the host
marched hand in hand with that of the priest and therefore of the
liturgy, the mass, in which the former was consecrated by the
latter. Involving as it did the routine embodiment of the supreme
holiness upon earth, the mass became the means of prayer *par
excellence*. Whatever the spiritual or material benefit sought by the
supplicant, there was no more powerful and accessible means of
intercession with God than the mass. The fourteenth century
therefore witnessed the introduction, not merely in England but
across Europe, of 'votive masses' – what the Protestant Reformers
were later to call 'private masses', which means not private in the
modern sense, as in excluding the public, but private as to their
'intentions'. That is, the votive or 'private' mass was offered by the
priest for the sake of the particular intentions of a private
individual or a group. Specific liturgies were devised for specific

categories of intention. Thus a late medieval missal would contain votive masses in honour of the Trinity, Our Lady, or the Five Wounds of Christ, or else for peace, the harvest, or the dead. The burgeoning demand for these votive masses changed the topography of the parish church. In addition to the high altar on which the parish priest celebrated high mass on Sundays and feast days, side-chapels and side-altars proliferated around the nave in order to accommodate the huge numbers of masses required by the faithful. It was this huge demand, also, which spurred the rise in the numbers of those ordained to the priesthood in this period.

Perhaps the most widely requested of all the votive masses was that for the dead. Chantries and obits were devised to finance the stipends of the priests who were to celebrate them. Until the early fourteenth century, most chantries were founded in monasteries, but thereafter they tended to cluster in secular colleges or parish churches,[35] perhaps reflecting the greater inclination of founders to secure some educational or pastoral benefit to the wider community along with the intercession for their soul. Lincolnshire chantries become numerous from the later fourteenth century (except in Lincoln itself, where many predated 1300).[36] While most masses for the dead were celebrated at side-altars, the more elaborate chantry foundations provided not only stipends for priests and doles for the poor to add their prayers to his, but also the costs of running, furnishing, and even building new chapels in the church.

At their most pious or ostentatious, founded by kings or great lords, these chantries could take the form of major ecclesiastical foundations of a new kind, the college or collegiate church. From the early fourteenth century, the flow of religious foundations which had marked so much of the Middle Ages began to dry up, or at least to change direction significantly. When prayer was the main vehicle of intercession, the crucial variable in its effectiveness was the holiness of those offering it up. Clearly, those who had renounced the temptations of the flesh and the world for the life of the monastery were holier, and thus the most effective earthly intercessors. However, from at least Gregory VII's time theologians emphasised that the value of the mass did not depend on the holiness of the priest who offered it, but on the divine action itself: it was effective, it was said, *ex opere operato*, 'by the performance of the deed'. Now it was not the personal holiness of intercessors which counted so much as their priestly qualification. That said, holiness was an additional benefit, and one which many patrons valued and sought to stipulate. Nevertheless, priesthood itself became ever more important, and even the monasteries themselves had to adjust to the market, which they did by having ever more of their monks ordained as priests. Nunneries, of course, could not compete effectively in this environment (as women could not be made priests), and their finances consequently suffered in comparison to those of the male religious houses. But the most obvious consequence in the patterns of religious foundation was the rise of collegiate churches, hospitals, and grammar schools (at the expense of more traditional religious houses). Not that it was simply a change in devotional preferences which drove this change. There is a clear sense in the charters of these new institutions that an ecclesiastical foundation should pay a social as well as a spiritual dividend. Public utility is becoming a priority. Even the smaller chantry foundations reflected these changes, as they were increasingly in secular churches rather than religious houses, and often supplemented local pastoral provision, especially in towns where the parish system was stretched.

While the rise of the chantry represented the devotion of the individual, or more properly of the family, one of the most distinctive features of the 'rising tide of lay participation' in religious life in the fourteenth century was the rise of the devotional fraternity.[37] Although guilds were often founded with clerical encouragement or even at clerical instigation, there is plentiful evidence of the foundation of guilds by small groups of devout layfolk, usually though not exclusively men. Caroline Barron's survey of London confraternities in the later Middle Ages suggests strongly that the great age of the popular brotherhood commenced only after the Black Death, and was in part stimulated by the need for mutual insurance against the costs of Christian burial, a need felt more acutely at a time of crisis mortality and its consequent social and economic disruption. Only five London confraternities can be shown to have been in existence before 1348, with another five formed in 1349–50, and then another 74 by 1400.[38] Lincolnshire and Yorkshire evince a similar pattern, with fraternities proliferating in the later fourteenth and fifteenth centuries.[39] The government, anxious lest popular fraternities might be a cover beneath which sedition could be fomented, began a nationwide survey of these groups in 1388. Over 500 returns survive,[40] yet few gilds demonstrably dated from before 1350. However, we should beware of the reductionist notion that the rise of guilds was some subconscious response to the psychological pressures of the Black Death. On the contrary, the motives of founders were predominantly devotional. And, when their devotion was spurred by crisis or epidemic – as was sometimes the case – their response was entirely conscious and rational.

Some devotional guilds became institutions of civic political importance, like the Corpus Christi guilds in York, Boston, Coventry, and Leicester, St George's in Norwich, or Holy Trinity in Lynn. The great guilds of York and Boston clearly enjoyed a still wider social appeal, and were often joined by notables from the surrounding area, bishops, abbots, peers, knights, and gentlemen.[41] Like the consistory in Calvinist cities of a later era, they could take a place in the civic *cursus honorum*, with office-holding in these essentially voluntarist organisations serving as a training and a trial for office-holding in the city itself. In some cases, the guild administrative structure ended up becoming the city government. When guilds reached these levels of significance, joining them was not so much voluntary as a sign and prerequisite of social success.

The social appeal of urban fraternities offers the insight that their membership was predominantly drawn from the artisan sector: exactly the same group among which Lollardy (as we shall see) was to exert its greatest appeal. Out of about 600 laymen who joined the Stratford guild between 1406 and 1431, we know the occupations of 100. The 33 distinct occupations represented are a mixed bag of urban and rural trades, 17 of them with but a single representative. Of the rest, bailiffs and seneschals lead the way (12), followed by servants (9), gentry landowners (9), carpenters (7), millers, and butchers (5 each). Excluding landowners, their officials, and servants, we find nearly 70 men in what we might broadly label the artisan and trading classes. Given the scale of entrance fees (which seem to have fallen in stages from 20s to 6s a head), the members were, for the most part, necessarily comfortably off.[42] When we can identify the occupations of Lollards, which is no more often, we find a similar spread of occupations.

Devotional guilds were closely associated with another of the distinctive features of late medieval piety, sacred drama. Although the mystery and miracle plays owe at least as much to the emergence of vernacular religious literature, all three phenomena form part of the growing lay involvement in the religious life – Miri Rubin has remarked on the dependence of guild piety on a 'knowledgeable, partly literate laity', and it has recently been suggested that some craft guilds may have been established in order to stage plays. The earliest recorded reference to a Corpus Christi play comes from 1377 (at Beverley), around the time when the guilds were beginning to flourish.[43] Most of the surviving plays were probably composed by clerics of one kind or another, yet their performance was clearly in a lay, albeit sacred, context. This lay dominance is suggestively embodied in the way that, around 1470, the Corpus Christi play in York (which was in any case organised by the city council) actually displaced the clerical Corpus Christi procession to the following day![44] It is again evidence of the symbolic centrality of the body of Christ that these great dramatic cycles were not focused narrowly upon the sacrament, but ranged over the entire field of Christian doctrine and sacred history, from the Creation to the Last Judgement. The dominance of East Anglia in the English dramatic tradition is paralleled by a similar dominance in the field of church architecture and adornment. Its literary culture was also fertile, the richest in provincial England.[45] The cycle plays clearly depended on sophisticated urban guild organisations; the non-cycle plays more typical of the dispersed semi-urban settlements of East Anglia. East Anglian plays were often fund-raising events.

Paradoxically, the increasing lay role in religious life resulted in a parallel increase in the role of the secular clergy. The widespread endowment of chantries and parish funds, guilds and obits, led to a vastly increased demand for priests, while better educational provision in colleges and grammar schools improved the supply. The result was a surge in clerical recruitment. These changes were matched by the growing prominence of secular clergy among new saints and their higher esteem in literature – John Shorne and Chaucer's Poor Parson being cases in point. With more and more of the most able recruits choosing secular status rather than joining the monks or friars, one is left with the context in which Wyclif himself emerged, and in which the Wycliffite assertion of the absolute moral superiority of the secular priest over his regular counterparts becomes merely the radical expression of a wider consensus.

Where the vigour of lay religious interest and the rise of the secular clergy came together was in the parish. Growing lay involvement in the parish has been charted by Beat Kumin, and follows a rise which parallels that of the voluntary confraternities. Parochial office-holding as churchwarden or parish clerk was in itself politically important. The parish, like a confraternity, held and administered funds and even properties for communal benefit. And it often exercised a certain oversight over at least the lesser guilds and the 'lights' which operated in the parish church.[46] Pious fraternities have been seen by some historians as rivals to the parish, but they were mostly based in parish churches (though some were based in mendicant churches). But more recently, historians have seen evidence of considerable cooperation between guilds and parishes in building and decorative projects, and even in pastoral provision.[47] The confraternity was an adjunct to the parish rather than a rival.

We can deal in a similar way with the suggestion that a growing sense of elitism and individualism among the gentry was leading them to withdraw from the parish church into private chapels in the later Middle Ages.[48] On the contrary, the indisputable rise in individual and family piety among the gentry ran hand in hand with a commitment to (and perhaps even a sense of responsibility for) parochial religious life. The gentry tomb, the gentry chapel, even the gentry aisle, became common features of fifteenth-century parish churches, combining a declaration of piety with a claim to social precedence. It must be conceded that as long as monasteries and friaries were competing for gentry loyalty, the parish was not the unique focus for their attention that it would become after the suppression of religious houses in the 1530s. Yet there is every indication that even before this, the gentry were a decisive force in parish life. The largesse of the local squire was a crucial element in parochial festivities, as we know from Roger Martin of Long Melford.[49] Much parochial patronage was already in the hands of the gentry (more was to follow the dissolution of the monasteries), and there is no evidence as yet to suggest that gentry patrons were any less likely than episcopal patrons to exercise their patronage to secure capable parsons and vicars for the churches under their aegis. As we shall see, the example of Lollardy itself confirms the extent of gentry influence over parish religion.

The centrality of the parish to religious practice and everyday life cannot be exaggerated. With the churchyard around and the tombs and memorials within, with the evidence all over it of parish, fraternity, and gentry involvement in its construction and adornment, its careful reflection of the hierarchies of the village or town in the standing or seating of the faithful on Sundays and feast days, in the processions around the church on the same occasions, and in the chapels and aisles around the nave, with the blessed sacrament continually reserved above or near the high altar, with an ornate font to symbolise entry into the community, and a doom picture to remind everyone of their place in the eternal scheme of things – with all this, the medieval parish church was one of the most symbolically rich communal structures in history. Law and power, as well as liberty and fraternity, clustered around it, but we should not bring the anachronistic libertarianism and individualism of the twentieth century to bear on the understanding of the nature of community in the fourteenth and fifteenth centuries. We would not like to be transported to such a community, which we would find restricting and intrusive. But we should not assume that fifteenth-century parishioners would have experienced this community as twentieth-century academics would. When Wyclif's doctrines finally burst upon the English people in the 1380s, they were to offer a radical reconstruction of everyday religious experience which, while retaining the essential parochial structure from the past, was to amount to a wholesale demolition of all that was sacred. Almost every distinctive aspect of late medieval Christian practice was to be challenged by Wyclif's teachings. It is hardly surprising that his teachings attracted but little support. Historians should rather be seeking to answer the question of how he attracted even such little support as he secured.

2

JOHN WYCLIF AND HIS THEOLOGY

England, then, was remarkably free from heresy, especially from popular heresy, when, in the 1350s, John Wyclif came to Oxford, one of the greatest universities in Europe, to embark upon an academic and clerical career. For many years that career was typical of the able and successful academic of the age. He was a junior fellow of Merton College by 1356, and served briefly as Master of Balliol (1360–61) until his presentation to that college's best living, Fillingham (Lincolnshire), disqualified him from office. This appointment was of course intended not to serve the spiritual interests of the parishioners of Fillingham, but to finance his continued career within the university, as was the canonry in the collegiate church at Westbury-on-Trym to which he was papally 'provided' (at the university's request) the following year. Wyclif had by now completed the arts course, and although he continued to fulfil his statutory obligations by lecturing in logic and philosophy, his studies were directed towards his doctorate in theology. Along the way he met a galling and expensive setback in the later 1360s. Having been appointed master of the new Canterbury College in 1365, his position was legally challenged and he was displaced in favour of a monk. The costs he incurred in this unsuccessful case compelled him to exchange Fillingham for the less remunerative benefice of Ludgershall (Buckinghamshire). According to William Woodford, an Oxford Franciscan who was to spend much of his life refuting the teachings of Wyclif and his followers, this episode left him with a lasting bitterness against monasticism.

In about 1372 Wyclif finally attained his doctorate and, like most men who reached this eminence, had reasonable expectations of high office in Church or State (although, as ever, lawyers tended to fare better than theologians in the rat race). He was already a controversial figure in Oxford, where his philosophical 'realism' had embroiled him in academic disputes. But it is unlikely that his views attracted any attention outside the university. For a brief moment it looked as though Wyclif's career would follow the accustomed path. In 1374 he was included on an English embassy to Bruges, to discuss clerical taxation with papal representatives. His presentation by the King to the lucrative rectory of Lutterworth (Leicestershire) that same year was presumably meant both to finance and to reward this service. But at this point his ascent seems to have stalled. He was back in England by September, and was not involved in the second round of negotiations next year, which concluded largely to the satisfaction of the papal rather than the royal side. One is tempted to conclude from Wyclif's undoubted talents as a preacher and a polemicist that he was not cut out to be a diplomat.

A later story had it that Wyclif's animus against the established Church was fuelled by his disappointed hopes of the diocese of Worcester.[1] It is tempting to dismiss this as a libel put about by unscrupulous opponents, but characters and careers have been shaped or warped by less, and Wyclif was unquestionably the sort of man to bear a grudge. He may indeed have entertained high hopes. The see of Worcester was vacant from 1373 to 1375, and his three clerical colleagues on the embassy to Bruges all became bishops within the year. While there is no contemporary evidence to link him with Worcester, he was in line in 1374 for the wealthy prebend of Caistor in Lincoln cathedral – to which he had procured a papal 'reservation' (i.e., a warrant entitling him to claim it when it next fell vacant). In the event he was frustrated even of this, by a rival whom he later described as an 'idiot'. There is thus a disconcerting timeliness about the course of events which lends credence to what would otherwise seem mere backbiting. On the eve of his trip to Bruges, Wyclif was on the brink of great things. On his return, he was a man with a great future behind him. He watched his erstwhile colleagues ascend effortlessly into the hierarchy, while his own hopes of Caistor were cruelly dashed. His failure to reach even the first rung of the ladder is remarkable given his intellectual talents. But, as R. G. Davies has argued, administrative skill and experience were the main criteria for ecclesiastical promotion.[2] Wyclif had little administrative experience, and the brevity of his tenure as Master of Balliol suggests that he may have had commensurately little skill.

After his return from Bruges, Wyclif returned to Oxford and began to air for the first time his radical views on property and ownership, in a course of lectures which were almost immediately circulated in manuscript as *De civili dominio* (1375–76). These lectures were notable chiefly for their bold contention that clergymen should not own property. It was hardly surprising that they aroused controversy, and evoked a swift reply from Woodford. It was not possible to question something as fundamental as ecclesiastical property without inviting instant and bitter hostility at the highest level. The Benedictines (the wealthiest of the religious orders, and thus the most threatened by Wyclif's views) soon informed their man at the papal curia, the English monk and rising star Adam Easton. By November 1376 Easton was writing back to the Abbot of Westminster for further details of Wyclif's teachings, and he set to work not only to lobby for papal sanctions against Wyclif, but also upon a massive defence of the *status quo*, the *Defensio ecclesiasticae potestatis*.[3]

Wyclif's abrasive manner and increasingly radical ideas ensured that he received no further advancement. However, a venerable historiographical tradition, taking its departure from the chronicles of Thomas Walsingham and the *Acts and Monuments* of John Foxe, has laboriously constructed a political career for him in the mid-1370s. This tradition, canonised by H. B. Workman,[4] emphasises Wyclif's connection with John of Gaunt, Duke of Lancaster. It envisages an unholy alliance of principled anticlericalism with princely ambition, in which Wyclif provided the ideas for solving the financial crisis consequent upon defeat in France, and often presented these ideas in person before council, Parliament, and the London public. The myth of Wyclif's political career was badly dented in the 1950s when Joseph Dahmus showed that much of the evidence adduced for it was unreliable and hard to interpret.[5] Yet despite Dahmus's refreshing scepticism, the traditional version was emphatically restated in George Holmes's account of the Good Parliament.[6] At its most implausible extreme, this tradition has seen 'Wycliffite support at the heart of the royal administration' and proposed that 'Lollardy was broadcast because it was official

policy'.[7] In fact, a fair estimate of Wyclif's political importance in
the 1370s can be derived from almost any recent study of the
politics of those years. While his alleged political involvement is
almost always invoked – once – Wyclif rarely gets mentioned again.[8]

John Wyclif's connection with John of Gaunt is first attested in
February 1377, when he was summoned to appear before the
bishops at St Paul's, and Gaunt, assisted by the Earl of Northumberland, burst in upon proceedings and broke them up in acrimo-
nious disarray. It is upon the interpretation of this episode that
understandings of the relationship between Wyclif and John of
Gaunt hinge. Walsingham, our main authority, himself embroiders
the episode with vague allegations of collaboration, claiming that
Wyclif had been preaching throughout London against the
clerical interest, talking of Gaunt recruiting Wyclif to his Council,
and hinting that Wyclif's preaching was designed to attract the
Duke's attention and win favour.[9] It has been inferred from this
that Gaunt had brought Wyclif to London to preach his radical
doctrines over the winter of 1376–77 as part of his own political
campaign against the clergy.

Historians have sought corroboration for this in a summons of
Wyclif to the King's Council in September 1376, which has been
taken as an invitation to participate in the formulation of royal
policy. However, there is nothing in the text or context of the
summons to justify this interpretation.[10] Although Wyclif later
boasted of his status as a king's clerk, he never pretended to the
status of a royal councillor and was hardly the sort of man to have
modestly concealed such a distinction.[11] In fact, the summons was
probably related to a dispute about Wyclif's canonry at Westbury-
on-Trym, which Edward III had bestowed the previous year
upon someone else, presumably under the impression that it was
vacant. In December 1376, the dispute was quite properly
resolved in Wyclif's favour.[12] His appearance before the Council,
however, not only accounts for Walsingham's comments about his
preaching in London (there is nothing remarkable in his having
seized the opportunity to fulfil the obligations of a doctor of
theology in preaching to the people), but also explains how he
came to the attention of the Duke of Lancaster, for there is no
evidence of any prior connection between them.

Wyclif's summons before the bishops in February 1377 has
generally been interpreted as an attempt by them to hit back

at John of Gaunt by humiliating one of his clients.[13] However, Walsingham's account suggests that Gaunt's intervention came as a surprise to the bishops – which would hardly have been the case had Wyclif been openly speaking to the ducal agenda for several months.[14] On the contrary, the episcopal hearing should be taken at face value, as a response to the publication of Wyclif's radical book about ecclesiastical property, and perhaps also to his airing of his views in London pulpits.[15] If his ideas were already causing concern at the papal curia, it is hardly surprising that they provoked investigation at home. What requires explanation is not the episcopal initiative, but Gaunt's intervention. Possibly, having recently made Wyclif's acquaintance, he saw a potential human investment and was acting to protect it. More probably, he was out to humiliate the bishops.[16] By stepping in to protect Wyclif he was simply rubbing their noses in the fact of his political dominance. His move was, in fact, a misjudgement, as the London mob rioted against him and his supporters – not, one suspects, from any especial resentment against Wyclif, of whose teachings they probably knew next to nothing, nor even from any deep sympathy with the clergy, but from a simple hatred of John of Gaunt and his arrogance, of which this episode was such an egregious display.

Over the next few years, Wyclif enjoyed the protection, but not the patronage, of the Court. Although he can hardly be seen as a policy-maker or a royal councillor, the extremism of his views had its uses. Nobody put Wyclif in any kind of position where he could do real damage, but he was allowed to air his views at opportune moments, acting in effect as a stalking-horse for more moderate policies. Having a Wyclif around helped concentrate the minds of the bishops on the fiscal needs of the Crown. At no point in the 1370s or 1380s did any magnate or councillor show any support for Wyclif's policy of radical expropriation of the clergy. Wyclif had no political career, although he was not without political significance.

Wyclif's opponents may have been stymied in England, but were having more success at the curia. Adam Easton procured from Gregory XI a bull of 22 May 1377 condemning a series of 19 propositions extracted from Wyclif's De civili dominio – 11 of them also cited in Easton's own treatise on ecclesiastical power.[17] Further bulls instructed the English bishops to ascertain whether Wyclif really held these views, and if so, whether he was prepared to recant them. In the meantime, after the accession of Richard II in June, Wyclif himself provided occasional advice on ecclesiastical issues at the government's request. He produced a trenchant memorandum against papal taxation of the Church of England, apparently for a 'great council' (a body something between a parliament and the King's Council, at which bishops and lords supplemented the usual councillors). As the memorandum reiterates many of his contentious teachings, the council was probably the occasion on which Thomas Brinton, Bishop of Rochester, told him that his teachings had already been condemned in Rome.[18] This might explain why at the end of the memorandum there is a note that the council enjoined Wyclif to keep silent upon the matters discussed in it. The papal bulls seem to have arrived later that year, and to have been promptly leaked to Wyclif, for he dashed off a brief response, which he circulated at the parliament (presumably that of autumn 1377).[19]

The powerful combination of Wyclif's friends at Court, his support in the university, and the university's resentment at external interference meant that the measures against him could not be implemented. When the papal bull reached Oxford just before Christmas 1377, confusion reigned over what to do about it. Although the vice-chancellor put Wyclif under house arrest, his supporters, perhaps with backing from the Court, soon obtained his release. Under pressure from the Pope, the bishops summoned Wyclif before them a second time in March 1378. But proceedings were again impeded by secular intervention, this time in the form of a message from the young King's mother, Princess Joan, delivered by Sir Lewis Clifford.[20] This secured Wyclif's release, and before the curia was able to react to this setback, proceedings against Oxford's hottest intellectual property ran into a far more serious obstacle: the Great Schism. Gregory XI died in 1378, and his successor, Urban VI, promptly alienated enough of his cardinals to permit the election of a plausible alternative, Clement VII, who established a rival papal curia back at Avignon. The French associations of the Avignon papacy made it almost inevitable that England would line up behind the Roman claimant, and the mere fact of schism took the immediate pressure off Wyclif. Both pontiffs had more important things to do than deal with dissident Oxford dons.

The papal condemnation of his views was the turning-point in Wyclif's career. Although John of Gaunt continued to afford him some protection, the condemnation seems to have terminated his limited political usefulness. The one exception to this came later that year, when, at the invitation of Simon Burley (the King's tutor), Wyclif appeared before the House of Commons to justify a breach of sanctuary committed at Westminster Abbey by royal agents.[21] Here, one suspects that the Crown's hand was forced. What other English theologian could have been persuaded to mount a public defence of such a flagrant breach of church custom and taboo? But Wyclif was by this time out on a limb, and had nothing to lose by publicly espousing a cause with which his theological principles in any case predisposed him to sympathise.

In the meantime, theological opposition to Wyclif hardened in 1378 as he suddenly began to speak out against transubstantiation, the papacy, and the mendicant friars. His views were condemned by a commission of Oxford theologians over the winter of 1380–81, but, characteristically, he responded in May with a trenchant justification of his teaching.[22] It was the Peasants' Revolt of June 1381 which made his position untenable. The commonplace connection between heresy and sedition (to which Wyclif himself subscribed) was invoked, and his teachings were made the scapegoat for the rising – rather ironically, given the high view of royal authority which he voiced in his *De officio regis* (1379). He seems to have left Oxford shortly afterwards, and spent the rest of his life in retirement at his Lutterworth parsonage. Things went from bad to worse in 1382 when William Courtenay, prominent in the attacks on Wyclif back in 1377, became Archbishop of Canterbury. Courtenay summoned a church council at the London Blackfriars in May 1382, and this body formulated a sweeping condemnation of Wyclif's doctrines. This may have precipitated his stroke – his curate later recalled that Wyclif had been paralysed for the last two years of his life. He seems to have agreed to moderate his language, and in return to have been allowed a peaceful retirement. Some have seen in this remarkably restrained treatment of a heretic the last dividend of John of Gaunt's 'good lordship'. It may equally have been the tentative approach of an ecclesiastical hierarchy reluctant to proceed to extremes against a man who, for all his eccentricities, was very much one of their own in a situation for which there was no local precedent. Wyclif's uncharacteristic readiness to compromise, however, did not last. Whatever the physical effects of his stroke, he continued to write, or dictate, strident manifestos and vitriolic attacks on his opponents. These embittered, obsessive, and repetitive documents are deeply apocalyptic, yet his was the sort of apocalypticism which expects persecution rather than anticipates paradise. Judging by his productivity, he must have been active until the moment when, on 28 December 1384, a second stroke deprived him of the power of speech and led to his death three days later.

Wyclif's Philosophy

Although the doctrines which were to leave their mark upon English history were worked out only in the twilight of Wyclif's career, his ideas were always distinctive. His abrupt descent into heresy from about 1378 needs to be understood in the context of the philosophical principles to which he was wedded, as well as of his personal circumstances. Gregory XI's judgement against him, followed by Gregory's death and the succession of Urban, evoked an apocalyptic response from Wyclif, which explains the sudden tautening of his theological bowstrings at this point.[23] The death of the Pope who had so recently condemned him seemed like a providential vindication: 'Blessed be the Bridegroom of the Church', he wrote, 'who has slain Gregory XI and scattered his accomplices, whose crimes have been exposed to the Church by Urban VI.'[24] Encouraged, Wyclif briefly hoped to win over Pope Urban, but the ensuing schism between rival popes at Rome and Avignon was to him a sign and an opportunity: a sign that the papacy's authority in the Church was spurious; and an opportunity not only to continue teaching despite the condemnation, but also to pursue the implications of his philosophical principles in directions which papal canon law had hitherto closed off. Wyclif himself testifies to the impact of these events on his theological development: 'Blessed be the God of truth', he wrote of the schism in about 1379, 'who ordained this dissension so that the truth of this faith might shine forth.'[25]

In order to understand his later theology, it is essential to grasp the nature of his philosophy. Wyclif himself was convinced that true philosophy was a prerequisite for sound theology, and in a late work, the *Opus evangelicum* (1384), he laid down five principles that he considered essential for the proper understanding of scripture:

(i)   a knowledge of 'universals' (the 'logic of holy scripture');
(ii)   an understanding of 'accidents';
(iii)   a proper understanding of the 'eternity' of God, that is, a realisation that God exists 'outside' time, so that past and future are to him the same as present;
(iv)   that all created things exist eternally in the mind of God; and
(v)   therefore that all created things are, in their 'essence', everlasting and unchanging (even if their material forms, their 'accidents', are not).[26]

Wyclif's five principles are phrased in technical terms which require a little elucidation if his theological position is to be understood today. Medieval philosophy was deeply concerned with the problems of existence and knowledge. There were, broadly, two schools of thought about these problems. 'Realists' (a somewhat confusing name in the light of twentieth-century understandings of realism) held that things existed because they shared or 'participated' in some underlying and ultimate reality (an 'idea' or 'universal'), an ideal model of a thing, to which all particular examples of that thing were mere approximations: earthly photocopies, as it were, of heavenly originals. This was essentially the 'metaphysics' (understanding of reality) taught by Plato. 'Nominalists', however, following (and developing) Aristotle's critique of Plato, denied the reality of these 'universals', and maintained instead that there were only things, which were known to the human intellect by a process of 'abstraction' from sensory data (or 'accidents', another term with a meaning totally different from its modern usage). Thus whereas for 'realists', all chairs were imperfect copies of an ultimate and eternal chair; for nominalists, all chairs were different. The dominant philosophy at Oxford, in which Wyclif was brought up, was nominalism. But Wyclif reacted against this and became a vociferous exponent of 'realism'. His affiliation to a minority philosophical school probably does much to explain his combativeness.

Along with other Christian theologians (such as St Augustine) who espoused 'realism', John Wyclif regarded 'universals' or 'ideas' as existing eternally in the mind of God.[27] Real things were for Wyclif metaphysical 'substances' which derived their reality from sharing in the 'ideas' or 'universals' conceived in the mind of God, and therefore themselves shared the eternity of those 'ideas'. These things were made known to the human intellect by means of their 'accidents' (properties and dimensions, in our terms), which were perceived by the senses. These 'accidents' had no reality in themselves: they were simply the ways in which real things were manifested to the senses. Human minds were able to know things by receiving illumination from the mind of God. Thus human knowledge itself was a sort of sharing or participation in the ultimate and perfect knowledge of God.

The Bible

Wyclif's affiliation to a minority school in philosophy may have made him a maverick, but it did not make him a heretic. However, his philosophy was intimately and explicitly connected with his theology, and thus with his heresy, because of his profound conviction that his philosophical views were not only endorsed, but exclusively taught by the Bible and were essential to understanding it. This is the true significance of one of his catchphrases, the 'logic of holy scripture'. He was not speaking in some metaphorical way about the message of scripture. He meant quite literally that the Bible endorsed a particular school of logic – realism – and thus condemned the nominalist logic of the schools.[28] He first seems to have made this link between logic and scripture around 1370, at the time he was turning his attention from the arts to theology. His sense of the biblical character of his philosophy helps explain why he came to see his move from nominalism to 'realism' in terms of a religious conversion: 'Blessed be God, who has freed us from the superficial snares of words in order to direct our mind's eye to penetrate to their meaning.'[29]

Wyclif's biblicism, which became evident in his determination to lecture upon almost the entire Bible (a project which occupied him for much of the time from 1370 to 1376[30]) was extreme, even by the standards of the Middle Ages. In the early days, he espoused a naive literalism about the sacred texts, which was based on his Platonic concept of eternal ideas (in his view, the Bible was one of those ideas). This gave him serious problems. One of his earliest opponents, John Kenningham, impaled him on an obvious dilemma with a question about the truth-value of a lie recorded in the Bible, and then laughingly doubted that he would turn the other cheek if he was struck in the face.[31] In his later writings, Wyclif mitigated his naive literalism, but still maintained that the Bible, as the purest expression of God's mind to the human race, contained all truth, as much in matters of logic or philosophy as in matters of faith and morals, and consequently that nothing could qualify as truth unless it could be ascertained from the Bible. Wyclif's mature views on scriptural authority and interpretation were developed in his *De veritate sacrae scripturae* (1378), the first of his books to diverge dramatically from traditional theology. Here he brought his concept of the 'logic of Holy Scripture' on to a more public stage.

Wyclif's sense of the peculiar authority of scripture was well adapted to fourteenth-century England, which, as M. T. Clanchy has shown, was, irrespective of actual literacy levels, now thoroughly imbued in the public sphere with the values of a literate culture.[32] That cast of mind which in secular affairs gave written law and documentation moral priority over custom and memory would be open in spiritual matters to the preference of the scriptures, the written word of God, over the oral tradition and custom of the Church. 'No law, act, or document is valid unless authorised by the Bible', Wyclif announced in 1375.[33] The legalistic phraseology of his claim is a perfect illustration of the lawyerly mentality which had already done so much to promote literacy in England. Farr has argued for Wyclif's wide, if at times shallow, knowledge of the English common-law tradition, and for its influence on many aspects of his practical reform programme.[34] Wyclif's doctrine could hardly have been conceived, let alone promulgated, in a society which had not attained the degree of respect, at least in theory, for literacy and written law which characterised fourteenth-century England. One might also remark on the poetic justice by which Wyclif's doctrine ascribed such authority in ecclesiastical affairs to the king, given that the rise of the literate, legalistic culture on which his teaching depended was itself largely a product of or response to royal government. It is worth noting in this context that the Lollards' favourite English term for the scriptures was the 'law of God' – a term which soon achieved wider currency, but which the Lollards popularised.

Lordship in Grace

Theories of being and knowledge and eternity might prove controversial within the university, and a high view of the role of scripture might excite debate, but Wyclif's radical ideas took on a broader significance only when they moved out of the realm of pure philosophy into that of theology. His lifelong opponent, the Franciscan friar William Woodford, had (among others) attacked some of Wyclif's views as early as 1373. But it was only in 1376, when Wyclif published his doctrine of 'dominion in grace', of what we would call ownership and rights, that bitter controversy flared up. Given the inseparability of the administration of justice from the possession of landed property in medieval society, and thus in Wyclif's analysis, it is more appropriate to call his doctrine 'lordship in grace'. For it was definitely medieval lordship which was in Wyclif's mind as he constructed his arguments. His view of justice was that the 'just' was that which accorded with the will of God, the immutable exemplar of justice. Accepting, like all scholastics, the Aristotelian definition of justice as rendering to each their due,[35] his conclusion was that God willed each to have their due: reward for the virtuous and retribution for the vicious. Every right to a thing was a right through which God ordained that the thing should be held or possessed.[36] It therefore followed that God could not will to reward the sinful by granting them goods. This would stand, in Wyclif's view, neither with divine truthfulness nor with divine immutability. As the sinner is a person who resists God's will,[37] any goods held by a sinful person are held against God's will, which means that they are held illegally. Those in the wrong have no rights: every sinner is a thief.[38]

Although this doctrine figured in all condemnations of Wycliff-ism, it never made any impact at the political or the popular level. This is rather surprising, in that a theory as radical as this might seem to undermine all human property rights. The explanation lies in the fact, pointed out by R. L. Poole over a century ago, and recently endorsed by J. I. Catto, that Wyclif's theory of lordship in grace was worked out with a very specific purpose in mind: to justify the right of the state to tax and even to confiscate church property.[39] Although in 1376 he cautiously limited the power of expropriation to circumstances in which either the Church was abusing its property or the obligations of ownership were dis-tracting the clergy from their evangelical mission, the idea that ownership as such distracted the clergy from their mission and contravened the will of Christ lurks just beneath the surface. The idea that the clergy should abstain from involvement in temporal affairs and administration is explicit, and canon law is criticised to the extent that it upholds ecclesiastical property and forbids kings to interfere with it. The theory of lordship in grace is simply the theological infrastructure for the polemic. However, in common with most medieval theologians, Wyclif regards the injunction and example of poverty which Christ gave to his disciples as an 'evangelical counsel' or a 'counsel of perfection' rather than as an absolute commandment or precept. This meant that it was not morally binding, but that those who aspired after a greater spiritual perfection in this life (notably the clergy) should be more inclined to observe it.

As with other aspects of his thought, so too with respect to ecclesiastical property Wyclif's ideas were transformed by the apocalyptic combination of his condemnation by Gregory XI, that Pope's death, and the subsequent papal schism. For in the *De ecclesia*, published in 1379, he came down far more firmly against ecclesiastical property. In the context of an argument which sets out to show that occasional almsgiving is more meritorious than 'perpetual alms' (the legal convention which both described and justified the endowment of the Church), he bases his case on an argument from the Old Testament, where it was frequently laid down that the priests of Israel were to have no hereditary possessions, but were to be supported by the tithes and offerings of the people.[40] If the priests of the Old Law were forbidden from holding property, he argues, then *a fortiori* the priests of the New Testament (who must be more perfect than those of the Old) should hold themselves still more aloof from earthly riches. He goes on to exhort the clergy to poverty and self-denial in imitation of Christ, his apostles, and the primitive Church, tracing all the evils of the contemporary Church to worldliness and seeing the renunciation of worldly wealth and power by the Church as the condition of healing the schism.[41] Wyclif's absolute argument against the 'civil dominion' of the clergy, primarily directed against the exercise of temporal power, elides into an argument against the 'lordship' of the clergy, interpreted as a matter of landholding – reasonable enough, given the intimate connection between landholding and power. By the time that he composed his *Trialogus* (1382–83), his views had hardened further. Property is now inextricably entangled with temporal business, from which the clergy must abstain. Endowment of the Church is contrary to the ordinance of Christ; temporal lords who offer it sin gravely, as do clergy who accept it; and expropriation of the Church is now a moral obligation which the king and his subjects infringe by failing to fulfil.[42]

Predestination and Necessity

One of Wyclif's most notorious doctrines was that everything which happens, happens by absolute necessity. He stated this so flatly and repeated it so often that it is hardly surprising that his own contemporaries and later scholars took him to be denying human free will.[43] However, as Anthony Kenny has shown, Wyclif's teaching on predestination was expressed in conventional scholastic terms, and was not vastly different from that of Thomas Aquinas.[44] His doctrine has been misunderstood because of his idiosyncratic use of accepted terminology. His use of 'absolute necessity' reflected his insistence on the eternity and immutability of God and of the divine ideas of created things (the third and fourth of his basic principles of sound theology). As God always knows everything, even what is humanly speaking in the future, whatever happens must do so in accordance with God's knowledge, otherwise God would be wrong (which is impossible by definition). Therefore, as things cannot possibly be otherwise than God foresees them, Wyclif talks of 'absolute necessity'.[45] However, in his earlier writings Wyclif qualified this doctrine by spelling out the compatibility of human free will with this predestined necessity, making it pretty much what other scholastics (such as Aquinas) tended to call 'conditional necessity'. In his later writings, Wyclif frequently reiterates his doctrine of 'absolute necessity', only occasionally and briefly qualifying it. Nevertheless, he clearly states that God does not necessitate sin, that free will is essential to the concept of sin, and that human free will is compatible with divine predestination.[46]

Wyclif, like Aquinas before him and Calvin after, stood firmly in the Augustinian tradition of Christian theology, which laid considerable emphasis on divine predestination. But his teaching did not anticipate the Calvinist doctrine of 'double predestination' (i.e., that God symmetrically predestines the elect to heaven and the damned to hell). Wyclif followed the medieval consensus in distinguishing God's 'predestination' of the 'elect' to heaven from his 'foreknowledge' (*praescientia*) of the punishment of the 'reprobate' in hell. The point of this distinction was to justify the claim that the salvation of the elect was entirely due to divine action while the fate of the damned was entirely their own fault and not to be blamed on God. Thus God actively intervened to save the elect, but passively permitted the damned to bring about their own destruction. Likewise, rather than anticipating the Calvinist doctrine that the elect attain a certainty in this life of their own election and salvation, Wyclif held, with Augustine and the medieval consensus, that even among the elect, only a few would ever attain such certainty, and then only by a special revelation.[47]

The Church

What was distinctive about Wyclif's doctrine of predestination was the way he applied it to the definition of the Church. In his view, the Church was the congregation not of the faithful, but of those predestined to salvation. His doctrine of divine ideas made the traditional view of the Church on earth ('Church militant') as a mixture of saints and sinners quite untenable. As an eternal divine idea, the true Church could not change or admit within itself any impurity. His doctrine of divine immutability led him to the same conclusion. God always loves the Church, and as he is immutable, the Church which he loves must always be the same (otherwise God's love would change with every change in the Church). Because, after the end of the world, the Church will consist exclusively of the elect, so even before the end, the elect must, in fact, be the true Church which God loves. Thus Wyclif had to confine the Church to those predestined to eternal life. The 'foreknown' who would incur eternal damnation could never be members of the true Church, although they might appear to be its members, or even its ministers, in this life.[48] Given Wyclif's adherence to the scholastic commonplace that nobody could know whether or not they were predestined to salvation, the corollary of his definition was that in this life nobody could know whether or not they were really members of the Church. As the medieval organisation of society was based on the idea that the Church was a visible institution, and Wyclif's theory made the

true Church invisible, his theory had immense potential consequences for the medieval Church.

The impossibility of ever identifying the Church or its members
left no room for autonomous spiritual authority within it. If the
'foreknown' did not belong to the Church, they could scarcely
legislate for it in matters of faith and morals. And if not even the
elect could be sure that they were members of the true Church,
neither could they be sure that they were rightfully exercising any
authority (spiritual or temporal) of which they seemed to be
possessed. Moreover, Wyclif's doctrine of lordship in grace made
any putative authority utterly insecure. If a bishop, or even a pope,
was in a state of mortal sin, he was for the time being deprived of
all rightful authority, and was therefore incapable of lawfully
exercising any teaching office even if such an office really existed.
Wyclif's theology thus undermined any kind of hierarchy in the
Church, and tended instead to favour the 'charismatic' model of
leadership – indeed, the thrust of his theology curiously anticipates
the modern distinction between 'charismatic' and 'hierarchical'
leadership drawn by Max Weber. Authority within this understanding of the Church becomes a mere adjunct of grace. Hence
the common Wycliffite and Lollard argument that the true vicar
of Christ on earth, the true pope, could be none other than the
holiest – that is, the most Christ-like – person on earth, irrespective
of sex, rank, or state of life.

The 'tradition' of the Church, which had long been so powerful
in Catholicism, was completely overturned by this theology. For
the notion of tradition depended on notions of authority and
succession, especially among the bishops. But if neither the true
Church nor its spokesmen could be identified with certainty, the
concept of the institutional Church as the guardian and authoritative interpreter of scripture, the arbiter of doctrinal disputes,
was vacuous. Canon law and the writings of the fathers, the accumulated wisdom of the Church through the ages, were at once
stripped of binding authority. Scripture alone remained as the
reliable and sufficient rule of Christian faith and life – a conclusion
at which Wyclif had, in any case, already arrived by other means.
Although he continued to cite the early fathers and even medieval
authorities when he felt it useful, by 1378 he had lost confidence
in both tradition and the visible Church as reliable vehicles of
truth.[49]

The Papacy

Wyclif's rejection of official Church authority, inspired by that authority's condemnation of his doctrines in 1377, was taken further in the *De potestate pape* (1379), in which he took up the now familiar medieval dissident identification of the papacy with Antichrist. His adoption of this theme may have resulted from the Great Schism, which perhaps inspired apocalyptic imaginings. It came to a climax in the final section of his *Opus evangelicum*, a section also known as the *De antichristo*.[50] Before 1377, Wyclif had recognised papal primacy in spiritual affairs even as he had maintained the subordination of popes to kings in temporal affairs.[51] As late as the *De ecclesia* (1378–79), he conceded a vestigial primacy to the Pope.[52] Peter always remained for him 'the prince of the apostles', and he could still praise certain popes (e.g. Nicholas IV, who had taken the Franciscan side in the controversy over evangelical poverty). But any primacy was clearly 'charismatic' rather than 'hierarchical': if a pope was to be praised, it was as a good Christian, rather than as the incumbent of a divinely sanctioned office.[53] Once Wyclif had become disenchanted with the papacy, his doctrines of predestination and lordship in grace combined to produce powerful arguments against papal claims. If only those in a state of grace could rightfully exercise authority, then a sinful pope (in other words, a pope with whom Wyclif disagreed) had no valid jurisdiction. And if only those who were predestined were really members of the Church, and there was no way to identify the predestined in this life, then no one could ever be sure that an elected pope was even a member of the Church, let alone its earthly head.

Faith and Salvation

Wyclif's emphasis on scripture and predestination have a great deal to do with the abiding perception of him as a forerunner of the Protestant Reformation of the sixteenth century. It is therefore especially important to realise that in his theology of salvation, Wyclif deviated but little from the scholastic consensus of the medieval Church. First and foremost in this was an understanding of the New Testament as law, the 'lex Christi' or 'law of God', an understanding revealed in the commonest Wycliffite synonym for scripture, 'law of God'. For Wyclif, as for the scholastics, Christianity was a new law which ordered human behaviour towards the gaining of eternal life, with grace being granted to people in order to enable them to live according to that law. Wyclif did not reckon that one could be certain of one's own predestination barring a special reve-lation. One could hope, but not know.[54] Wyclif also agreed with the scholastics (against the later Reformers) that the Command-ments were not impossible for people to observe.[55] He accepted the scholastic understanding of faith as a habit (implicit faith) expressed where possible or appropriate as an act (explicit faith). For all his deviations from the scholastic consensus, Wyclif still worked within the scholastic intellectual universe. Where Luther would later seek to eliminate any possibility of human cooperation in salvation, Wyclif continued to see the individual's salvation in terms of a cooperation between divine grace and human good works, even if the action of grace was primary and indispensable.

The Eucharist

As we have already observed, the effect of the papal condemnation of Wyclif and of Wyclif's consequent repudiation of papal spiritual authority was to loosen the restraint of canon law on the working through in theology of his philosophical principles. This led almost at once to a dramatic break with both church teaching and popular piety over the eucharist. His denial of the doctrine of transubstantiation, which he announced for the first time in his treatise *De eucharistia* (1379–80), was a stab at the heart of late medieval Catholicism, which focused above all on the 'Corpus Christi', the body of Christ made really present under the out-ward appearance of bread whenever a priest consecrated bread with Christ's words, 'This is my body.' Wyclif's denial of this central doctrine, and his consequent critique of much religious practice dependent on it (he criticised the feast of Corpus Christi itself[56]), soon became the defining feature of his heresy, not least for his enemies, who found it easy ground on which not only to secure his formal condemnation, but also to isolate him from popular sym-pathy. But Wyclif himself acknowledged and indeed asserted the critical significance of the controversy over eucharistic doctrine, although he also alleged that his opponents were motivated in their condemnation of his eucharistic doctrine by the desire to punish him for his attacks on religious orders and ecclesiastical endowments.[57]

Transubstantiation – the miraculous process by which the 'substance' of bread was inwardly transformed into the real body of Christ despite retaining all the 'accidents' (appearances and physical qualities) of bread – had quickly been spotted as something of a problem for Wyclif's philosophical principles. In the early 1370s John Kenningham had tried to refute those principles by arguing that they logically required a denial of transubstantiation. Wyclif himself, while resolutely affirming transubstantiation, was already troubled by the concept of accidents surviving without their original substance,[58] and in one of his early writings he promised to deal with the problem fully at a later date.[59] Yet his complete orthodoxy on the eucharist in the early 1370s is evident not least in the total absence of the issue from the papal condemnation of 1377. As Paul Strohm has recently pointed out, the psychological importance and technical complexity of eucharistic theology made it easy ground on which to convict an enemy of heresy.[60] Had Wyclif been vulnerable on this ground in 1377, his enemies would never have allowed his eucharistic views to escape censure in Gregory XI's bulls. As transubstantiation enjoyed the support not only of a general council of the Church, but also of the only scholastic for whom Wyclif had any real respect, Aquinas, it is hardly surprising that he felt no urge to challenge the consensus of the Church upon this issue.

It was only in the wake of his condemnation by the papacy that Wyclif was led to reconsider his position on the eucharist. By condemning him and his views on lordship in grace, the papacy had revealed itself as the tool of Antichrist, and in the apocalyptic scenario which this entailed, the visible Church, corrupted and enslaved by Antichrist through its endowment with property, ceased to be an authoritative teacher. Thus any restraints on the development of Wyclif's theology were removed. In his *De eucharistia*, Wyclif finally examined the theology of the eucharist in the light of his basic principles, though surely in a far more radical way than he could ever have expected.[61] The views which he laid out in the *De eucharistia* were to be reiterated, reformulated, expanded, modified, and defended in a number of later works, notably the

De apostasia (late 1380) and the *Trialogus* (1382–83), but they were
never to be retracted or fundamentally altered.

In his writings on the eucharist, Wyclif devotes far more space
to refuting the teachings of his opponents than he does to establishing and explaining his own.[62] His main problem with the official
doctrine was one of which orthodox theologians were well aware.
Thomas Aquinas had formulated it as the main objection in his
own discussion of transubstantiation. The problem was that of
'accidents without a subject'. 'Accidents' were not thought to have
any reality in themselves, but were thought to be inherent qualities
of 'substances', based in subjects in such a way that the mind, by
perceiving the accidents, could intuitively know the presence of
the underlying subject. In the case of a consecrated host, however,
these accidents could not be inherent in the substance of Christ's
body, unless people were prepared to say that Christ was small,
round, and white. As they were not inherent in the bread (which
had been transformed into Christ's body), the accidents were left
hanging. And this was impossible according to the Aristotelian
physics which provided the terms of the discussion. Orthodox
theologians blandly parried this thrust by invoking God's omni-
potence: the survival of the accidents without a subject was a miracle.
For Wyclif, however, the notion of accidents without a subject was
not just *practically*, but *logically* impossible. All theologians agreed
that what was *logically* impossible (e.g. a 'square triangle', i.e., a
'three-sided plane figure with four sides') was impossible even for
God. In Wyclif's view, accidents without a subject were impossible
by definition, logically impossible.[63] He had many other specific
objections to transubstantiation. But the problem of accidents
without a subject threatened his entire view of reality. To suggest that
there was not really any bread where the roundness and whiteness
of a consecrated host indicated that there was bread amounted in
his view to making God a liar, and tended to make people doubt
the evidence of their senses. As the roundness and whiteness
certainly did not belong to the body of Christ, it was far from clear
what they actually were. Hence the question with which he liked
to tease his opponents: 'What is the round white thing?'[64]

Wyclif played endless variations upon these themes, but was
rather less forthcoming about his own interpretation of the eucharist. And he had a problem. If God could not be made a liar by the
doctrine of transubstantiation, neither could Christ have been lying

when he said, 'This is my body.' But if the eucharistic bread was still what it looked like, namely bread, how could he have been telling the truth? Unfortunately, Wyclif's answer is far from clear, and understanding it is impeded not only by his own recondite phraseology, but also by recent misunderstandings of what he was trying to do when he maintained that Christ's words were true. His insistence on this last point has led several commentators to conclude that he shared with his opponents a basic belief in the 'real presence' of Christ in the sacrament of the eucharist.[65] In fact, Wyclif maintained (still more confusingly) that it was his opponents who did not really accept the truth of Christ's words. And he himself could only insist on the truth of the words 'This is my body' by introducing a special new sense for the word 'is' in that sentence. This sense he described variously as 'habitudinal being', 'habitudinal predication', and 'respective denomination'. What the long words meant was that the bread remained bread in reality, but that it was Christ's body according to its signification, its power, and its effects.

Once Wyclif had jettisoned transubstantiation, he found himself not only heading for a new clash with the Church authorities, but also challenging broad swathes of religious practice. He took issue, for example, with the popular concept of 'seeing God' which was the focal point of the eucharist in everyday religion. The idea that witnessing the elevation of consecrated host at the mass was 'seeing their maker' was (although theologically suspect even in official terms) ingrained in popular culture.[66] Wyclif's insistence that the host was still mere bread, and that Christ's presence was a matter of grace rather than substance, made nonsense of this popular practice and language. His attack on eucharistic practice also sat well with his attack on ecclesiastical property.[67] In Wyclif's day, the main reason for adding to the endowments of the Church was to finance the celebration of Mass for the benefit of the souls of the dead. He was now able to identify doctrinal error about the eucharist as a theological counterpart to moral error about ecclesiastical property.

Sacraments and Signs

In his *Trialogus*, Wyclif enumerates the customary seven sacraments of the Church. However, the importance he attached to predestination as the sole condition of Church membership meant that the role of the sacraments in his theology was greatly reduced. From being in themselves the means of delivering grace and salvation to the faithful, they become mere signs of that grace, valid only for the elect. In effect, only the predestined really receive sacraments, and only predestined priests can really administer them. He sees the sacraments as not absolutely necessary, compared with faith, and points out the danger in caring more for signs than for the signified.[68] In his latter years, Wyclif came to see the ritual profusion of late medieval Catholicism as a burden, and warned that the Church was overburdened with signs and rituals, especially by friars. This critique threatened the whole sacramental system around which the ritual life of the medieval Church was constructed.

Wyclif accepted the unarguably scriptural basis of baptism, but blurred both the medieval emphasis on its absolute necessity for salvation and the traditional view that it cleansed from all sin. Both these tendencies reflect his doctrine of predestination, as he reckoned that the predestined would be saved irrespective of receiving baptism in water, while the reprobate could not possibly benefit from it.[69] Above all, where for the medieval Church baptism was what made people members of the Church, for Wyclif this function was fulfilled exclusively by predestination. With respect to confirmation, he questioned both its necessity and the episcopal monopoly on administering it. He was deeply sceptical of the scriptural foundation for the sacrament of 'extreme unction' (anointing with holy oil, mostly administered to those on the point of death), and certainly did not regard it as necessary, though conceding that it might be a sacrament when administered by a worthy priest to one of the elect. Marriage he regarded as a sacrament ordained for the lawful procreation of the human race, but he endorsed the traditional preference for virginity over matrimony, holding that it was more certain of God's blessing and that God did not really join together all those who went through the formalities of a wedding.[70]

On the sacrament of confession or penance Wyclif had rather more to say, albeit mostly in a polemical vein. His emphasis on the importance and inscrutability of predestination renders the medieval practice of auricular confession almost redundant, and certainly far from compulsory (though he allows that it can be helpful in particular cases). Contrition alone can secure forgiveness, but only the elect can be truly contrite. There is no need for confession to a priest, because neither priests nor anyone else can tell who is predestined, and thus who is truly contrite; nor, even among the contrite, could they possibly know how guilty and how contrite they were. Only Christ could truly absolve, and therefore priestly absolution was a devilish and blasphemous presumption. Even when it is useful, confession can be made just as well to a layperson or to God. Wyclif's hostility to auricular confession in practice was exacerbated by what he saw as its exploitation for immoral purposes and financial gain, as well as by its association with the friars.[71] The friars had not only worked out most of the theology of the sacrament, but dominated its administration, especially among prominent sectors of society such as the gentry and the urban elites. The sacrament was therefore crucial to their social standing and influence.

Wyclif's understanding of the Christian life retained a place for a special priesthood set apart by sacramental ordination, even though his doctrines on confession and communion massively reduced the sense of sacred power inhering in priests, who could no longer forgive sins or bring about Christ's physical presence on earth. But Wyclif's vision of priesthood was of an elite of virtue rather than power, a select group of Christians distinguished from the laity by a more faithful imitation of Christ and a deeper knowledge of the Christian law laid down in the scriptures. Priests were above all to preach, and to practise what they preached by living lives of poverty and service. Neither marrying nor holding property, they were to be free of the web of worldliness which entangled the laity. Basing his argument on scripture, Wyclif emphasises that in the early Church there were only two orders: priests and deacons. 'Bishop' was for him just another word for 'priest'. He recommends abolishing the lesser orders (such as subdeacons and acolytes),[72] and disapproves equally of the higher ranks, such as archdeacons and cardinals. Hierarchy itself is for Wyclif a symptom of the corruption of the Church by endowment and thus by avarice and ambition, and his treatise *De blasphemia* (late 1381) is among other things an extended polemic against the entire Church hierarchy. There is for him no distinction within the priesthood, neither of jurisdiction (priests should have none) nor of sacramental power. All priests are equal, and any priest can

administer any scriptural sacrament.[73] Wyclif even anticipates the
later Protestant doctrine of the priesthood of all believers
(although in his case it would be better termed the 'priesthood of
the predestined'): 'all holy men and women who are members of
Christ's body are priests'.[74] But this was not as radical as it sounds.
The only sacrament he allowed laymen or women to administer
was baptism, in an emergency – a concession which simply endorsed
the custom of the medieval Church.[75] Wyclif upheld St Paul's
prohibition on women preaching, which eliminated them from
any public ministry.[76] His priesthood of the predestined was
mystical rather than ministerial.

Christian Life

Wyclif's rejection of transubstantiation set him on a collision
course with the friars, who had done more than anyone else to
make that doctrine the official teaching of the Church. Worsening
relations with the friars are evident in the *De eucharistia* and *De
symonia* (early 1380), while the *De apostasia* puts them beyond the
pale.[77] Earlier in his career, he had enjoyed some support from
friars, who had their own traditions of writing on evangelical
poverty. But, from 1379, they stood in his eyes as perpetrators of a
gross blasphemy and promoters of a new idolatry. Even more
than the papacy (with which he sees them as being in an unholy
league[78]), they are the target of his abuse, charged with ambition,
avarice, hypocrisy, heresy, and schism – in short, with substituting
a religion of their own for that of Christ. Wyclif's later works, especially those written after his retirement from Oxford, are bulked
out with seething abuse of the friars. The friars are blamed for
preaching Despenser's crusade to Flanders in 1383, for calling it
heresy to translate scripture into English, for preaching transubstantiation, for burdening the laity with excessive religious ceremonies, for alienating people from their parish priests, for
abusing confession, and even for an attempt on the life of John of
Gaunt in 1384. Wyclif seeks to portray them as seditious, a *tu
quoque* response to their association of his heresy with the Peasants'
Revolt. He appreciated the importance of their cosy relationship
with the English elite (his opponent William Woodford, for example,
was confessor to Margaret, Countess of Norfolk), and did his best

to undermine it by sheer invective. But in breaking with the friars, Wyclif left himself without any obvious constituency among the clergy, limiting the potential influence of his message. He came to classify the established clergy in four 'sects': the 'Caesarean clergy', that is, secular priests in the political service of the Crown or in possession of land; the monks, who held property and followed the rule of Benedict or its derivatives on it; the canons, who followed the rule of Augustine; and the friars.[79] In effect, he declared war on the entire clergy. His gift was for making enemies, not friends.

Wyclif's doctrine of the Church radically altered the relationship of the faithful with the dead. As only the predestined were true members of the Church, and the decree of predestination was fixed from eternity, there was no point praying for particular individuals: either they were saved or they were damned, and nothing could alter their fate. Hence Wyclif criticised showy funeral rites,[80] and rejected prayer for particular dead people, and indeed for particular living people, arguing that perfect charity had no respect for persons and could therefore not be restricted to preferred individuals. Prayer could only be general, essentially for the coming of God's kingdom and the doing of his will: a surrender to the divine will rather than an attempt to sway it. To pray for a particular person without a direct divine command (such as in the legend of Pope Gregory's prayer for the soul of the Emperor Trajan) was to risk, as it were, trespassing upon God's good will, lèse majesté. The illegitimacy of conventional prayer for the dead was confirmed in Wyclif's eyes by its major role as an inducement to endow the Church.[81] With prayer for the dead all but eliminated, the doctrine of purgatory was radically altered, and that of indulgences ceased to make any sense. Indulgences drew his fire on any number of counts, as they depended on papal authority (and he emphasised that the Pope could not possibly know whether God sanctioned his indulgences), were often rewards for participation in crusade or pilgrimage or other activities of which he disapproved, and were usually preached and distributed by his mortal enemies, the friars. Finally, as even their supporters could find little in the way of direct scriptural evidence for indulgences, it was not difficult for Wyclif to reject them as blasphemy and as 'groundless delusions'.[82] His retention of some concept of purgatory, however, of a purification of the soul after death before admission to paradise, reflected his essentially traditional view of the process of salvation.[83]

Wyclif brought his hermeneutic of suspicion to bear on the cult of the saints which flourished in the fourteenth-century Church. With deliberate irony, he chose the opening sermon in his sequence of sermons for the feast-days of the Church – known as 'sermons on the saints' – to announce his scepticism about canonisation.[84] As it was impossible to say whether any particular persons, other than those vouched for in scripture, were predestined or not, it was close to blasphemy for the Pope to claim to know that some-body had certainly reached heaven. Subsequently, Wyclif argued that as the saints were humble and devoted to God alone even in this life, then, when they had reached heaven, the last thing they would want would be praise and worship addressed to them rather than to God.[85] The cult of relics (which Wyclif perceptively links to the cult of the consecrated eucharistic host), the main-tenance of shrines, and the practice of pilgrimage were dismissed as rituals lacking scriptural foundation. He warns against a blind zeal for relics and the associated commercialism, as well as an excessive trust in miracles. The miracles proclaimed to lend cred-ibility to the cult were dismissed by Wyclif as human or diabolical frauds.[86] He did not entirely rule out the intercession of the saints, but he compared it most unfavourably with the mediation of Christ, and left his readers in little doubt as to his own prefer-ences.[87] The unacceptability of the cult of the saints as a whole was underlined for him by its intimate links with the wealth of the Church, visible as much in the luxuriant decoration of shrines and churches as in the exploitation of pilgrimage as a source of income.

Royalty and Reform

The explosion of creativity in Wyclif's theology in the later 1370s, once the shackles of canon law had been struck from his thinking, had two further important consequences. The first was to erode the traditional distinction between Church and State (or 'kingdom' as he termed it). The second was to convince him that the Church – the organisation of Christian life according to the principles laid out in scripture – was in dire need of reform. When the true

Church had been reduced to the body of the predestined, entirely indeterminable in this world, it effectively lost all those functions of law and government which it usually exercised in medieval society. It needed no legislative power, as Wyclif contended that all the laws needed to regulate Christian life were laid down in the Bible. And it had no public power or authority, partly because its kingdom was not of this world, and partly because nobody could ever be sure that someone claiming to exercise such authority was, in fact, a member of the Church. The collapse of the Church into the kingdom is most evident in Wyclif's analysis of the Church Militant, which he divides not, as canonists would, into 'clergy' and 'laity', but into the traditional tripartite structure of the social order: *oratores*, *bellatores*, and *aratores*; those who pray, those who fight, and those who work.[88]

By thus collapsing the Church into the kingdom, making them not even two aspects of one thing, but simply one thing (his doctrine of lordship in grace meant that social organisation itself was a grace of God, so that lawful social order could only arise in a Christian society), it was inevitable that Wyclif should look to the King as the primary agent of reform. He therefore came up with a version of theocratic kingship in his treatise *De officio regis* (1379), which in one sense looked back to the kingship of the earlier Middle Ages, but in another looked forward to the royal supremacy of the early modern era. It was the king who was to undertake the reform of Christian life by stripping the clergy of their possessions and pretensions. As the Bible laid down all the law that was really necessary to govern a Christian society, the king was of course to be guided in this task by theologians, and was to ensure among other things that the Church produced a steady supply of theologians for this purpose.[89] This royal supremacy before its time was a vision which might well have proved attractive to a strong king anxious to tax the clergy as heavily as possible to pay for his wars. As Michael Wilks has argued, Wyclif's teachings were evidently designed to appeal to the King and indeed to the landed families, as they alone were in a position to promote his reform programme.[90] However, the radical implications of Wyclif's theology for religious life and popular devotion combined in the event with the landed classes' anxieties about social disorder and revolution to ensure that the programme never came anywhere near to being considered practical politics.

The Peasants' Revolt and the Condemnation of Wyclif

If the implications of Wyclif's theology for late medieval Catholicism became apparent to his clerical enemies in 1378, it was
nevertheless some years before his teachings came to be seen as
a threat to society at large. It was in the messy arena of politics,
rather than the rarefied atmosphere of speculative theology, that
Wyclif found himself in deep trouble, thanks to the Peasants'
Revolt of 1381. The display of popular hostility to the regime of
Richard II which convulsed south-eastern England in the summer
of 1381 was on an unprecedented scale. Traditional grievances
about rents had been given a sharper edge by the recent labour
legislation with which the landed classes had sought to escape the
inevitable economic consequences of the Black Death (labour-
shortage meant higher wages).[91] The revolt was by no means
without its religious dimension. Anticlerical agitation and action
were characteristic of such risings, and this was no exception.
Abbeys were attacked and their records destroyed. Priests and
monks were beaten up or even lynched. The rebels murdered
Archbishop Simon Sudbury of Canterbury. The obscure hedge-
priest John Ball was credited with preaching the message of
radical social and economic readjustment in the name of divine
justice behind which the peasants marched.

An ancient and still influential tradition credits Wyclif's ideas
with some responsibility for the Peasants' Revolt. Wycliffites
themselves do not seem to have thought this. Nicholas Hereford
actually tried to persuade the Duke of Lancaster that it was the
preaching of the four orders of friars which had stirred up the
rebels.[92] The suggestion that heresy inevitably entailed sedition
was the most powerful weapon in the hands of the hierarchy for
securing the assistance of the temporal arm against their enemies,
so in this respect the revolt was a godsend. None of the surviving
accounts of the peasants' grievances and demands betrays any dissatisfaction with the religious services offered by the Catholic
Church. There was no sign at all of the Wycliffite critique of the
real presence, the cult of the saints, or pilgrimage. Even the preju-
diced monastic chronicler Thomas Walsingham, who saw the
revolt as a providential judgement on the English elite for their
shameful failure to deal with Wyclif more promptly, failed to
discern any Wycliffite significance in the semi-literate verses and

letters which passed for the manifestos of the rebels: a fact which is equally revealing irrespective of whether these documents were clever parodies by which the peasants expressed their contempt for the literate culture of their oppressors, or crude forgeries by which the authorities expressed their contempt for the illiterate culture of the rebels.[93] This makes it all the more surprising that the hierarchy was able to convince the government that Wyclif's teachings underlay the rebellion. But, as McFarlane argued, the association which was made owed more to the general sense of insecurity which the rebellion aroused in landowners. After such a shock, any threat to the established order of society was likely to call down their wrath. And whatever its putative connection with the Peasants' Revolt, Wyclif's theology certainly promised a radical change to the established order.

Spurred on by attitudes such as Walsingham's to a realisation of their obligations in the wake of the Peasants' Revolt, the bishops summoned a provincial council of the English Church at the London Blackfriars in 1382. This body, assisted by lawyers and theologians from Oxford and Cambridge, delivered a comprehensive condemnation of Wyclif's doctrines. Ironically, it is to the repressive measures which followed the council that we owe most of our knowledge of the real, if limited, diffusion of Wycliffite teachings outside the academic context in which they had been conceived.

3

THE EARLY DIFFUSION OF LOLLARDY

That Wyclif's ideas should have spread beyond the academic environment in which they were originally conceived was far from inevitable. It was not usual for the squabbles of the schools to trouble the outside world. Indeed, the theory that popular heresy was inspired by Wyclif, despite the fact that it was widely held at the time, has been called into question for precisely that reason. J. A. F. Thomson concluded from his work on later Lollardy that the popular heresy was too diverse to be viewed even as a single movement, much less as a movement derived from the teachings of a single theologian.[1] The anti-Wycliffite case depends on counting all dissent as 'lollardy' and then noting that there was a reasonable number of dissenters whose views bear no relation to Wyclif's. There is something to be said for this approach, in that 'lollardy' is nothing more than a synonym for 'heresy' or 'dissent' in the records of this period. However, it is not merely imposing an alien interpretative framework on to the data to observe that there is a larger group of 'lollards' whose views are similar to those of Wyclif and his immediate disciples, who tend to cluster in particular areas, often areas which can in turn be connected with those disciples; and a smaller number of stray individuals, often isolated cases from places far removed from dissident communities and with no known links to Wyclif's disciples, whose views are extremely heterogeneous. The former represent a Wycliffite movement, the latter are eccentrics or misfits fortuitously swept up in the panic over the former.

54

However, recent work on the earliest manifestations of Lollardy, by such scholars as Anne Hudson, Charles Kightly, and A. K. McHardy has tended to endorse the traditional view, which was also upheld by K. B. McFarlane.[2] With every new study, the case looks more secure. Nor should this surprise us. The character of Wyclif's doctrines made them much more likely than most academic theology to propagate outside their cloistered nursery. His teachings were not mere run of the mill speculation about high and dry theological questions: they were challenges to large areas of ecclesiastical and devotional practice. Moreover, Wyclif felt the need to reach a wider audience. He frequently voiced his sense of the importance of taking the message to the people in their own language, and both he and his disciples put that into practice. Although scholars are no longer as ready as they were a century ago to attribute to Wyclif himself the vast array of Wycliffite tracts in English, it is quite likely that he composed some of them and it is quite certain that many others are but translations or paraphrases of his Latin works.[3]

Lollard Preachers

Important though pamphlets and placards were in an age of rising literacy, the primary medium for new ideas was preaching, as it still would be 150 years later for the ideas of the Reformation. The manuscript treatises of Wyclif's time, like their printed counterparts subsequently, could inform, supplement, and consolidate the preaching effort, but could hardly replace it. Wyclif knew the importance of preaching, which he made the primary task of all Christian priests, and not simply of bishops or friars.[4] This was itself a revolutionary view in an age that saw the priest chiefly as a sacramental functionary. The non-preaching priest – by far the most common kind – was to him a contradiction in terms. Wyclif himself was apparently a preacher of some talent. He has left us enough sermons to indicate that preaching was a vocation as well as a principle, though they are preserved in Latin rather than the vernacular. It is perhaps to his preaching rather than to his writing that we should attribute his personal influence. His Latin writings are far from lucid to the uninitiated, couched as they are in an awesomely technical scholastic terminology: it is difficult to envisage them making many converts.[5] The sermons certainly seem more accessible than the treatises. We know that he preached in London in the early 1370s, presumably fulfilling the obligations and satisfying the requirements of his doctorate in theology. However, from the time of his first papal condemnation his direct influence was probably confined to Oxford University. After his enforced retirement to Lutterworth, he continued to pour forth a torrent of pamphlets, aimed especially at the friars, now his bitterest enemies, but as they were still in Latin, they were meant for an academic readership. If Wyclif's ideas did reach out to a wider public, it was through some other channel than the preaching of the doctor himself.

It is impossible to be certain about when Wyclif's radical ideas began to spread outside the university. The earliest independent evidence for Wycliffite preaching to the people comes from early in 1382, but this date so obviously reflects official anxieties stirred up by the Peasants' Revolt that it can tell us nothing about when such preaching started. The Peasants' Revolt of 1381 was an explosion of popular discontent fuelled by the Statute of Labourers (the repressive wage legislation which sought to prevent men benefiting from the labour shortage brought about by the Black Death) and ignited by the imposition of the Poll Tax (a levy on every adult male, irrespective of wealth, raised in order to pay for the failing war in France). The authorities of Church and State were quick to make an association between Wycliffite teaching and popular rebellion. Modern scholarship has not, in fact, detected any such connections: reports and records of the 'ideology' of the rebels show no traces of distinctively Wycliffite doctrines. However, even if the official view of the revolt can be discounted as a characteristically human preference for conspiracy over contingency in political explanation, it is less easy to dismiss the evident belief that Wyclif's ideas had already spread beyond the confines of Oxford. Having finally secured the condemnation of Wyclif's doctrines in May 1382, the authorities managed to sweep up a clutch of leading Wycliffite preachers so promptly as to assure us that they had already been so active as to become notorious.

Sensitised to dissent by the chaos of the previous year, during which the Archbishop of Canterbury had been lynched, the ecclesiastical authorities not only summoned Wyclif to answer before them in 1382, but also pulled in a number of his disciples found preaching around the country, particularly, though not exclusively, in the East Midlands around Leicester (on which Henry Knighton's virtually contemporary *Chronicle* provides fascinating detail). Bishop Buckingham of Lincoln was investigating the Lollards of Leicester by March 1382, before Archbishop Courtenay's provincial council met at Blackfriars in May. Leicester's proximity to Lutterworth (Wyclif's final home) and its contacts with Oxford through Philip Repingdon, a canon of Leicester Abbey, made it fertile ground for the new ideas. Repingdon, John Aston, and John Purvey all seem to have preached there.[6] Nicholas Hereford was preaching at Brackley (between Oxford and Northampton) around April 1382. He, John Aston, Robert Alington, and Lawrence Bedeman (all Oxford graduates) were preaching in northern Hampshire that same year, and Bedeman had already been in trouble for preaching in the Exeter diocese.[7] Cases from the next few years confirm that Oxford graduates were spreading the word. John Corringham, vicar of Diddington (near Huntingdon), abjured Wycliffite teachings in 1384.[8] Nicholas Hereford was preaching as far afield as Nottingham (1386) and Worcestershire in the 1380s, while Aston was at Gloucester (and probably Bristol too) in 1383 and in Worcestershire in 1384.[9] William Thorpe preached at London in 1386, and in northern England at some point in the 1380s. John Purvey was active in Bristol in the 1380s, as was Philip Repingdon around Leicester, notably at Brackley (a living held by his abbey of St Mary's, Leicester).[10] Almost all these dissident preachers can be shown to have had personal contact with Wyclif. The exception, William Swynderby, proves the rule. Swynderby, who was in trouble before Bishop Buckingham of Lincoln for preaching at Leicester in 1382, was not an Oxford graduate, but a well-established local holy man with a considerable popular following. However, a powerful argument has recently been mounted to the effect that it was Philip Repingdon who won him over to the new doctrines.[11] When Swynderby was prosecuted for a second time, in 1391, he was across the country in Hereford, having been active in the meantime throughout the Midlands (specifically around Coventry) and the Marches.

It is thus to the circle of Wyclif's academic disciples in Oxford that we should look for an understanding of the early spread of religious dissent. Such followers as Repingdon, Hereford, Purvey, Aston, and Thorpe gathered around the master in the 1370s (in

1407 Thorpe recalled having been involved with Wyclif's doctrine for 30 years or more).[12] The talented and idealistic young scholars who drank in his words actually went out into the regions and sought to pass on his message to the faithful, as they considered themselves bound to do. This is not to revive the nineteenth-century myth of Wyclif's 'Poor Preachers' with their russet gowns. Nobody now seriously believes that he or his followers established a formal organisation for the propagation of their views, a kind of order of preachers without vows. It is far more likely, as A. K. McHardy has argued, that they simply took advantage of existing ecclesiastical machinery than that they tried to supplant it.[13] Oxford Wycliffites, for example, who were presented by their colleges to benefices around the country could take the master's teachings with them to a wider audience. John Corringham had been presented to the vicarage of Diddington by his Oxford college, Merton, which held the rectory. Another Merton dissident was William James, who was preaching at Bristol in 1395.[14] Yet another fellow of Merton, Thomas Hulman, a supporter of John Aston who was compelled to recant, held the Merton chapel at Kibworth Harcourt (8 miles south-east of Leicester) from 1385 to 1388. In January 1414, when a few hundred aggrieved Lollards gathered in the name of Sir John Oldcastle (a prominent Lollard noble-man) just outside London (an episode sometimes dignified by the appellation revolt or rebellion), this village was among those which despatched a contingent.[15]

Even without such patronage, the graduate priest had great advantages. The graduate in theology was expected to preach: that was the purpose of his long and expensive training. As parish priests were mostly ill equipped for this task, the visiting preacher (usually a friar) was an indispensable figure in parochial, and especially urban, religious life. The increasing numbers of secular graduates from the universities increased the supply of that limited commodity, the preaching minister. Graduate clergy seem to have held the informal prerogative of preaching where and when they liked – with the permission of the parish priest, who would hardly be in any position to question what they said. Speaking in church with all the authority of the Church and of a superior education, they were ideally placed to disseminate new ideas – although many audiences may not have realised that they were new. One of the things which emerges very strikingly about the first generation of Wycliffite evangelists is their easy mobility. William Thorpe is found as far afield as Shrewsbury, Kent, and 'the North'; Thomas Drayton in Bristol, Buckinghamshire, and Kent; William Swynderby in Leicester, Coventry, and Herefordshire; and Richard Wyche is found in Newcastle, London, and the Welsh Marches. As even this knowledge is derived from stray and unsystematic records, we can be sure that they ranged further afield than we can say.

The Lollard Message

There is little direct evidence about what the earliest Wycliffite evangelists preached. Sometimes, we have specific articles of faith which particular individuals were invited to recant. But these give only an incomplete picture. However, a reliable impression can arguably be derived from the *English Wycliffite Sermons* recently edited by Anne Hudson and Pamela Gradon. The 294 sermons forming this homiletic cycle survive in 31 complete or partial manuscripts, and therefore constitute the most widely copied Lollard text after the English Bible itself. Their authorship remains uncertain, but their modern editors have shown that they were almost certainly compiled at Oxford in the reign of Richard II, during the formative phase of Lollardy. They exhibit substantial textual and doctrinal parallels with the Latin sermons of Wyclif, and, though never mere translations, are mostly faithful representations of his teaching. The frequent copying of these sermons assures us of their importance in early Lollardy. However, as the manuscripts survive largely in the university environment in which they were compiled, we may conclude that it was only in this first phase of the movement that they were significant, as works of this scale and complexity would rarely if ever have been available outside. But whether they were designed to be read aloud, or simply to guide preachers in the construction of their own sermons, they probably give us a reasonable conspectus of the early Lollard message.

What is most remarkable about the sermon-cycle is the virtual absence of Wyclif's most socially radical doctrine: lordship in grace is hardly so much as mentioned. On the principles of salvation the sermons are entirely scholastic, emphasising the cooperation of the human will with divine grace, and even invoking the scholastic dictum that God gives grace to those who 'do what lies within them'.[16] There is an understandably strong emphasis on the duty of the clergy to preach, irrespective of episcopal licences or prohibitions. There is not, however, much emphasis on Bible-reading of the sort found in later Protestantism, although the reading of the scriptures certainly became a Lollard practice. The sermons give clear expositions of epistles and gospels, ranging from close paraphrases to exotic allegories. It has often been said that there was much more to Lollardy than the rejections of Catholic beliefs and practices which are given prominence in the interrogations of suspected heretics by ecclesiastical officials. This claim is not borne out by the sermons, which confirm the negative impression of Lollardy conveyed by the heresy trials. Attacks on the friars, prelates, and papacy occur with monotonous regularity, as in Wyclif's own later writings. The wealth and simony of the clergy are subjected to withering criticism, and moral exhortation itself frequently collapses into an indictment of hypocrisy aimed primarily at the clergy. When it avoids this, it consists of entirely conventional encouragement to follow Christ, avoid sin, and perform the corporal and spiritual works of mercy. For example, the allegorisation of Christ's seven last words on the cross into censures of the seven deadly sins is a typically medieval exercise in scriptural interpretation.[17] The only teaching ever presented on the subject of the eucharist is the denial of transubstantiation (and in these sermons, Wyclif's recondite eucharistic theology was reduced to a flatly figurative interpretation of Christ's words). Scorn is poured upon the cult of the saints in all its manifestations. Confession to a priest is rejected in favour of general confession before the community and specific confession to God alone. Indeed, moral rectitude is emphasised at the expense of religious ritual in general.

Given the nature of the Wycliffite sermon-cycle, it is hardly surprising that few of Wyclif's more subtle and speculative teachings took root among the Lollards. Few seem to have espoused lordship in grace, or to have adopted his harsh teaching on predestination, despite the attraction that fatalism has often held for rural communities: later Lollardy leans more to Pelagianism (an excessive trust in the unaided powers of human nature, especially of free will) than to predestination. Wyclif's nuanced account of the eucharist was soon forgotten. On the ground, Lollardy became a principled rejection of 'traditional religion': the cult of the consecrated host; the Corpus Christi procession; the veneration of devotional images and relics; pilgrimage; auricular confession, individual penances, fasting, indulgences; prayers and masses for the dead; prayers for specific individuals or purposes; ornate ritual in services from evensong to funerals; church music; miracle plays; the use of candles, ashes, and holy water. This might seem to lend weight to Andrew Brown's observation that Lollards tend to have been found in places where traditional religion was especially flamboyant or luxuriant, and may thus have been at heart a reaction against the excesses of popular ritualism.[18] But as traditional religion seems to have been luxuriant almost everywhere, the observation is of little explanatory value.

Lollardy and Patronage

In explaining the rise of Lollardy it is not enough to identify early Wycliffite preachers and to establish a likely profile for their message. It is also necessary to investigate the social structures that helped bring the message to popular attention. Here, as Anne Hudson has written, it is to 'the collaboration of Wyclif's academic disciples with the Lollard gentry that we should look to explain the rise of Lollardy'.[19] Foremost among these men were the 'Lollard knights', known to history primarily through the chronicles of Thomas Walsingham and Henry Knighton. The Lollard knights were a small and apparently cohesive group of men, many of them 'chamber knights' prominent at the King's Court, whose personal ties were confirmed by K. B. McFarlane's researches among their wills, in which they variously figured as each other's beneficiaries or executors. Sir Thomas Latimer, Sir Richard Sturry, Sir John Cheyne, Sir Lewis Clifford, Sir William Neville, and Sir John Montague (later Earl of Salisbury) are among those named in the chronicles.[20] The example of Sir Thomas Latimer shows the potential of this group: he used his influence in Leicestershire and Northamptonshire to promote Lollard preachers and teachings; he was in trouble for possessing heretical literature as early as 1388; and he maintained dissident clergy such as John Woodward at his manor of Chipping Warden (about 6 miles north-east of Banbury), and Robert Hook in his own home village of

Braybrooke (about 17 miles south-east of Leicester), where a Lollard tradition survived into the early fifteenth century. Of the other knights named in the chronicles, John Montague is said to have harboured Nicholas Hereford at Shenley (Hertfordshire, between Barnet and St Alban's). Suspicion against Sir Richard Sturry, one of Richard II's chamber knights, was so strong that in the 1390s the King compelled him to forswear Lollardy.[21] In a similar fashion, Archbishop Arundel induced Lewis Clifford to renounce a specific schedule of Lollard beliefs early in the reign of Henry IV. It is not clear whether Clifford's extenuating plea of 'simplicity' was merely disingenuous or, just as probably, reflected a genuine unfamiliarity with the precise mapping of doctrinal boundaries.[22] And John Cheyne instituted a Lollard, Thomas Drayton, to the living of Drayton Beauchamp in 1414.[23] However, as J. A. F. Thomson observed, although the close personal ties between the Lollard knights are easily discerned, their shared values are rather harder to make out. While Latimer probably was a committed Lollard, the others were more ambiguous, active in mainstream channels of piety as well as connected with Lollards.[24] As in the early days of any new religious movement, the boundaries were neither firmly drawn nor impermeable. Thus the 'Lollard' phraseology of Latimer's will is echoed in the will of Thomas Arundel, Archbishop of Canterbury and hammer of the Lollards, while even Latimer's will, despite its omission of religious bequests and masses for the dead, calls upon the Blessed Virgin Mary and the saints in a manner hardly to be called Wycliffite. However, in assessing the importance of the 'Lollard knights', it is worth recalling a distinction which used to be drawn by the medieval Church between heretics and 'favourers of heretics'. If the 'Lollard knights' make at best ambiguous heretics, there can be no doubt that they were, at times, favourers of heretics.

One of the most important patrons of Lollardy was Sir John Oldcastle, Lord Cobham, whose original power base was in the Welsh Marches. Oldcastle was probably already a Lollard before he attained the highest ranks of county office-holding as MP for Herefordshire in 1404 and Sheriff in 1406–07. He had been brought up at Almeley, where Swynderby had preached in the 1380s, and perhaps owed his beliefs to that most charismatic of Lollard evangelists.[25] Oldcastle found refuge for a while among his childhood haunts after his escape from the Tower, and the local bishop was still concerned over heresy in Almeley as late as 1433.[26] The Severn Valley provided much of the support for the Oldcastle Rising, and Worcester was the home town of John Badby, the first layman to be burned for Lollardy (5 May 1410). Once Oldcastle had married the heiress of the Cobham estates in 1408, Lollard influences began to be felt in Kent as well. His chaplain was in trouble for preaching Lollardy in the Hundred of Hoo, the isolated villages lying north-east of Rochester on the marshes and mud-flats between the Medway and the Thames. Oldcastle was also connected with the important early Lollard preacher Richard Wyche: the two were clearly together in 1410 when both wrote letters to Hussites in Bohemia on the same day.[27]

There are other signs of early gentry patronage of Lollard preachers. William Swynderby probably enjoyed the protection of John Croft, Esq., of Croft near Leominster in the early 1390s, and Croft himself had to abjure heresy in 1395. Another Herefordshire potentate, Sir Robert Whitney (who served the county as JP and MP), owned a copy of one of Swynderby's sermons, and was a kinsman of Perrin Clanvowe, daughter-in-law of the Lollard knight Sir John Clanvowe.[28] Thomas Tyckhill, a gentleman lawyer and Crown official in Derbyshire, had a Lollard preacher (one William Ederyk) as his domestic chaplain from 1411 to 1414.[29] The chaplain of Sir Roger Acton, a prominent Shropshire figure, preached against images in 1407. Sir William Beauchamp of Gloucestershire, who had links with some of the Lollard knights, presented to Kemerton, a benefice within his gift, an Oxford theologian named Robert Lychlade, who had been expelled from the university in 1395 for his loyalty to the legacy of Wyclif.[30] In short, although in many cases the extent of the lay patron's knowledge of and commitment to dissent is far from clear, the picture which emerges from the fragmentary evidence is of a sizeable group of gentlemen who were prepared to use their influence to advance preachers of unorthodox opinions.

The town of Northampton provides evidence of the importance of both local political patronage and links with Oxford in the early growth of Lollardy. A petition of grievance addressed to Richard II in 1393 by a townsman named Richard Stormesworth accused the mayor, John Fox, of harbouring Lollard chaplains and fostering Lollard preaching. As Stormesworth was embroiled in a feud with Fox, whom he hoped to supplant as mayor, his allegations must be treated with some caution. Nevertheless, Fox was said to have kept as his domestic chaplain one Richard Bullock, who, according to Stormesworth, had already been convicted of heresy in a church court. Besides this, he was said to have harboured both James Collyn, a London mercer's apprentice who had abandoned his trade for Lollardy, and Thomas Comberworth, who, as Stormesworth correctly reported, had been convicted of heresy before the university court at Oxford (in fact, in 1385). Fox had also sent to Oxford to hire preachers – presumably Lollard preachers – for Lent. If this was not enough, he was said to have encouraged three Lollards – Mr William Northwold (a former Archdeacon of Sudbury then living in St Andrew's Priory, Northampton), Robert Braybrooke (or Braibrok, a chaplain, not to be confused with the Bishop of London of that name), and an unnamed 'Parson of Wynkpole' – to preach in the town.[31] Despite the obvious animus, there is enough circumstantial detail and corroboration to support Stormesworth's picture of a local boss using his political muscle and trading links to promote heresy and intimidate opponents. Later that same year, presumably acting on instructions from the King's Council, Bishop Buckingham struck at the Northampton Lollards: among the names he turned up was that of Robert Braybrooke.[32]

Geography of Early Lollardy

Although the discussion of gentry patronage has already cast some light on the early geography of Lollardy, it is interesting to summarise what can be ascertained about how widely the doctrines were sown. Most English regions were reached by early Wycliffite preachers: of England's 20 largest towns around 1400, over half had certainly seen Lollard preaching or the presence of Lollards by 1430; and given the scantiness of the evidence, it seems fair to conclude that the others had done so too.[33] But Lollard communities and traditions were not established everywhere. In 1408, royal proclamations evince concern for the spread of heresy in London, Bristol, Coventry, Warwickshire, Leicestershire, and East Anglia.[34] Lollard groups were mostly found in the south and east, although even in these regions they were few and far between. Indeed, although the geography of Lollardy can be conveniently divided into regions, this runs the risk of misrepresenting the little that we know. The evidence we have is for a few individuals widely scattered among a small number of settlements and estates on a limited number of occasions.

It is hardly surprising that Lollardy soon appeared in some of the villages around Oxford, doubtless thanks to the university's influence. A gentleman named Thomas Comberworth, of Kidlington, was prosecuted in 1385, and a band of Lollards from that area was indicted following the Oldcastle Rising.[35] The Thames Valley, as the arterial route from Oxford to London, was perhaps the next most likely area to show signs of Lollard activity, although there is, in fact, only the slenderest of early evidence for this. Together with the nearby regions of East Berkshire and South Buckinghamshire (Chiltern Hills), this area was the main seat of Lollardy in early Tudor times, and there is some evidence of early Lollard stirrings. There was Lollard preaching at Odiham, a few miles south of Reading, in 1382, while Reading itself yielded a suspect in 1412, when a Lollard from nearby Wokingham abjured.[36] Some half a dozen men from Amersham turned out on behalf of Oldcastle, while 1428 saw the abjurations of a layman from Amersham and a clergyman from Chesham.[37]

London itself offered an irresistible target for Wyclif's followers. Hereford, Aston, and Repingdon attempted to appeal to the London crowd against the condemnation of their master in 1382, and the first two were preaching there again in 1386, probably together with Thorpe. The following year saw what Walsingham interpreted as a Lollard riot in the city, led against his former brethren by an apostate Austin Friar named Peter Patteshulle.[38] Richard II prohibited unspecified conventicles in the city in 1392, the year in which James Collyn fled to Northampton on account of his beliefs. There were certainly Lollards in London in 1395 when the Twelve Conclusions were posted at Westminster Hall and a number of Londoners were arrested on suspicion of heresy. If definite evidence of particular heretics in London is hard to come by, this can be put down to the anonymity of the big city. William Taylor, an Oxford academic, was in trouble for what he preached in London in 1406, and a significant number of citizens and denizens were implicated in the Oldcastle Rising, which was, after all, organised from London – not to mention the importance of the stationery trade around St Paul's in the copying of Lollard texts. Altogether, we can safely say that London soon became an important Lollard centre.

South of London the story remains hard to piece together. In Kent, few signs of Lollardy are found until Oldcastle's arrival, although William Thorpe was active there in 1405.[39] Heresy was thus certainly being spread in the diocese of Rochester, although there is no direct evidence of heresy on the Downs, where it was to prove ineradicable, until the 1420s when William White emerges on the scene. William White and Hugh Pye fled from prosecution in Kent in the later 1420s, which indicates that the measures taken were quite intense, although they left no other trace. There may be some connection here with the execution of five men at Maidstone in 1437–38. Although the men were hanged, drawn, and quartered rather than burned, they were convicted 'for heresyes and destroyers of the Kinges peple'. This may mean nothing: the instinctive connection of heresy and sedition tends to confuse the issue. But it may be significant that the victims came from Tenterden, where White had preached, a place notorious for Lollardy in early Tudor times. Another Lollard priest, Thomas Drayton, had taken up a benefice nearby at Snave in 1422, and was cited for heresy in 1425.[40] Maidstone, too, was home to several Lollards in the early sixteenth century. As for the other southern counties, Sussex, Surrey, and Hampshire yield even less than Kent. As we have seen, there was Lollard preaching at Odiham (Hants) in the 1380s, but the episcopal registers of Winchester and Chichester give no reason to believe that heresy was a problem in this region at the end of the fourteenth century.

The first sign of Lollardy in East Anglia comes from Essex, where there was an abjuration in 1400: John Becket of Pattiswick near Braintree had preached against the veneration of images, the validity of sacraments performed by sinful priests, and clerical celibacy. A Lollard chaplain was preaching in places as far afield as Thaxted and Maldon in 1402, while Thaxted, Pattiswick, and Colchester all produced followers of Sir John Oldcastle in 1414.[41] There had been some concern over heresy at Colchester as early as 1405, and in 1429 a Lollard was burned there.[42] Essex was of course in the diocese of London, whereas Norfolk and Suffolk made up the diocese of Norwich, but Essex Lollardy seems to have looked in both directions, paying little attention to diocesan boundaries. The earliest documented case of heresy in Norwich diocese was when John Edwards, a Lollard chaplain from the diocese of Lincoln, recanted various charges of heresy at Norwich on 12 April 1405.[43] The unsuccessful proposal of Richard Dereham for the diocese of Norwich in 1407 maintained that his quali- fications as a theologian and preacher were indispensable for a diocese in which heresy was rife, but the first indisputable evi- dence for this comes only in the 1420s, when White and Pye took refuge in the Norfolk Broads.[44] Given the later practice of Lollards, it is likely that they chose this region because heresy was already established there, although there is no doubt that White advanced it much further. Bishop Alnwick's vigorous prosecutions in the 1420s nipped a mass movement in the bud, but Lollards were still turning up in the Waveney basin a hundred years later: here, too, lasting traditions were established.

Elsewhere, East Anglia's religious peace was little disturbed. The diocese of Ely saw no recorded proceedings against heresy until the later fifteenth century. Cambridge prided itself on its immunity from heresy (although there were one or two hints of sympathy with Wyclif among the Cambridge Austin Friars), and was more notable for its opposition to Wycliffism.[45] The early Lollard preacher at Diddington near Huntingdon (in the Lincoln diocese) seems to have made no lasting impression. And when the Bishop of Lincoln's commissary inquired into heresy in the archdeacon- ries of Huntingdon and Bedford (roughly coterminous with the counties) in 1417, all he unearthed was a village cunning-man telling fortunes in Alconbury Weston. A warrant was issued at some point for the arrest of John Langley of Pulloxhill (between Luton and Bedford) on suspicion of heresy, but beyond that these counties yield nothing.

The east and north Midlands witnessed considerable Lollard activity in the late fourteenth century, most of it under elite patron- age. As G. H. Martin has argued, Philip Repingdon seems to have been able to use the ecclesiastical influence of the abbey of St Mary's, Leicester (which was 'corporate patron and rector' of the city's churches), to promote Wyclif's teachings there in the early 1380s. Knighton's *Chronicle* shows that the full range of Wycliffite teaching was disseminated there: attacks on the friars and the bishops, on clerical wealth, indulgences, saints and images, and transubstantiation. The teachings seem to have appealed to the devout folk of the town. A lay hermit named William Smith and a priest named Richard Waytestathe lived just outside the walls in a chapel which they made a centre for a short-lived Lollard conventicle. However, after they shocked local opinion by chopping up an image of St Catherine for firewood, they were run out of the town.[46] Another prominent local Lollard was William Swynderby, again a hermit who already had a reputation for holiness before taking up Wycliffite doctrines and joining forces with William Smith. His preaching was mostly anticlerical rather than profoundly doctrinal at this stage, but was still enough to bring upon him a severe sentence, from which only the intercession of John of Gaunt saved him. It should not be concluded, however, that Gaunt had any particular liking for Lollards. Swynderby seems to have obtained his hermitage some time before through the patronage of Gaunt, who seems simply to have been fulfilling a good lord's obligations in protecting a client whose offences at this stage were not doctrinally radical.[47] However, the support which Swynderby enjoyed from the mayor and burgesses of Leicester, who were presumably better acquainted with his current beliefs, suggests that Wycliffite sympathies were widespread in the city.[48]

Heresy also spread early elsewhere in the region. The city of Nottingham was troubled by dissent for a couple of decades. Nicholas Hereford preached there in the 1380s, and a local chaplain, John Stoke, was arrested for preaching heresy in the city in 1388. Four Lollards renounced their views in the presence of Thomas Arundel at Nottingham in September 1395, and three of these men had previously been in trouble before the King's Council in 1388.[49] William Ederyk was preaching heresy in Derbyshire in the early fifteenth century, and activities in those counties seem to have been linked to the Lollard centres of Leicester and Northampton (see above, pp. 63–4).

After the reconciliation to Catholicism of Philip Repingdon and Nicholas Hereford, the movement seems to have lost much of its impetus in the east Midlands, though our knowledge of heresy during the early fifteenth century in the sprawling diocese of Lincoln is hampered by the fact that records of proceedings against dissent have demonstrably been lost. Philip Repingdon (Bishop of Lincoln, 1405–19) had already acquired a reputation as an inquisitor by the time of Archbishop Arundel's interrogation of William Thorpe, and his successor, Richard Fleming (1420–31), was sufficiently troubled by the threat of heresy to found Lincoln College at Oxford in order to train priests in response to it. The editor of Repingdon's register concluded that Lollardy was a major concern for the Bishop.[50] Sample warrants and commissions transcribed in his register show that a major investigation was undertaken through much of the diocese in the wake of the Oldcastle Rising. Yet, while the documents testify to his zeal against heresy, they give us remarkably few names. Stray allusions are found in other sources to Repingdon's proceedings against specific heretics. For example, we learn from proceedings against one William Emayn in the diocese of Bath and Wells in 1429 that he had appeared before Repingdon four times on suspicion of heresy before betaking himself to Bristol. Yet no traces of this survive in Repingdon's registers.[51] The conclusion must be that Repingdon, like his successors in the diocese, recorded proceedings against heretics in court books separate from his episcopal registers, and perhaps separate also from the normal consistory court records. William Smith of Corby was presumably voicing Lollard opinions when he inveighed against the use of candles and torches at the elevation as vain pomp, but this was hardly mainstream stuff, and in any case he abjured.[52]

The frequent arrest of Margery Kempe on suspicion of heresy during her perambulations of England in the later 1410s shows how sensitive clerical noses were to hints of doctrinal deviation. Her survival (not to mention the fact that heretics who abjured were not executed) suggests that heresy investigations were more than mere witch-hunts. Her success in vindicating her innocence shows that the authorities were not in the habit of conjuring Lollards out of thin air for ulterior social or political motives.

The last of the regions in which Lollardy made a significant impact was the west Midlands and the Marcher country towards Wales. We have already seen how the new doctrines took root under gentry patronage in Herefordshire, and the Severn Valley nurtured Lollards at several points. Shrewsbury was an early focus. A dozen heretics from the town were gaoled as early as 1395, and William Thorpe was preaching there in St Chad's soon after Easter 1407, to the intense annoyance of the town council.[53] But it was above all at Bristol, which long remained a centre of dissent, that Lollard teaching made its impact. There is clear evidence of concern about Lollardy in Bristol as early as 1401, when Archbishop Arundel wrote to the canon of Bedminster in Salisbury Cathedral about heretical preaching, presumably in the parish of St Mary Redcliffe, which was attached to the prebend of Bedminster, and was the main focus for Bristol dissent thereafter. Similar concern for Bristol's orthodoxy was expressed by the Vicar General of Bath and Wells in 1408. The seeds were doubtless sown by John Purvey, who was active in Bristol around the turn of the century, and with other prominent Lollard clergy such as Thomas Drayton and William Taylor turning up (in 1416 and 1420 respectively), the city was clearly of the first importance to the movement. The first local follower recorded in Bristol was Richard Devenish, a weaver of Temple parish who abjured in April 1413, but we can be sure that there had been others for some years. The same part of Bristol produced a clutch of abjurations in the aftermath of the Oldcastle Rising, to which Bristol had sent some men.[54] The prominent involvement in these affairs of Christina More, widow of a Bristol alderman, suggests that in Bristol, as in Northampton, the movement enjoyed the support of powerful elements in the urban elite.

There seems to have been virtually no Lollard penetration north of the Trent, except for the occasional migrant from southern England. William Thorpe had certainly preached in the North in the later fourteenth century, and Richard Wyche was preaching in Northumberland in 1400.[55] But neither seems to have had a lasting effect. Thomas Langley's lengthy episcopate saw only one case of heresy, when the Carmelite Prior of Newcastle revived the ancient controversy between the friars and secular priests. But he was not accused of any specifically Lollard opinions.[56] There is no evidence at all for Lollardy in Wales, and precious little in the West Country. Near Yeovil, a chaplain named John Bacon had brought down interdicts on a handful of parishes for unlicensed Lollard preaching. And he may have been linked to the contumacious vicar of North Petherton, said in 1409 to have been excommunicated under the previous bishop (Henry Bowet, 1401–07).[57] But the long and devoted episcopate of Edmund Lacy at Exeter (1420–55) produced no more evidence of heresy, and it is barely plausible to suggest that such a dedicated pastor would have missed any significant threat to the orthodoxy of his flock.[58]

Social Distribution of Early Lollardy

If Lollardy were to have flourished, it would have required considerable support among the gentry and even at Court, the true seats of local and central power. In the very earliest stages, this seemed possible. As we have seen, Wyclif himself enjoyed some favour at Court in the 1370s, and it was probably the good lordship of John of Gaunt that shielded him from the full consequences of the condemnation of his teachings in the 1380s. The 'Lollard knights' played an important part in the early diffusion of the new doctrines, and were well-placed at Court themselves. Even as late as 1414, gentlemen could be found in the movement. Nevertheless, Lollardy does not seem to have held a disproportionate appeal for the gentry. Only small numbers of gentlemen can be shown to have dabbled with Lollard beliefs, and only in the early years of the movement. This is hardly surprising. The gentry were more deeply implicated, by ties of both family and politics, in the ecclesiastical structure of England than were less exalted layfolk. Family chapels were already a feature of many parish churches, and funeral monuments in church testified to a family's wealth and social eminence as well as to its piety. Gentry families were the main source of abbots and prioresses for the hundreds of religious houses across the land. The ministrations of the Church were evidently welcome to the gentry, who spent lavishly on the practice of their faith. In short, the late medieval Church seems to have done a good job of satisfying their religious aspirations.[59] The relative failure of Lollardy to penetrate this sector of society, despite a good degree of overlap between the spiritual concerns of Lollardy and of zealous orthodoxy, severely limited its potential. The gentry controlled a great deal of parochial patronage, which could have been deployed to increase the reach of Lollard preachers. Latimer and Oldcastle show how useful this might have been. But on the whole, the parochial connections of the gentry probably pulled them the other way, reinforcing their commitment to the *status quo*. And whatever gentry sympathy with Lollardy there may have been seems to have evaporated after the Oldcastle Rising. Hardly any gentlemen, and not a single knight, can subsequently be identified as a heretic. Not until the 1530s was heresy once more to mobilise support among the ruling elites.

The Lollard failure among the gentry was a fair reflection of its failure among friars. Wyclif himself had recognised the enormous influence which the friars had over England's elite. But his frontal assault on them simply did not damage their position. His best-known early opponent, the Franciscan William Woodford, for example, was confessor to the Countess of Norfolk (who in 1399 was buried in the London Greyfriars), and wrote one of his works against Wyclif while staying at Framlingham Castle in 1396 as a guest of the Countess of Arundel. Kings themselves usually had friars as their confessors: Friar John Woodrow was confessor to Edward III in his latter years, while the Dominican Thomas Rushook was confessor to Richard II, and John of Gaunt's confessor was the Carmelite Walter Diss. The leading friars were often of gentry or wealthy bourgeois origin. Roger Dymmok, another influential opponent of Lollardy, was of the family which furnished the hereditary champions of the king, and would himself have fulfilled that function at Richard's coronation had he not chosen the religious life. Many of the gentry chose burial in the grand churches of the friars, especially those of the Dominicans and the Francsicans in London, and even if this was as much for social as for spiritual reasons, then these reasons were equally effective in strengthening the bonds between the two groups.

Despite the limitations of its appeal at the highest levels, Lollardy tended to attract those securely established in society rather than the oppressed or dispossessed. From the knightly and gentle sympathisers through the graduate clergy and the lawyers to the merchants, artisans, yeomen, and tenants, Lollards were generally secure and even comfortable – predominantly what would later be called the 'middling sort'. The majority of those who turned out to support Oldcastle in 1414 were from such back-grounds.[60] Of the 51 male Lollards whose names are recorded in the Norfolk proceedings of 1428, the occupations of 26 are known: apart from four priests and a servant, all were craftsmen, and only one seems to have been wealthy (and he was the master of the solitary Lollard servant). L. R. Poos has found a similar profile among those 67 Essex Lollards whose occupation is recorded. There were no labourers among them except for 8 pardoned after Cade's Rebellion of 1450; and their identification as Lollards depends on an equation of sedition with heresy which must be considered dubious in this case.[61] Excluding the figures for Cade's

Rebellion, the remaining 30 Lollards were all craftsmen and clergy-men. Although by no means all Lollards were literate, the premium which a bible-reading religion inevitably laid on literacy ensured that it was likely in a predominantly oral culture to go over the heads of the lowest in society. The social spread of Lollardy thus narrowed over time, for the gentry and wealthier clergy seem to have lost interest early on, while Lollardy does not seem actually to have sunk on the social scale. Those few labourers and servants found among the Lollards mostly came in on the coat-tails of their employers. This social distribution may be reflected in the lack of any significant millennial expectations among the Lollards (Lollard apocalyptic was pessimistic, expecting persecution rather than revolution[62]) and in the consequent absence of social protest. This is a point of no little interest, as Wyclif's radical ideas on property and ownership might easily have lent themselves to a movement of popular discontent, but, in fact, did not do so.

The social limits of Lollardy may have owed something to the ritual barrenness of the new dispensation. When comparing Lollardy with popular religious movements such as Hussitism in fifteenth-century Bohemia or Lutheranism in sixteenth-century Germany, one is struck by the way in which the more successful movements created new symbolic acts with which to unify and motivate their followers. In both cases, vernacular liturgy and communion under both kinds became slogans and symbols. Wyclif and Lollardy had nothing like this to offer. The nearest thing was the English Bible, and in a society of limited literacy this would inevitably restrict its popular appeal, as would the sheer expense of books. The experience of the Reformation suggests that iconoclasm could also become a ritual gesture of wide appeal, but again Lollards seem to have been slow to turn their iconopho-bia into action. Even the notorious attack on the Rood of Dover-court by some East Anglian Lollards in 1532 seems to have been inspired by an evangelical preacher, Thomas Rose.[63] Wyclif was offering religion without ritual, which for most countryfolk would have amounted to no religion at all. As J. I. Catto has pointed out, his attack on the real presence struck at the heart of popular Catholic devotion, which in practice revolved around a visual experience of the eucharist.[64] Had Wyclif offered communion in both kinds as a devotional alternative, he might have countered traditional piety with a powerful symbol. But unlike Luther and

Hus, his theology left little for the eucharist to do. As it is, reading aloud in private houses seems to have competed at some disadvantage with the multimedia approach of the late medieval parish church and community.

The appeal of Lollardy lay for the most part in precisely the same quarter as that of the literate lay piety which arose at about the same time. Adherents of both came mostly from the ranks of the religious (whom a later age would call the godly), those clerics or laymen who took the obligations of faith seriously. But the fact that heresy is likely to appeal first and foremost to religious people is a truism which frequently renders futile the search for the sociological basis of new religious movements. Neither the emergence of Wyclif's theology nor its diffusion depended on the rise of a literate lay culture – for the theology itself required nothing more than the university environment while its diffusion was primarily a matter of preaching. Nevertheless, the emergence of such a literate lay culture probably helped extend the reach of Wyclif's ideas, as the sort of people who read Richard Rolle and Walter Hilton might be equally attracted to writings by other clerks of a similar background, writings which, however, conveyed a rather different spiritual message.

Lollard Texts

Despite the imposing bulk of surviving Lollard literature, the promulgation of Wyclif's teachings was an oral rather than a literary process. Lollard books, especially English books, were unquestionably important in that process, but there are few if any signs of that common Reformation phenomenon, the convert made through reading. Surviving heresy investigations indicate that most Lollards did not themselves own books. Very few are specifically charged with the possession of forbidden literature. Significantly enough, those who did own books often had several, and were usually leaders in their Lollard community. They seem to have passed on their doctrines by preaching and teaching from their texts. Communal reading aloud rather than private meditation was the purpose of much of this literature. It follows that literacy need not have correlated especially closely with Lollardy. The work of L. R. Poos on Essex, for example, has suggested that the middling sort among whom Lollard ideas met with their readiest reception were not significantly more literate than other sectors of society. As long as there was a lay or clerical leader who could read a New Testament or a moral tract, there was enough literacy to beget a Lollard group.[65]

The impressive statistics relating to Lollard literature, and especially the Lollard Bible, have been taken as evidence of a sophisticated organisation capable of, among other things, huge efforts of copying and distribution. However, this argument breaks down under scrutiny. The most widely copied text was the Bible. But the well-known figure of around 250 surviving manuscripts of all or part of the Lollard Bible must be interpreted with care. Only around 20 are complete Bibles, while around 100 are copies of the New Testament or the Gospels. The rest are scattered groups of books, many of them doubtless originally part (or intended to be part) of complete Bibles. The scribal effort this represents, though still enormous, is rather less than that which the bare figure of 250 manuscripts might suggest. Until much more research has been done upon the materials and palaeography of the manuscripts, it will not be possible to reach reliable conclusions about the extent, duration, and significance of that scribal effort. But before Archbishop Arundel imposed strict limits on the translation and circulation of the Bible around 1410, it was perfectly legal to copy the English Bible. It is likely that a great many of the surviving copies were produced in the late fourteenth or early fifteenth centuries, and that much of the market consisted of devout clergy and layfolk of impeccable orthodoxy. For example, one of the earliest known owners was John Bount, a wealthy merchant of St Mary Redcliffe, Bristol, who bequeathed a copy of the Gospels in English in 1404. This led Charles Kightly to see a possible connection with the Lollards of that parish. Yet as Bount's will also left legacies to the Bristol friars, it is more likely that his devotion was orthodox.[66]

Even after Arundel's restrictions came into force, the vernacular scriptures were not absolutely prohibited. Nor was the Wycliffite translation in itself heretical: it was for the most part a faithful, even stilted, rendering of the Latin Vulgate. Its only plainly heretical aspect was the so-called 'general prologue', which explicitly challenged official church teaching on transubstantiation. But this prologue is found in only 11 copies.[67] It would be folly to suggest that only texts which included this prologue were in dissident hands, but it does allow us to fix one extreme to a range of possibilities, with at the other extreme the notion that most texts do, in fact, represent original Lollard owners and copyists. What is clear is that many loyal Catholics had copies of the scriptures in English. Indeed, it is hard to be certain that any known owners of surviving copies were Lollards at all.[68] One of the most famous readers of the Lollard Bible was the anti-Lollard polemicist Reginald Pecock, Bishop of Chichester, who was himself condemned for heresy on entirely other grounds. Yet, as Anne Hudson has pointed out, it is remarkable that even when it was open season on Pecock, he was never criticised for using the Lollard Bible.[69] Indeed, two of his leading opponents, Ive and Eborall, seem to have licensed the use of an English New Testament by a laywoman. Other known owners of the scriptures in English included the royal family, Duke Humphrey of Gloucester, the Carthusian priory of Sheen, the priory of Syon, Fotheringay College, Sir William Weston (last English prior of the Knights of St John), John Lacy (a Newcastle Dominican), the Dominican priory at Cambridge, Roger Walton (an early sixteenth-century parish priest), and Dame Anne Danvers. By the 1520s it was possible for Thomas More to maintain – wrongly – that one of the English versions of the Bible predated Wyclif and was therefore exempt from Arundel's restrictions. He added – probably rightly – that many bishops permitted people to own the scriptures in English.[70] What the huge number of vernacular biblical manuscripts indicates is not the strength of Lollardy, but the thirst for the vernacular scriptures among the literate and pious laity.

Other Lollard texts were less theologically or devotionally ambiguous than the Wycliffite Bible. Many original Lollard treatises survive in unique exemplars, and some of these were probably never even intended for wider distribution. Among the more frequently copied texts were the encyclopaedic scriptural commentaries and the Lollard sermons. But exemplars of these texts survive predominantly in the libraries of Oxford and were presumably compiled not so much for public circulation as for the benefit of students and preachers. Our best evidence for what was read in Lollard communities comes from the records of church courts. But while these allude quite often to suspect books in the possession of Lollards, they rarely give details of the titles in question. Mostly the texts mentioned were portions of the scriptures. Sometimes, they were perfectly orthodox texts. For the rest, the commonest Lollard texts were expositions of the Ten Commandments (presumably quite short) and concise polemical treatises against transubstantiation and the cult of the saints. Even then we often have problems in correlating surviving texts with recorded titles. One of the most commonly mentioned titles, *Wycklyffes Wycket* (almost certainly not written by Wyclif), survives only in a sixteenth-century printed edition – no manuscripts are known.[71] Remarkably little of what was potentially a rich Lollard library seems in practice to have circulated.

Where were Lollard manuscripts copied? It is clear from the proceedings relating to Oldcastle that the London stationery trade numbered Wycliffite sympathisers among its ranks. Suspicion first fell firmly upon Sir John when some heretical English books belonging to him were found during a search of an illuminator's workshop in Paternoster Row, next door to St Paul's Cathedral. When he later escaped from the Tower of London, he was harboured by a Smithfield parchment maker.[72] In any case, the number of surviving Lollard manuscripts shows that the book trade, which was based in London, offered fertile ground for dissident teachings. It would be going too far to see the stationery trade, or even a section of it, as the skeleton of a putative Lollard organisation. But a significant number of recorded names and occupations of early Lollards show connections with the trades of writing and copying. Apart from priests and chaplains, who were presumably literate, we find suspected Lollards with such names or occupations as 'parchmenter', 'scriptor', and 'scrivener' in places as far afield as London, Lincolnshire, Norfolk, Oxfordshire, Nottingham, Bury St Edmunds, Daventry, St Albans, and Hereford. To what extent the London stationery trade continued to cater for the Lollard market after the Oldcastle Rising is unclear, although in the immediate aftermath both Oldcastle himself and John Purvey were sheltered for a time by its members.[73] Few surviving Lollard manuscripts can be securely dated much later than this. On the other hand, Lollard handbills and texts could still be widely copied and distributed as late as 1431.[74]

Lollard literature, despite its bulk, is not the best starting point for an assessment of the social and historical significance of Lollardy. On the contrary, an excessive concentration on the literature solely because it happens to survive is almost calculated to

distort our understanding of the movement. The survival of
Lollard texts reflects to a large extent the literary preferences of
post-Reformation collectors and librarians.[75] John Bale's catalogue
of British authors is rich in information on orthodox preachers
and scholars of the fifteenth century, many of whose works have
since disappeared. But Lollard texts represented the intellectual
patrimony of the early modern Church of England, when the
Anglican view of the past was shaped almost exclusively by John
Foxe. A bundle of Lollard tracts was far more likely to survive
the Reformation weeding of monastic and collegiate libraries
than was a bundle of orthodox sermons. Bale himself records
many lost works by members of his own religious order, the
Carmelites. Yet the only one he is known to have preserved was
the *Fasciculi Zizaniorum*, a collection of documents relating to
Wyclif assembled by Friar Richard Lavenham for polemical
purposes, and put to rather different polemical use by Bale and
John Foxe. To put the statistics into perspective, it is worth
recalling that the text most likely to be found in the hands of
a late medieval English layman (or woman) was the (Latin) Book
of Hours. Over 700 manuscript Books of Hours produced in, or
for, England between 1300 and 1500 still survive today. Many
more must long since have disappeared, and in the early Tudor
period this figure must be supplemented by over a hundred
printed editions.[76]

Lollardy and Lay Piety

The fact that many surviving Lollard texts were copied before
Arundel's censorship was effectively implemented enables us to
put in slightly different perspective something which has often
been observed by scholars, namely the conflation in certain religious
texts of 'orthodox' with 'deviant' themes, and the juxtaposition in
particular manuscripts of 'orthodox' and 'deviant' works. M. T.
Brady's penetrating studies of the *Poor Caitif*, a devotional treatise
compiled around 1400, illustrate this perfectly. Although since
the time of John Bale (who ascribed it to Wyclif) this treatise has
been credited with Lollard associations, it contains no suggestion
of heretical teaching. However, six of the 23 manuscripts in which
it survives also contain Lollard works or extracts alongside it. And

Brady has shown that the original treatise itself draws on a group of Wycliffite vernacular compilations such as the Glossed Gospels and the Floretum. Yet none of the texts drawn from these sources is itself heretical, and none of these compilations, not even the Lollard Bible itself, was condemned until 1409. Thus the *Poor Caitif* was probably compiled by a person of orthodox convictions with access to a range of vernacular reference works of Lollard provenance – presumably therefore at Oxford, where these works themselves were compiled and kept. It constitutes evidence of the narrowness of the gap that could separate heresy from Lollardy, of the circulation of devout and dissident texts within one and the same milieu.[77] This in turn explains why, as Margaret Aston has shown, such unexceptional works as *Dives and Pauper* and *Prick of Conscience* were occasionally deemed suspect in the eyes of some heresy-hunter, and why the Lollard Bible itself was often to be found in perfectly orthodox hands. Orthodox and dissident texts were being compiled and copied in one and the same milieu, at least before 1410, and such writings shared both general objectives and perceived audiences.

An appreciation of the extent to which conventional and Lollard piety could overlap in the decades between the Blackfriars Synod and the Oldcastle Rising helps us to make sense of the conflicting views which historians have expressed about the 'Lollard knights' and the impact of Lollardy at Richard II's Court. On the one hand, there is some evidence to justify the identification of certain knights by Walsingham and Knighton as heretics or favourers of heretics. They promoted or protected Lollard clergy and owned Lollard texts. On the other hand, the most obvious common factors which McFarlane found between these men – the contempt for funeral pomp and vivid revulsion from the sinful flesh which they expressed in their wills – were shared not only with each other, but also with Archbishop Arundel, whom nobody could possibly mistake for a Lollard.[78] When this is added to the facts that their wills can also display conventional Catholic confidence in post-mortem intercession, and that two of them (Clanvowe and Neville) died in unlollardly fashion on pilgrimage or crusade in the Near East (hardly a Lollard activity), while another two (Sturry and Clifford) forswore Lollardy, it becomes apparent that we cannot simply endorse the crude judgements of the early chroniclers.[79] McFarlane therefore concluded from this that elements of Lollard spirituality had penetrated the orthodox domain.[80] A better explanation is perhaps that Lollardy was appealing to the same interests and impulses as more orthodox spiritual movements. We can see signs of this in another feature of religious life at Richard II's Court, one pointed out by Anthony Tuck, namely the interest in Carthusian spirituality. Although Tuck uses this to argue against the plausibility of Courtly interest in Lollardy, the Carthusians were in fact the one religious order occasionally exempted from the strictures and despoliatory manifestos of the Lollards.[81] The Carthusian emphasis on simplicity and renunciation was, after all, not far from Lollard ethics. Nicholas Hereford, Lollard evangelist turned orthodox ecclesiastic, retired to end his days in the Coventry Charterhouse in 1417. In a sense, the Carthusians themselves, who were at the heart of the vernacular devotional literature of the time, were part of a broader spectrum of piety in which Lollardy was another band of colour.[82] It was not that Lollardy was penetrating orthodox spirituality, but that it was a deviant form of it. Both forms of spirituality might gain a hearing in the same circles, whether at Court or elsewhere.

This perspective on the relationship between lay piety and Lollardy offers us an explanation of another curious feature of our limited evidence concerning the spread of Lollardy: the fact that any unconventional display of piety, whether unusual in kind or merely in degree, could strike the unsympathetic as smacking of heresy. Thus the irrepressible Margery Kempe frequently aroused suspicion through her extravagant religiosity, even though much of that religiosity consisted in acts or attitudes diametrically opposed to those of the Lollards. In the realms of fiction, Chaucer's Poor Parson was dismissed as a Lollard by the Host whom he had rebuked for taking God's name in vain. To those whose religion was more mundane and conventional, religious enthusiasm was suspect *per se*. Pious distaste for idle swearing was not far removed in many people's minds from the Lollard repudiation of all oaths. This must not be taken the wrong way. The charge of hypocrisy is the first recourse of those whose conscience or *amour propre* is wounded by the public display of religious conviction. But it does suggest that the popular mind saw something in common between the Lollards and the devout.

Lollardy as a Movement

Except in its early years, Lollardy seems to have remained barely if at all organised. The production of large quantities of Lollard texts, and the half-cocked planning that culminated in the abortive Oldcastle coup, must have required a degree of coordination, and even of command structure. But once the coup had been nipped in the bud and the government had acted vigorously against potential sympathisers in the shires, it is more appropriate to talk of a Lollard 'network' than of a sect. After the failure of the rising, Oldcastle himself managed to evade capture for several years, presumably fleeing from house to house. But a network is one of the loosest forms of organisation, and after Oldcastle's execution there is little sign of coordinated collective effort. The so-called Lollard Rising of 1431 was little more than the distribution of subversive leaflets by a small group of zealots or opportunists.[83] Talk of 'gathered churches' among the Lollards seems even more inappropriate: the 'gathered churches' of the French Huguenots in the sixteenth century existed on a wholly different plane of formality, organisation, and record-keeping. Nor can a wedding feast at a Lollard house justify talk of 'Lollard sacramental activity'.[84] Taking into account the close and generally pre-existing personal connections that bound Lollard groups together, it seems that the household was the basic unit of Lollard survival, with the doctrine often spreading along family networks.[85] This may go some way to explain the apparent Lollard preference for the sacrament of marriage over those of baptism and the eucharist. There were Lollard communities, and there was a Lollard tradition, but it is misleading to talk of Lollard schools in the sense of institutions for formal and regular instruction.

Nor is the evidence for a distinctive Lollard ministry any firmer. Of course there were leaders – evangelists or prophets, if you will – among the Lollard communities: men like William White in Kent and then Norfolk in the 1420s, or Father Hackett in London and Essex a century later. Most of them were clergymen episcopally ordained within the Catholic Church; others were, formally, lay-men.[86] But the qualifications of Lollard leaders were charismatic rather than hierarchical. They owed their pre-eminence to their education, or at least to their articulacy. There is no evidence of formal appointment, calling, or ordination to ministry within the

Lollard communities. Nor would Wycliffite theory seem to have required such formal means. The common Lollard tenet that the most just person on earth was the true pope shows that the theory, as well as the practice, of Lollard ministry was charismatic. There seems, moreover, to have been an inchoate doctrine of the priesthood of all believers among the Lollards, which might have rendered any formal ministry redundant.[87]

The claim that Lollards ordained priests, originally made by Thomas Walsingham, has been accepted by a number of recent historians. However, that claim was founded on only one case, from the diocese of Salisbury, and the details of this case, which survive in the Salisbury episcopal registers, suggest a rather different story. What we find is the tale of the mock ordination of a miscreant named William Ramsbury who, whatever his religious views, was more interested in exploiting the financial and sexual opportunities available to an unscrupulous priest than in making God's law known to his people. Although some of the beliefs he was persuaded to abjure are couched in Lollard terms, they seem to betray a coarse scepticism about the profession he parodied so successfully for four years rather than the Wycliffite theology credited to him by his interrogators. His most distinctive tenet, that it was licit for a man to have sexual relations with any woman, be she wife or widow, virgin or nun, for the propagation of the human race, was hardly a recommendation for the doctrines of which he stood accused. Indeed, his judges doubtless appreciated the value of parading this low-life as a Lollard. It seems that Walsingham, like many later historians, was generalising from inadequate evidence. Walsingham makes another reference to ordination, but it, too, is unsubstantiated.[88] There is an allegation in the Norwich materials that William White ordained a follower to a eucharistic ministry, but White denied this charge – needless perjury for what was not a capital offence when he was admitting heretical doctrines for which he would, in any case, be burned.[89]

Lollardy and Politics

The association of heresy with sedition, which had been a commonplace of Christian thought since at least the age of Innocent III, enabled the hierarchy, in the wake of the Peasants' Revolt, to purchase the support of the lay authorities in their own campaign to silence Wyclif and suppress his followers. The success of their stratagem is evident in the chronicles and literature of the time, which systematically conflate religious with political dissent. This makes such sources a pitfall for historians, who may see in them proof rather than prejudice. There is an alluring tidiness in the idea that religious dissent had close links with the political upheavals of the period. But one of the most remarkable things about Lollardy is its almost complete irrelevance to those upheavals. Lollards, for example, made no special contribution to the events of 1399, when Richard II was deposed and replaced by Henry IV. Despite the attempts of some historians to depict Lollardy as a Court-centred and aristocratic movement, the handful of favourers of heresy found at Richard II's Court do not justify this claim. On the contrary, as Nigel Saul has recently shown, Richard's Court was a focus of fashionable orthodox piety.[90] Nor did the case against Richard so much as hint that he had been soft on heresy.[91] It would be pleasing to find the Lollards either among Henry's supporters or later among Ricardian loyalists, but, in fact, both sides repudiated heresy. Henry IV lent his backing to campaigns against Lollardy almost at once, in order to bolster his own feeble legitimacy by support for orthodoxy. But he had more to fear from the friars – the sworn enemies of the Lollards – than from the Lollards themselves.[92] The role of the friars as popular preachers ensured them a public role at times of political tension, and several friars were executed in the early years of Henry's reign for predicting a Plantagenet restoration.

Nevertheless, it was the Lollards who immediately found themselves under further pressure in the wake of the Lancastrian usurpation, as Henry IV gave the royal assent to a statute, *De haeretico comburendo* ('On the burning of heretics'), which regularised the customary medieval penalty (recommended by canon law) of death by burning for relapsed or unrepentant heretics. This may have been part of a broader campaign to bolster his dubious legitimacy (in this case by publicly fulfilling the coronation oath to protect the Church). Or it may simply have been a *quid pro quo* to Thomas Arundel, Archbishop of Canterbury, who with his relatives had done so much to promote Henry's cause, and who, even in Richard II's reign, had been perhaps the most zealous of the bishops in the suppression of dissent. Either way, the driving

force of this policy was certainly Arundel, and Parliament passed
the statute in response to a petition from Convocation. The law
itself was perhaps more symbolic than draconian, as arguably it
made no practical difference to the fate of heretics. The man often
seen as its first victim, William Sawtry (a priest from Lynn in
Norfolk), was in fact executed under customary procedures
shortly before the Act received royal assent. Its real importance
lay in its unequivocal demonstration that the Crown stood
squarely behind the Church in the defence of the faith, which in
turn helped deprive Lollardy of the elite support essential for its
continued growth. There was to be only one more victim in Henry
IV's lifetime, John Badby, who was burned in 1410. The proceedings against both Sawtry and Badby were highly public affairs,
conducted before Convocation in London in a fashion which was
obviously designed to maximise their impact and to put the royal
rejection of Lollardy beyond any possible doubt. Henry, Prince of
Wales (later Henry V), presided in person over Badby's execution, abandoning him to his fate after a fruitless last-minute
appeal to him to recant. Burnings were to remain relatively rare
events under both the Lancastrians and the Yorkists (although
they were to become more frequent under the Tudors): enough
to be a deterrent, yet hardly a reign of terror. More friars than
Lollards were executed in the name of Henry IV.

The Oldcastle Rising

The hierarchy's identification of heresy with sedition was gloriously
vindicated in the attempted coup mounted by, or in the name of,
the disgraced Lollard peer and career soldier Sir John Oldcastle
(latterly Lord Cobham). Oldcastle himself had been a thorn in
episcopal flesh for some years. His presence as a knight of the
shire in the 1407 Parliament, and as a baron in the Parliaments
of 1409 and 1410, coincides with the circulation of bills and peti-
tions for the disendowment of the clergy. When, in the reign of
Henry V, Oldcastle might perhaps have hoped to gain some real
political influence as a former boon companion of the young
King, Archbishop Arundel was able to produce decisive evidence
of his heretical convictions, which the old soldier himself was unable
to deny and unwilling to recant. Arundel was clearly out to get him:

there is excessively happy timing in the detection of Oldcastle's chaplain on the opening day (6 March) of Convocation in 1413, followed promptly by the discovery of compromising manuscripts belonging to the baron in a nearby illuminator's workshop. Doubtless, Arundel made the most effective use possible of information received. This discredited Oldcastle himself, not least in the eyes of Henry V. Oldcastle was arrested, and Henry himself twice urged him to recant before allowing Convocation to initiate formal proceedings against him. Oldcastle was committed to the Tower, and on 23 September 1413 he appeared before Convocation to be given two days to submit. Appearing again on Monday 25 September he was obdurate, and was convicted of heresy. Even now, Henry V did his best to save the knight, and in the ensuing delay Oldcastle made his escape from the Tower of London on 19 October. He hid, typically, with a parchment maker.[93]

The coup or demonstration which was then organised in Oldcastle's name is the best commentary on the numerical weakness and political impotence of Lollardy. A few hundred zealots and hirelings arrived at a rendezvous in St Giles's Field early in the morning of 10 January 1414.[94] Their numbers pale into insignificance even beside the relatively low turnouts for such Tudor revolts as those of Sir Thomas Wyatt (1554) or the Northern Earls (1569), both of which brought several thousand men into the field. Many sympathisers and supporters sent unfortunate parties to Oldcastle's aid, yet drew back from committing their own persons. Others ignored the call altogether. The purpose of those who turned out is now far from clear. As Paul Strohm has recently argued in a forceful exegesis of the documents in the case, the Lancastrian regime was probably better informed about the rising than the rebels themselves. If events were not necessarily, as he suggests, 'invented', then they were certainly 'extensively managed'. Certainly the machinery of repression seems to have been in place before the riotous assembly in St Giles's Field even gathered. Yet the presence on the day of men such as John Purvey, once a chaplain to Wyclif himself, and a leading Lollard until his death in custody a few months after the rising, lends credence to the traditional understanding of the event as a manifestation of Lollard activity.[95]

Oldcastle's part in events has also become less clear. Was he the hidden paw, the mastermind conspicuous by his absence on the

day, but hunted for years once the full truth was known? Or was
he the victim of his supporters as much as of his opponents, an
unwitting figurehead trapped by friends and enemies in a role he
had never sought? Whatever the truth, the regime was in
complete control of events as they unfolded on 10 January 1414,
and controlled the later understanding of those events still more
completely.[96] Oldcastle himself became a mythic figure of diabolical cunning, rather like the Jesuit Henry Garnet in the wake of
the Gunpowder Plot (with which this rising has much in common). In each case, a well-informed and well-organised regime
was able to exploit an ill-conceived conspiracy of hotheads in
order to complete the discrediting and demonisation of a religious
minority. And in the injunction for national prayers and processions of thanksgiving which were issued after the rising had been
thwarted, we can see something of the same desire to use national
deliverance to bolster national identity.[97]

Henry V's commissions of oyer and terminer in the aftermath
of the revolt were set up in only 22 of England's shires, in a revealing
distribution which excluded Wales, Cornwall, and the North, as
well as the Eastern Counties (which, with the exception of East
Anglia, broadly confirms the geography of early Lollardy sketched
above).[98] It appears therefore that Strohm's further interpretation of the affair as a put-up job designed to bolster Lancastrian
legitimacy goes too far.[99] For Lancastrian legitimacy stood in most
need of buttressing in Wales and the North, whence the most
threatening opposition to Henry IV had emerged. Moreover,
several shires for which commissions were issued produced few or
no returns: Derbyshire, Devon, Dorset, Hampshire, and Somerset.
As they were close to areas where Lollardy made no real impact at
all (the North and the far West), we should conclude not that they
were courageously defiant of royal interference, but that they
simply had nothing to declare. On the other hand, suspects were
later to be found in significant numbers in two counties omitted
from the Oldcastle commissions: Norfolk and Wiltshire.

In the years following the Oldcastle Rising, the political and
organisational aspects of Lollardy guttered out. The Lollard networks seem to function for a few years in succouring and con-
cealing Oldcastle himself, and in the way in which those linked
with Lollardy, but less directly implicated in the rising, stand bail
for their more reckless colleagues and, it seems, help them out of

trouble. But the echoes of the rising soon die away, and with them the active Lollard networks. What remains is altogether less functional, slight connections between one community and another, enough to allow Lollard suspects or convicts to slip from one jurisdiction to another, but with neither the ambition nor the resources for anything beyond survival. Oldcastle himself survived on the run until late in 1417. Once captured, he was brought to London and, on 14 December, burned hanging in chains. The crude symbolism of the punishment (which was later represented in a woodcut in Foxe's *Acts and Monuments*, reproduced on the cover of this book) summed up the identification of heresy and sedition which the Oldcastle Rising itself had sealed.

From Henry Beaufort's sermon at the opening of the Leicester Parliament (May 1414) onwards, heresy and sedition were to be spoken of in one breath. Indeed, for Beaufort, Lollardy was essentially a matter of disobedience to established law, and he played endless variations on this theme on subsequent occasions.[100] Guided by his eloquence, the Leicester Parliament passed a statute calling upon royal officials and servants of all kinds to give the ecclesiastical authorities the fullest assistance in hunting out heretics.[101] An undertaking to this effect was henceforth written into the oath which men swore on taking up such offices. Episcopal registers across the land testify to the vigour with which heresy was hunted out over the next decade (although the numbers actually found remained small).[102] Years later, the association of treason with heresy was still useful to the government in settling accounts after Cade's Rebellion. Many of Cade's followers were labelled as Lollards in order to facilitate the procedures leading to their execution, though there is no evidence that the rebels had any specifically religious aims.[103] As for the rising of 1414, it was a reckless and desperate act that sealed the fate of Lollardy. In the words of J. A. F. Thomson, the pious gentry, who were otherwise potential recruits for the zealous and principled reformism of Wyclif and his followers, now found that they were 'king's men first and religious radicals second'.[104] As Arundel and Henry V responded to the challenge or spectre of heresy with a measured programme of devotional reading, orthodox preaching, and clerical reform, Catholicism proved itself more than adequate to the spiritual needs at least of the rulers, and probably also of the ruled, in late medieval England.[105]

4

SURVIVAL AND REVIVAL

By 1430, the expansive phase of Lollardy was well and truly over. This is as plain in intellectual as in social terms. No new Lollard treatises were compiled after this date, and there is little evidence even for the continued copying of old texts. Thomas Netter had completed his monumental refutation of Wyclif, and nobody afterwards thought the task worth repeating – except Reginald Pecock, whose innovative attempt to refute the Lollards in the vernacular around the middle of the century struck his clerical contemporaries as a cure far worse than the disease. Nor is there any solid evidence of Lollard traditions being established any-where new after this time. Cases of Lollardy are recorded from time to time in most of the areas already known for heresy, in a pattern which probably reflects rather the varying zeal of the bishops or of the local ruling elite than the innate strength of the movement. It has been argued that Lollardy suffered a sharp decline in the mid-fifteenth century, as very few Lollards turn up in ecclesiastical records between 1430 and 1480, followed by a dramatic revival under the early Tudors. Yet this is probably an optical illusion. Despite the paucity of records in this period (for which many episcopal registers are lost, and for which very few ecclesiastical court books survive), there are clear signs of the persistence of Lollardy in most of the areas where it had already become established.

The question of Lollard numbers is perhaps the most difficult of all those raised about this shadowy movement. Historians tend either to minimise Lollardy on the basis of the small numbers recorded in the admittedly scanty evidence that survives, or else to base vague claims about its popularity on the admitted inadequacy of the poorly preserved records of sporadic and inefficient investigations. Thus Thomson concludes that heresy was confined to the Midlands and the South, whereas Hudson hints that the poorer records for the North and other apparently unaffected regions may conceal a very different reality.[1] Clearly, not even an approximate figure for Lollard strength in the fifteenth century can be produced. However, a sensitive interpretation of surviving evidence, combined with some allowance for the possibility of now lost records, can permit us at least to sketch the distribution of Lollardy, and to estimate whether it was statistically significant or insignificant on a national level.

Geography of Later Lollardy

In the vast diocese of Lincoln, which produced so many early Lollards, dissent seems to have declined during the fifteenth century. The well-head of Lollardy, Oxford University, had seen Lollards as late as the 1420s, but none thereafter. Even at the time of the Oldcastle Rising, Oxfordshire support had come from the surrounding villages rather than the university town itself. It had taken a long time for purges which began in the 1380s to reach their objective, but events such as the flight of Peter Payne to Prague in 1413 and the burning of William Taylor in 1423 illustrate the virtual impossibility of surviving as a Lollard in Oxford after the implementation of Arundel's Constitutions, which, having been formulated there, were promulgated from London in 1409. They also mark the elimination of the academic leadership of the Lollard movement.

Leicestershire and Northamptonshire seem likewise to have been largely clear of heresy after 1414. The gentry of Leicestershire, some of whom had been implicated in the early phase of Lollardy, now stood aloof, with the single exception of Thomas Noveray, a minor gentleman from Illston-on-the-Hill (a few miles from Kibworth Harcourt).[2] Some suspected Lollards were examined at Leicester in 1424, and a few were induced to do penance, but that seems to have been the end.[3] Royal intervention in Northampton in the 1390s seems to have done its work swiftly. Despite the early strength of dissidence in the east Midlands, no evidence of an enduring tradition is found there. The Chilterns, in contrast, turned up a good crop of heretics whenever the Bishops of Lincoln troubled to delve at all deeply. Lollardy was firmly entrenched around Amersham and Chesham.[4] Indeed, in the early sixteenth century, as much as a tenth of the population of the area may have had Lollard beliefs or sympathies. These well-established dissident communities had some connections with those of London, which helps account for the outcrops of Lollardy found along the Middlesex section of the Thames Valley around Staines and Uxbridge – although it has recently been shown that these groups also had connections, by way of the Carder family, with the Lollards of Tenterden in Kent.[5]

The other counties of Lincoln diocese – Lincolnshire itself, Bedfordshire, Huntingdonshire, and Rutland – had seen only one or two isolated cases, if that, in the years up to 1414, and nothing thereafter. Episcopal inefficiency cannot plausibly be invoked as an explanation of how Lollardy might have continued unnoticed, as the Bishops of Lincoln were highly sensitive to the heresy, which had originated in their diocese, and which certainly survived in strength in its southern parts. If they could pick up the scent from distant Buckinghamshire, they would not have missed widespread Lollard activity under their noses. Poor record-keeping can hardly be the explanation, as the Lincoln diocesan records are among the best for the period. It would be strange indeed, if there were ever any court books relating to large-scale investigations elsewhere in the diocese, that only those relating to Buckinghamshire should have survived long enough to fall into John Foxe's hands.

The Kentish Weald also held numerous dissenting communities. Although there is little direct evidence from the fifteenth century, records survive of a major assault on heresy in Canterbury diocese in 1511–12, part of a nationwide hunt which also found dissidents in the Chilterns, Coventry, and Berkshire. Fifty-three suspects were investigated. Most abjured, but five were burned as obdurate or relapsed heretics. Half of the suspects came from around Tenterden, and the rest clustered around Maidstone, Stapleford, Ashford, and Canterbury itself. In the cases of Tenterden and Maidstone, the early sixteenth-century records provide clear indications of an older tradition of heresy. Half of those examined in 1511–12 came from the Tenterden area, and William Carder vouchsafed that his mother had fled Tenterden about 40 years before 'for fere of the saide heresies' – presumably for fear of prosecution.[6] This suggests not only that Lollardy was already established there, but also that Canterbury was among those dioceses (others were London and Hereford) which launched enquiries into heresy around 1470. William White's similar flight from Kent in the 1420s, and the flurry of executions for heresy and sedition which broke out in the county around that time, may indicate another clampdown for which records no longer survive.[7] We can therefore conclude that court books for heresy investigations in fifteenth-century Kent have very probably been lost.

Outside Kent, Lollardy made no further advances in the South or the South West. Chichester diocese, roughly coterminous with the county of Sussex, seems to have remained untouched by it. A certain caution is necessary here, as only two medieval episcopal registers survive. Fortunately, the earliest of them is that of Robert Reade (1396–1415), and the absence of any heresy cases suggests that Lollardy made no headway here in the crucial and sensitive years during which Reade occupied the see, a time of flux when Wycliffite preachers were bolder and less discreet than they were later to become. The brief episcopate of Richard Praty (1438–1445) yields no cases, nor do any turn up in the surviving *sede vacante* records at Canterbury. Despite its proximity to London, Sussex was not even among those shires for which commissions of oyer and terminer were issued in the aftermath of the Oldcastle Rising. The only known heretic in the diocese was Reginald Pecock, himself its Bishop from 1450 until 1457, and he was convicted, ironically enough, on the basis of his own writings against heresy. His deep concern with this problem probably owed more to his years as Master of Whittington College in London (1431–44). The college had been founded by the famous Lord Mayor of London with a specific view to improving the education of the laity in the Christian faith, and London, thanks to the anonymity characteristic of a populous city, was always a relatively safe haven for Lollards.[8]

In the diocese of Salisbury, which covered Berkshire, Wiltshire, and Dorset, Lollardy enjoyed better fortunes. There were signs of heresy in Salisbury itself around 1400, but it does not seem to have taken root there. The very detailed early fifteenth-century ecclesiastical court books which testify to the intrusive moral regime of Dean John Chandler show us plenty of sexual misconduct and ritual transgression, but no heresy. Wiltshire was not among the counties for which commissions of oyer and terminer were issued in the wake of the Oldcastle Rising, though Berkshire was. One might conjecture that dissent spread down into Berkshire from southern Oxfordshire and Buckinghamshire, and perhaps also across from London, following the trade routes to Bristol and the west country. The extensive researches of A. D. Brown found only 16 cases of heresy in the diocese recorded in the century following the Peasants' Revolt. To these can be added the stirs relating to what is sometimes called Jack Sharp's Rising in 1431, when Lollard bills were posted in Salisbury and Devizes, and Thomas Puttock, a priest of Westbury in Wiltshire, was executed. An episcopal commission against heresy issued in the early 1470s shows that the problem did not go away. Heresy cases become far more numerous in this diocese under the Tudors, but again cluster in Berkshire, around Newbury and Reading. Only one or two cases are found from Dorset and Wiltshire, with nothing to suggest that Lollardy had deep roots in those counties. Apart from the clusters in eastern Berkshire, the cases were scattered, and the fact that heresy investigations were recorded in the episcopal registers indicates that these, rather than separate act books, were the preferred document of record for such cases in the diocese, and that therefore no large-scale prosecutions took place. Heresy was certainly an abiding presence, but far from a massive one.

The diocese of Winchester (covering Hampshire and most of Surrey) has an almost complete run of episcopal registers (except for the lengthy episcopate of Cardinal Beaufort), but they contain little evidence of heresy. Records of investigations in Lincolnshire, Salisbury, and London dioceses allude once or twice to Lollards from Winchester, but these men seem themselves to have been stray figures involved in the more flourishing dissident communities outside the diocese. Cardinal Henry Beaufort personally presided at the trial of one Lollard, and asked his episcopal colleague and neighbour, Praty of Chichester, to head an investigation of heresy in his diocese, a task which he was presumably prevented from undertaking himself by the burdens of his high royal office. The records relating to the Oldcastle Rising confirm this silence. A commission was issued for Hampshire, though not for Surrey, but the only indictments or pardons relating to the diocese were for people in Southwark and the Surrey suburbs of London, which were included in a commission for the capital. When occasional heretics were unearthed in Winchester diocese, they came mostly from the Odiham area or from Southwark. In the former case, the links with the Lollardy of nearby Newbury and Reading in Salisbury diocese are plain, and in the latter the influence of London is equally clear.

The different scale of the Lollard problem for the bishops of Salisbury and Winchester is best illustrated in the career of Thomas Langton, Bishop of Salisbury from 1485 to 1493, then translated to Winchester, which he held until 1500. Bringing to his new diocese the zeal that he had shown in searching out 17 heretics during his eight years at Salisbury, his seven years at Winchester yielded only five suspects. One was clearly mad and another eccentric (neither of them from places with any known Lollard connections), while the remaining three – all from Southwark – did penance for nothing worse than possessing illicit books. If they were indeed Lollards, they were clearly orientated towards London rather than the rest of the diocese.[9] The episcopate of Langton's successor, Richard Fox, saw the nearest thing to a major purge against Lollardy in the history of the diocese. One man was burned and ten others abjured in 1513–14, with one group clustered around Kingston-on-Thames and the other around Dogmersfield in Hampshire. Linked with dissidents in Reading, Uxbridge, and Tenterden, they seem to have been of recent origin. The remainder of Fox's episcopate (if anything more vigilant after he retired from royal service in 1517) gives no reason to believe that his diocese had an enduring problem with heresy.[10]

The South West remained almost immune from Lollardy throughout the fifteenth century and beyond. Commissions were issued for the counties of Devon, Dorset, and Somerset (though not for Cornwall) in the wake of the Oldcastle Rising, but these counties provided no recorded supporters for the rising, and virtually no evidence of heresy thereafter. Lollardy left no trace, for example, in the bulky and detailed register which marks the vigilant episcopate of Bishop Edmund Lacy of Exeter, a man whose devotion to his pastoral duties was so intense as to earn him, after his death, popular veneration as a saint.[11] Lollard bills were scattered in Frome (in Somerset, near the Wiltshire border) during the disturbances of 1431, but that is the closest thing to heresy seen in the South West until the Protestant Reformation.

East Anglia was the scene of Lancastrian England's largest documented heresy investigation, the Norwich heresy trials of 1428–31, which saw 60 people charged with sundry offences against the beliefs and practices of the Church (although six of them were casual offenders swept up in the panic[12]). About 50 came from villages or small towns in the Norfolk Broads, especially around Beccles, Bungay, and Loddon, although in most cases only one or two households per settlement were involved. According to the records, the chief figure in this movement was William White, a priest, but as he had only fled to this region from Kent in 1428, he must already have been aware that 'known men' were to be found there. Some of the cases show signs of contacts with Lollard groups further south, in Colchester and perhaps Ipswich. They were later to be found around the Suffolk border and down into Essex, which provided many of London diocese's heresy cases. Lollardy in Essex was found chiefly, though not exclusively, between Colchester and Chelmsford, where it was still firmly rooted in early Tudor times.[13] Narrative sources indicate that Lollards continued to be burned in East Anglia in the late fifteenth and early sixteenth centuries. While some cases are recorded in the episcopal registers, others certainly are not, so it may be inferred that there were later court books (like that for the 1420s) which are now lost.

The situation in the other East Anglian diocese, Ely, was very different. The only recorded cases of heresy in the fifteenth century involved three men from Cambridgeshire who abjured in 1457. They may have been investigated during the panic which accompanied proceedings against Reginald Pecock at that time, and the precise nature of their offences is not known. The presence of Cambridge University in the diocese must have severely limited the impact of Lollardy there. Not only did Cambridge pride itself on its immunity from the heresy which the elder university had begotten, but the benefices of the diocese were often filled by Cambridge graduates who would be better placed than the average rural clergy to detect dissent. Moreover, Ely diocese was small, and episcopal supervision (except under the indolent placeman James Stanley) correspondingly that much more close.

The west Midlands (Gloucestershire, Herefordshire, Shropshire, Warwickshire, and Worcestershire) had seen a good deal of Lollard activity in the early years, but after the 1420s saw practically none

outside the urban centres of Bristol and Coventry, and the isolated
Forest of Dean, where cases of heresy are reported from the
1470s, the 1490s, and the early sixteenth century. The episcopal
registers of Bath and Wells show that the problem was ineradicable in Bristol, where the parish of St Mary Redcliffe was notorious for Lollardy throughout the fifteenth century.[14] The vigorous
episcopate of Charles Booth (Bishop of Hereford, 1516–35) turned
up not a single case. Booth took a close personal interest in the
diocese he rarely left for any reason, and his register is a model of
careful administration and record-keeping. Nor is there much to
be said in this case for the conjecture that there were once separate
act books for proceedings against heretics, as Hereford previously
recorded such proceedings in the episcopal registers. If Booth
had faced a serious heresy problem, it would almost certainly have
manifested itself in his register, which contains several documents
relating to the clampdown on evangelical doctrines in the 1520s.
And it would probably have left some impression on mid-Tudor
evangelical literature. John Foxe was well informed about proceedings in Coventry, and would probably have heard had there been
serious purges elsewhere in this region under the Tudors. The
early success of Lollardy in this region had been heavily dependent
upon gentry support, but after the Oldcastle Rising the gentry of
these counties were solidly orthodox until evangelical teachings
began to make some converts in the 1520s.

Coventry, unlike most of the west Midlands, offers compelling
evidence of a continuous Lollard tradition. From the stray survival
of a Coventry act book relating to the proceedings of 1511–12
under Bishop Geoffrey Blythe we may infer that other such books
from earlier periods have been lost.[15] John Foxe certainly had access
to materials of this kind, for he reports a clutch of abjurations in
1485 and of burnings in 1519. As only one Lollard turns up in the
full series of episcopal registers from the fifteenth century, it
seems likely that earlier investigations regarding Coventry were
separately recorded as they were under Blythe. In 1449 a Coventry
man named John Cardmaker was burned at Smithfield for heresy,
having denied the real presence and attacked the cult of the
saints. Lollard bills had been posted in Coventry during the stirs
of 1431, and there were some executions there that year.[16] Going
still further back, Coventry had provided men in response to
Oldcastle's call. Yet if Coventry continued to harbour a Lollard

minority, this was apparently all that remained of the Midlands'
tradition so strong earlier in the century. In this particular case, it
is possible that religious dissent was linked with social dissent, as
Poos has argued was also the case in Essex. For Coventry under-
went sharp economic decline in the later Middle Ages, and this
experience was marked not only by regular proceedings against
heresy but by even more frequent outbreaks of disorder.[17]

Neither the North nor the northern Midlands figure in the
history of Lollardy in the later fifteenth century. The only convicted Lollard found in early Tudor Yorkshire, Roger Gargrave
of Wakefield, had learned his heresies from a Lincolnshire priest.[18]
Again, it remains theoretically possible either that the ecclesiastical
authorities in that vast region never realised what was actually
going on, or that records of systematic heresy investigations have
since been lost. But the first alternative seems implausible for
a region in which the personality of Margery Kempe made such
an impact. The region which put tens of thousands of men into
the field in 1536 over the relatively limited religious reforms of
Henry VIII would hardly have tolerated Lollard minorities in the
way that parts of Buckinghamshire, Essex, and Kent seem to have
done. The more dispersed nature of settlement in the North (few
towns of any size and many more hamlets than villages) and the
predominance of pastoral over arable agriculture meant that
there were fewer craftsmen and fewer schools, which in turn
meant less literacy – a prerequisite of Lollardy. The immense
power of the northern monasteries (which monopolised what
schooling there was) further reduced the potential for heresy. Even
in the relatively more favourable social and geographical condi-
tions of Yorkshire, monasteries and collegiate churches formed
an ecclesiastical establishment which must have made it very hard
for dissent to be propagated. The silence is overwhelming, and
the stray cases of heresy which appear in the surviving episcopal
registers for York not only militate against the likelihood that
separate court books recorded heresy purges, but are also too
obviously scattered for it to be maintained that the north Midlands
and the North harboured traditions of dissent.

The importance of geographical considerations in the history of
Lollardy can sometimes be seen in the way that suspect dissidents
came to the attention of the authorities. In the case of major investigations, such as those in Norfolk in the 1420s, or the Chilterns in

the early sixteenth century, the means of detection was determined official investigation. However, many of the cases recorded in episcopal registers were isolated, and therefore presumably reflect casual informing rather than systematic investigation. Often enough, the Lollards brought to abjuration had betrayed themselves by indiscreet remarks or behaviour. At the best of times they were not inclined to force their beliefs down other people's throats, but it must often have become difficult to avoid giving oneself away.

Many of these casually detected Lollards were recent arrivals, and had brought their distinctive attitudes with them. Edward Freez, for example, born in York of Dutch ancestry, went south in search of work and picked up Lollard beliefs in Colchester before finding himself gaoled for heresy around 1530.[19] Thomas Hygons was a carpenter from Woolaston in the Forest of Dean who was clearly connected with the Lollards of Lydney (a few miles away to the north-east). It was only when he moved to Micheldeane, far away to the north of the Forest, that a stray comment sympathetic to the heretics of Lydney got him into trouble with the authorities.[20] It seems unlikely that convinced Lollards should refrain from expressing their beliefs until they moved to a new home or workplace. More plausibly, there may have been a degree of tacit toleration of their reclusive deviance in those communities where Lollard minorities had become part of the scenery. Views which might not raise eyebrows in one's birthplace could become rather more shocking elsewhere. Derek Plumb's illuminating work on the Buckinghamshire Lollards of Henry VIII's reign, work which has reshaped our vision of later Lollardy, shows us a group which was thoroughly integrated into local society, and which was so numerous that it simply cannot have passed unnoticed by conformist neighbours.[21] Whenever the Bishops of Lincoln decided to crack down, they were able to penetrate the dissident movement at will, which shows that it was not well concealed. But when Lollards left those localities where they formed part of the landscape, they exposed themselves to the risk of detection by airing their views, even unconsciously, in communities in which such views were not tolerable.

This interpretation puts some of the tribulations of Margery Kempe into a different light. More than once this expressively devout lady so shook a local community that she was immediately suspected of heresy. Presumably, heresy was not socially acceptable in those communities (Leicester, York, Beverley, and Canterbury) where her piety aroused such unfavourable attention. So such communities probably harboured no tradition of dissent. Derek Plumb provides us with an interesting example of the process operating the other way round. The household of Francis Funge, a Lollard of Little Missenden, found itself under investigation in 1537 after churchwardens from a neighbouring parish, collecting door to door for their church funds, noticed a copy of the gospels in English lying around.[22] What was tolerable idiosyncracy in one parish could be unacceptable deviance a few miles away. This model offers an explanation for the curious fact that most of the Bristol Lollards known to history (other than those implicated in the Oldcastle Rising) are known because they were discovered away from Bristol, as far afield as Portishead, Gloucester, Salisbury, Birmingham, and Lincoln.

McFarlane noted years ago that Lollards flourished around diocesan boundaries, where evasion was easier.[23] We might add that Lollardy also survived better in less accessible regions. Physical geography can be as relevant to the understanding of Lollardy as political geography. The opportunities for concealment afforded by the Forest of Dean are illustrated by the case of Thomas Packer of Walford, who was wanted for heresy for several years but could never be apprehended. Lydney and Woolaston, to the south of the Forest, were remote from the diocesan administration.[24] The strong Lollard tradition in Bristol was never subject to effective repression because, although hardly remote geographically, the city was divided between two dioceses (Worcester north of the Avon, Bath and Wells south of it) and jealous of both. Moreover, Lollards came mainly from the parish of St Mary Redcliffe, which was just across the Avon from the city proper, and thus outside civic jurisdiction.[25] Most of our evidence for Lollardy comes from areas like the Chilterns (the southernmost region of the vast Lincoln diocese), the Forest of Dean (forested areas were notoriously hard to govern), the Norfolk Broads, and the Kentish Weald, which were either on episcopal borders, or relatively isolated, or both.

Conversely, a number of early Lollard preachers were picked up because they were active close to cathedral cities or episcopal residences. This in turn suggests that the later absence of evidence for Lollardy in most cathedral cities reflects reality rather than gaps in the historical record. The exceptions to this rule can be readily accounted for. London's uniquely dense population made it an admirable hiding-place, while Coventry was rarely visited by its bishops, who preferred their other seat at Lichfield. Coventry was a more powerful city, with a council more likely to resent and better able to resist episcopal interference. The example of Lichfield, a more traditional cathedral city, shows why heresy must have struggled in such places. The Lichfield records are exiguous in the extreme for the fifteenth century, but there is no sign of Lollardy in the single surviving volume of reports from the dean's visitations of the city in the 1460s. As with most such materials, the dominant theme is sexual misconduct.[26] Lollardy would have found it very hard to gain a footing in an urban society over which the dean maintained such close, even intrusive, supervision. As the town depended economically on the cathedral community (probably the largest local landowner) and remained in the bishop's manorial jurisdiction until the Reformation, Wycliffite teachings were never likely to find fertile soil there.

Another class of towns which seem to have been all but immune to Lollardy are the major monastic centres, such as St Alban's, Bury St Edmund's, Glastonbury, Gloucester, Malmesbury, and Peterborough. The unitary control of local government by an abbot who was both the feudal lord and the immediate agent of ecclesiastical jurisdiction (many such abbeys were, with their environs, exempt from episcopal jurisdiction) presumably lent itself to running a tight ship. Anticlericalism might flourish in places where political and social grievances would inevitably focus on a single institution, but heresy may have been simply too risky in such a context. Although Walsingham casts aspersions on the townsfolk of St Albans, who, having founded a guild of St Alban in 1377, sacked the monastery and its lordship in 1381, he provides no evidence of heretical beliefs among them.[27] His anxiety about heresy would have tipped into the paranoia on which it always verges had Lollards actually been detected within the jurisdiction of his own abbey. The great monastic towns may have been as successful in excluding the Lollards as they were in excluding the friars, who only rarely secured a foothold in these centres. Moreover, the importance of pilgrimage in the economies of monastic centres may have reduced the appeal of Lollard iconophobia and would besides have rendered Lollard views, if expressed, far more likely to be reported. There was one major exception to the rule, namely

Reading, which produced Lollards in significant numbers under the early Tudors. But, here, the countervailing influence was probably the relative strength of Lollardy to the north of Reading in Buckinghamshire, and to the west around Newbury, itself explicable in terms of this region's distance from episcopal centres and the confluence of trade routes there.

The case of London is *sui generis*. In such a large and densely populated city, a complex parish network full of jurisdictional peculiars and liberties, Lollards seem to have survived more anonymously than elsewhere. The case of Alice Cowper, tried for heresy with her husband William around 1510, illustrates this perfectly. Alice's views came to light when she had a bad fall in pregnancy. Her neighbours urged her to make a pilgrimage to a nearby shrine of St Laurence for the sake of the unborn child, but she replied with robust contempt for the practice, which she dismissed as a means for parting fools from their money.[28] This suggests that her neighbours were previously unaware of her Lollard convictions, for otherwise they would hardly have added insult to injury by proposing that she go on pilgrimage. Given her neighbours' role in betraying her, we can conclude that Lollards were not especially welcome in London, however easy they may have found it to hide there. Not the least significant aspect of this episode is that this Lollard couple's neighbours were obviously orthodox Catholics. Any Lollard 'community' to which the Cowpers were affiliated must have been diffuse in comparison with the irresistibly intrusive parish community of the average town or village. Evidence for Lollardy in fifteenth-century London is scarce, and mostly derives from the city chronicle tradition, which tends to record burnings rather than abjurations, although abjurations were presumably more frequent. With the Tudors, however, evidence becomes relatively plentiful. After the decision taken around 1510 to intensify action against heresy, Bishop Richard Fitzjames brought a substantial number of Lollards to book, and there were several burnings in the following decade.[29] Some of these cases are known to us from the episcopal registers, but others from now lost court books or visitation records. Fitzjames himself was acutely sensitive to heresy, suspecting even the dean of his own cathedral, John Colet, of doctrinal deviance. The paucity of evidence for London Lollardy prior to his episcopate therefore seems more likely to reflect either the disappearance of court books or a lack of inquisitorial zeal in his predecessors. Susan Brigden's analysis of the surviving evidence from Fitzjames's records portrays a tight-knit community whose members tended to marry among their own, were well furnished with books, and met regularly for bible-reading.[30] The endogamy and solidarity of this group are the marks of a well-established tradition rather than of a new growth.

Social Distribution of Later Lollardy

The received wisdom of a previous generation of historians was that Lollardy was predominantly 'proletarian' in character, an adjective as pejorative for some writers as approbatory for others. For once, we can truly say that recent research has proved the contrary. The analysis of the known social origins of late medieval Essex heretics conducted by L. R. Poos reveals a healthy number of craftsmen and tradesmen, and relatively few labourers. A similar pattern emerges from studies of Lollards in the dioceses of Coventry and Lichfield and of Salisbury.[31] The researches of Derek Plumb into the Lollards of Buckinghamshire, which have fleshed out John Foxe's summaries of now lost ecclesiastical records with the aid of wills and subsidy rolls, have shown us a group represented at every social level in the villages and small market towns of that region. Among those Lollards compelled by Bishop Longland to abjure in the 1520s were men worth £10, £20, and even £40 a year. No historian would any longer care to dismiss Lollardy as 'proletarian'. But the almost complete absence of Lollardy among the gentry and the clergy remains a serious limit on its social spread. Derek Plumb perhaps stretches the evidence in finding gentlemen among Foxe's Lollards. True, some were financially comparable to the lesser gentry, but, with the exception of the Durdants of Iver Court (mere gentry at best), none are described as gentlemen in surviving records. Nor are any clergymen found in this most numerous of Lollard communities. Plumb's Lollards hardly form part of the 'political nation'.[32] The Coventry evidence has been taken to show the appeal of Lollardy in higher strata of society, involving for example Alice Rowley, widow of a former mayor, and Dr James Preston, vicar of St Michael's Coventry and an Oxford DD. However, earlier interpretations of this evidence have recently been subjected to damaging criticism. While Rowley

certainly was a Lollard, neither Dr Preston nor the other prominent citizens named in the proceedings are likely to have had
heretical sympathies.[33]

With one or two exceptions, Lollardy after Oldcastle was confined
to the middling levels of the social structure. There were perhaps
a handful of Lollard priests, a few Lollards among urban elites,
and one or two among the minor gentry. But there were neither
suspects nor convicts comparable with Oldcastle or the 'Lollard
knights'. As with every observable feature of the Lollard phenomenon, the evidence, or lack of evidence, is susceptible of widely
differing interpretations. The likeliest is simply that heresy held
little attraction for the clerical and gentle population. But it has
recently been proposed that gentry disdain for Lollardy may be
an optical illusion, arising from the notorious difficulty of bringing
home criminal charges against gentlefolk in this era. Only, it is
argued, when a gentleman stepped so far outside the social consensus as to engage in treason, as in the case of Oldcastle and his
followers, was he likely to be troubled for his beliefs.[34] Under other
circumstances they would be virtually untouchable, especially by
the church courts. Moreover, the case goes on, the wide distribution
of English bibles, which were probably mostly in the hands of
gentry, bourgeois, and clerical readers, may in fact be evidence
for covert Lollard sympathies among the owners and their kind.
Ownership of the English scriptures might constitute *prima facie*
grounds for suspicion of heresy among artisans and labourers,
but clearly not among aristocrats and their ladies.

However, these revisionist hypotheses are flimsy enough.
While it is manifestly true that ownership of English scriptures
and, indeed, of English religious texts of any kind was socially
differentiated as grounds for suspicion of heresy, this may have
been perfectly justifiable. Moreover, it is an exaggeration to maintain that the gentry were entirely above the law, even the canon
law. For the church courts made notable attempts even in the
fifteenth century to impose stricter standards of sexual and marital
morality upon the gentry. These attempts may not have been
notably successful, but it is clear that they were made. In a society
whose tolerance for heresy was far lower than its tolerance for
adultery, it is unlikely that the church courts would have shied
away from pursuing heretics at any level. The unfortunate Reginald
Pecock might be evidence for this, although as a clergyman and

an author he was arguably far more likely than a layman to be troubled for doctrinal deviance. But bishops were themselves powerful figures in local politics, and it is hard to envisage Archbishops of Canterbury, for instance, who wielded massive power in Kent, where there was a firmly rooted dissident tradition, being intimidated by the prospect of proceeding against even substantial gentlemen for heresy should there have been any need to do so. An Archbishop of York whose retainers brawled with those of the Earl of Northumberland is unlikely to have shied away from confronting heresy among lesser landowners.[35] Examining the problem horizontally, rivalries among the gentry would have been an ideal mechanism for bringing religious dissent into the open. What better way to cripple a rival than to smear him with the charge of heresy, which was then by definition equivalent to sedition? As Maureen Jurkowski has shown, the Lollard smear was used around 1420 by the Derbyshire rivals of Thomas Tykhill, apparently with some success.[36] The equation of heresy with sedition was the ultimate deterrent to aristocratic Lollardy. Heresy was inextricably associated with social upheaval and disorder, precisely the values which the gentry were most concerned to oppose. Heresy disqualified from political office, and royal officials had to swear an oath against it. In considering the apparent lack of sympathy for Lollardy among the gentry, it is not so much the absence of charges or convictions as the absence even of rumours and suspicion which carries the weight of the argument from silence.

That Lollardy found its following chiefly among artisans is beyond doubt. Yet we should beware of assuming that this sector of society was deeply predisposed to dissent. For devout confraternities also exercised a particular appeal among artisans. Artisan interest in both Lollardy and orthodox piety may have reflected prosperity and leisure rather than any intellectual or temperamental preferences. Looking below the artisans and their like, we find ourselves among the humble labourers and the poor, for whom even membership of the sort of guild likely to have left us records was in most cases an expensive luxury rather than a rational economic and spiritual investment. This is not to deny that some of the other social characteristics of artisans, such as higher literacy rates, more moral independence as their own masters, and the business experience of trading and of minor office-holding in guild, parish, or civic administration, may have rendered them more likely to be reached by the Lollard message and better equipped to give it a hearing. But it is to maintain that none of these social characteristics need have predisposed them to Lollardy rather than to active engagement in conventional devotion through the lawful means of confraternity membership and administration, parish management and fund-raising, and public piety. In comparison with orthodox devotion, Lollardy was making an alternative, and ultimately more limited, appeal to what was essentially the same constituency rather than offering a degree of lay participation which was precluded in conventional parish life.

Gender Distribution of Lollardy

The very vivid pictures of some striking and talented women which emerge from the surviving records of Lollardy have led some historians to conclude that Lollardy had particular appeal for women, and that women were attracted to Lollardy because it offered them opportunities for self-expression and leadership denied them by the patriarchal structures of late medieval Catholicism. Women like Hawisia Mone and Margery Baxter were quite as familiar with the formal tenets of Lollardy as their male counterparts, and gave robust accounts of themselves and their beliefs under interrogation, obviously undaunted by the majesty and magisterium of the hierarchy.[37] Alice Rowley of Coventry occupied a prominent place in the Lollard community around 1500, and was in addition literate, perhaps a rare accomplishment at that time for a woman outside the cloister or the aristocracy. 'Mother Bocher' was clearly an influential figure first in Essex Lollardy, and then in Kentish Protestantism during the reign of Henry VIII.[38] Claire Cross has drawn together the material from across the history of the movement (1380–1530) concluding from her study of these 'great reasoners in scripture' that 'The attractions of lollardy for lay people in general and women in particular are not hard to understand'.[39] Derek Plumb has recently drawn attention to the prominence of women in early sixteenth-century Buckinghamshire Lollardy. Alice Collins of Ginge was liable to be called upon by Lollard friends to furnish them with recitations from scriptures which she had memorised.

Margaret Aston has even argued that there may have been Lollard 'women priests'.[40]

However, once the anecdotal evidence is set in a broader statistical perspective, as in the excellent recent study by Shannon McSheffrey, the case is altered. The surviving records of known or suspected Lollards show a heavy preponderance of men over women. Out of 955 suspected Lollards detected in those investigations for which sizeable quantities of data survive, 271 were women (28 per cent), 173 of them certainly related to a male suspect. This means that only about a third of the women detected are not known to have been related to male suspects (and the patchy nature of the evidence means that many of these women will, in fact, have been brought to Lollardy by family or household ties).[41]

Cross has conclusively demonstrated that the role of women in Lollardy was far from passive. However, as she declares, their activity took place predominantly within the family context, in accordance with the character of Lollardy as a 'family sect'.[42] Although she suggests that such women as the wives of William White and Thomas Man shared in the evangelical ministry of their itinerant husbands, the evidence for this is slim. John Foxe credits White's wife, Joan, with preaching the word, but the original records from which he seems to have worked do not bear out his claim. As for Thomas Man's wife, also nameless in the surviving records, she presumably abjured when her husband was sent to the stake, as she subsequently sank into obscurity. Foxe's account associates her grammatically with her husband in the conversion of several hundred people, but there is nothing to suggest that she played an active part in this work.[43] And although the authorities, as Cross shows, were for whatever reason more reluctant to burn women than men, it is hard to imagine them showing much mercy to women who had not only deviated from the orthodox faith, but also transgressed gender boundaries so egregiously as to exercise a public pastorate. Once more, the story of Margery Kempe provides a useful control, in that the hostile reception often accorded to her almost evangelical activities suggests that for a woman to venture on to such sacred ground was to invite trouble. The claim that Lollardy may have appealed to women through offering them opportunities for public ministry must be judged improbable.

Lollard women played their part within the movement, but largely within the domestic context. Although it was more common

for husbands to convert wives, there are several recorded case of
wives converting their husbands. But women themselves seem to
have acquired Lollard beliefs through household connections: if
not from their husbands, then from their parents or masters.
There is very little evidence for women coming to Lollardy outside
these power relationships. McSheffrey has pointed out how difficult it would be for married women in particular to gain access to
Lollard communities other than in their own homes or in the
company of their husbands. For a woman to be absent from home
at night (when many Lollard gatherings were necessarily held)
without her husband was to jeopardise her reputation and his
honour.[44] However, Lollard women exercised particular importance as mothers. As Claire Cross has shown, there are many
accounts of Lollard mothers teaching their children vernacular
prayers, passages from or summaries of the scriptures, and dissident
doctrinal tenets. Agnes Pykas, presumably converted to Lollardy
after her son had left home, summoned him from London to
Braintree in order to urge him to follow her example, which he
did. Lollard widows also figure more prominently in the history
of the movement. From Christina More of Bristol in the early
fifteenth century to Alice Rowley of Coventry in the early
sixteenth, widows are often found as hostesses of Lollard gatherings
or patronesses of Lollard groups. Christina More, the widow of
a Bristol alderman, maintained a Lollard chaplain and equipped
men for the Oldcastle Rising. Alice Rowley was the unquestioned
leader of a group of Lollards who, however, were themselves
predominantly female (as McSheffrey has pointed out). Although
there is nothing to suggest that Rowley's husband, William, was
a Lollard, his widow's inheritance of his social status seems to have
helped her establish her position of leadership in her community.

What is more debateable is whether the role which the surviving evidence allows us to ascribe to Lollard women with certainty
can justify Claire Cross's contention that Lollardy therefore
offered women scope for religious activity which was denied them
within the confines of late medieval orthodoxy. In fact, the two
main areas of female activity within Lollardy, namely the influence
of mothers over children and the relatively greater freedom of
action of widows, correspond closely to the position in the church
and society at large. The inculcation of traditional prayers in the
minds of small children was almost certainly largely the work of

mothers, literate or not. William Tyndale testifies to domestic catechesis in his controversy with Thomas More – 'And the father and the mother taught them a monstrous Latin paternoster and an ave and a creed' – even while anxious to emphasise that 'they understand them not'.[45] The fifteenth-century didactic poem, 'The good wife taught her daughter', is, as its title states, predicated on the mother's responsibility for educating at least her female children. It would tend to fall to the mother, rather than to the father, to show children how to tell their beads. We can base this claim on such diverse evidence as expositions of the Ten Commandments and of religious duties, which emphasise the role of mothers in such basic catechetical tasks, and in religious art, which often shows us, for example, St Anne teaching her daughter Mary to read. (Even if, as Eamon Duffy has suggested, we should interpret such pictures as Anne teaching Mary to pray, the fact that prayer is depicted as being taught with the aid of a book is in itself indirect testimony to an ideal of literacy, suggesting as it does a conception of prayer as a literate activity.)[46]

Although the social freedom of action of women was notoriously limited in the later Middle Ages, it is equally notorious that widows, as in the famous, if fictitious, case of the Wife of Bath, had certain advantages over the rest of their sex. This was particularly true for widows among the urban elite.[47] Christina More and Alice Rowley inherited their husbands' business interests and social status, and it was this which underpinned their prominence within their Lollard communities, not some putative Lollard openness to female activism and authority. Exactly the same opportunities were already available to Catholic widows in the urban elite or the aristocracy. Most widows clearly found conventional orthodoxy quite adequate for their spiritual needs and aspirations.[48]

Lollards themselves saw things differently from their modern historians. Like the early Protestant Reformers, they saw Catholicism as designed to appeal particularly to women. Michael Gamare of Wimborne St Giles (Dorset) is reported to have criticised the local custom by which 'women will come and set their candles afore . . . the image of Saint Giles'.[49] This was of course no compliment, but reflected a view of women as easily gulled. The cult of the saints was marked out as especially womanish, and although the evidence for male participation in that cult is plentiful, it is still likely that women might indeed have been disproportionately engaged in it.

We find more men than women on pilgrimages, yet women may have predominated over men in the domestic and local manifestations of the cult of the saints. And if the noblemen and gentry of late medieval England were pious enough, we often find still greater intensity of devotion in their wives or widows, women such as Lady Margaret Beaufort or Cecily, Duchess of York.

It is difficult to maintain that Lollardy offered most women more than they could find within the trammels of conformity. Orthodox piety afforded women opportunities such as licences to choose private confessors and maintain domestic altars, participation in Hocktide inversion rituals, membership of confraternities and guilds open or even restricted to women, the cult of the Blessed Virgin and of a host of other female saints, the role of godmother in the ritual kinship of baptism, specific roles in Candlemas rituals, and gender-specific provision such as midwifery and special relics to assist in labour and childbirth (the only two social structures for this difficult episode in a woman's life) and the 'churching' of women – not to mention the ultimate option of the religious life in a nunnery or as an anchoress. Almost all of these practices were repudiated by Lollardy, which might therefore rather be seen as restricting than as extending women's opportunities.[50] This is not to propose the late medieval Church as a pioneer of women's liberation. But it is to deny that we should seek to make Lollardy a pioneer of women's liberation either. The assumption, apparently traceable to modern feminist ideology, that dissidence was a more fulfilling female strategy than conformity remains, at least for the fifteenth and sixteenth centuries, just that – an assumption. The fact that Lollardy broke with traditional concepts of the sacred does not mean that it must therefore have broken with traditional concepts of the feminine. On the contrary, Lollardy may actually have anticipated the Reformation in toughening the patriarchal tendencies of late medieval Catholicism and in tightening, rather than relaxing, gender stereotypes.

The Dynamics of Lollard Communities

It has already been argued that Lollardy was not sufficiently clearly defined or tightly organised to be described as a sect. It was more of a network. Nevertheless, Lollards demonstrably enjoyed social connections with each other, and took part in shared devotional experiences, themselves perhaps too informal and inchoate to be termed ritual or liturgy, yet still testifying to a social spirit which can be properly described as community or tradition. Although the available data is entirely limited to nuggets in the hard rock of church court records, we can say a certain amount about how Lollards shared and enacted their beliefs, beyond the trivial facts that they did not hold regular services and that they seem mostly to have participated in the compulsory ritual life of the parish church.

One thing that soon appears from the records is that Lollards could be very mobile. Many Lollards can be named who travelled far from their birthplace in the course of their careers. There is no reason to presume, however, that they were disproportionately mobile. Recent research has emphasised that labour mobility in late medieval and early modern England was far higher than was once assumed in facile models of a stolid peasantry.[51] But it is worth noting that Lollardy did not impede labour mobility. Lollards do not seem to have sacrificed economic opportunities in order to stay in the relative security of their native communities.

Lollards were certainly mobile at the local level. The Kentish Lollards prosecuted in 1511–12 were drawn from a range of towns and villages (16 are named in the records), and the detailed depositions (of which there are all too few) show that dissidents from the surrounding villages were in contact with those in the urban centre of Maidstone. The Maidstone Lollard Edward Walker seems to have been a regional leader, and his home was visited by Lollards from Cranbrook, a good ten miles away. Robert Harryson, who came from Halden (near Tenterden), ended his days in a hospital in Canterbury, in contact with Lollards from Godmersham (six miles away).[52] The Lollards of Tenterden, Cranbrook, and the nearby villages were in touch with each other as well as with distant Maidstone and Canterbury. In short, it seems not inappropriate to describe early sixteenth-century Kentish Lollardy as a network.

Moreover, Lollards were able to move from a community in one county or diocese to another perhaps a hundred miles away. Trade routes marked the lines of communication – though, of course, religious beliefs have historically moved along trade routes, for reasons that hardly require elucidation. Thus, for example,

a Kentish Lollard who had abjured at Maidstone in 1495 was in
Coventry in 1512, having lived in the meantime in Northampton
and London.[53] In several cases this mobility was essential to survival.
We must be careful not to romanticise these cases as 'Lollard evangelists'. After the first generation, the leading Lollards were too
circumspect to justify such an appellation: they hardly shouted
from the rooftops. Such movement as we can trace seems to have
been between existing communities, rather than outreach to new
populations. Displaying dissident sentiments or behaviour among
unsympathetic strangers was often how travelling Lollards were
caught away from their homes. After the initial missionary phase
in the decades around 1400, the only Lollard we find boasting of
making converts is Thomas Man, perhaps the most widely
travelled Lollard in the history of the movement. His career took
him to places as varied as Amersham, Billericay, Chelmsford,
Colchester, Henley, Newbury, and Uxbridge, as well as to London,
Norfolk, and Suffolk. He boasted of having made 700 converts
during his career.[54] But we must be careful. Foxe paraphrases his
source (itself now lost), and was not averse to massaging his data to
make a point. The notion of conversion was central to Foxe's
understanding of Christianity, but not to the less evangelical
Lollard tradition. Although what we know of Buckinghamshire
Lollardy confirms Man's pivotal role, it does not suggest that
many people owed their dissident beliefs directly to him. Family
connections were still the main path of transmission.

Another feature of later Lollard life evident from the records is
that the transmission of Lollard teachings took place from the
1420s largely in an informal and domestic context. The early
decades of Lollard evangelism had ended with the system of
censorship and licensing established by Arundel's Constitutions
and enforced with the support of the secular magistrates from the
reign of Henry V. The publication and broadcasting of dissident
ideas was henceforth difficult and dangerous. Instead, Lollards
resorted to more private means of spreading the word. Margery
Baxter of Martham in Norfolk, for example, invited women
round to her house of an evening to hear her husband read from
the gospels. She also extolled the learning of Hawisia Mone, and
of the latter's nephew Richard Belward.[55] Richard Fox, the curate
of Steeple Bumpstead in the early sixteenth century, was converted
as a result of private conversations with one of his parishioners,

John Tyball, and himself influenced others beneath the secrecy of sacramental confession.[56] Parents, of course, taught their ideas to their children, as John and Agnes Grebill of Tenterden taught their sons Christopher and John in the reign of Henry VII. Other family or household connections could also play their part. John Grebill senior had been introduced to heresy by a weaver who worked for him, who read the gospels while he operated the loom. Agnes Raynold of Cranbrook, who abjured in July 1511, had formerly been a servant of William Baker, who abjured the month before. The London Lollards punished by Richard Fitzjames gathered in each other's houses, often by night, to listen to the scriptures.[57] The Durdants of Iver Court were accustomed to have the Epistles of Paul read aloud at meals.[58]

This generally domestic character might seem to be compromised by the references in certain records, notably the Norfolk heresy trials of the 1420s, to Lollard 'schools', a usage that has been taken by numerous commentators to indicate that the Lollards organised formal instruction on a regular basis at specific locations.[59] It should be observed, however, that talk of 'schools' is found in those parts of the records which reflect the thoughts of the persecutors, and not in those which bring us closer to the words of the victims and witnesses. It is the clergy of the official church who talk of schools, not those they are dealing with. Nor should this surprise us. The investigating clergy were for the most part university educated, and were thus predisposed to assume that sophisticated religious instruction could only be offered on a formal basis. But the recollections of fireside gatherings which come from the Lollards themselves show us something altogether less systematic. They differ only in content from the sort of gatherings which might have been held in other houses to listen to those *Canterbury Tales* or tales of Robin Hood to which Tudor Reformers of all complexions reckoned their countrymen were too deeply addicted.

Historians have been ready to assume the popular appeal of Lollardy, but less open to the possibility of popular hostility towards it. Yet there is evidence that neither the beliefs nor the behaviour of Lollards were much admired or respected in contemporary society. Apart from the host's contempt for what he jestingly takes as the Parson's Lollard hang-up about swearing, we have the less purely literary testimony of Margery Kempe to the way her combination of orthodox zeal with ebullient tactlessness could divide the communities she visited. Almost wherever she went, her extrovert devotion and her unapologetic campaign against blasphemy outraged clergy and laity alike. Her apparent usurpation of the priestly ministry offered an easy target: her habit of reproving vice and of telling instructive parables was simply too close to the preaching style and technique of the friars to whom she loved to listen. She was taken for a Lollard in places as far apart as Canterbury, Lambeth, Bristol, Leicester, York, Hessle (just outside Hull), Beverley, Lincoln, and Ely.[60] More importantly, although she often had supporters as well as enemies in these places, it was not because she was seen as a Lollard that support was forthcoming. On the contrary, those who thought her a Lollard wished to see her burned. She was of course an outsider in all these places, and thus more vulnerable, but it is still remarkable that the mere suspicion of Lollardy was capable of arousing such violent hatred. When one adds to this the stories of queues of devout churchgoers taking turns to place faggots on a heretic's pyre, one has good evidence of widespread social prejudice.

A Tudor Revival of Lollardy?

Such statistical evidence as can be amassed is certainly consonant with the view that there was a marked resurgence of Lollardy in Tudor England. For example, recorded investigations in the diocese of Salisbury, which had turned up 16 cases of heresy between 1380 and 1480, turn up growing numbers thereafter: 17 in the years 1485–93; 25 in the years 1493–96; and 70 in the years 1502–24. The distribution of heresy, however, remained strongly localised. Of the 17 cases from 1485 to 1493, a dozen came from around Newbury, and three more from the north-east corner of the diocese on the Oxfordshire border. The other two cases are almost certainly not Wycliffites. Richard Lyllyngston of Castle Combe appears to be an alehouse sceptic, while Joan Forde of Steeple Ashton expressed views best described as cant Donatism. Neither seems to have been part of any wider community of dissent.[61] The dioceses of Lincoln and London show a similar pattern: sporadic cases from 1380 to 1480, followed by more dramatic numbers thereafter. However, as is so often the case with data about Lollardy, particularly statistical data, the figures turn out to be less revealing, and arguably less impressive, when examined more closely. The crucial question remains whether the statistical growth represents a real increase in the numbers of Lollards, or a real increase in the interest of the authorities in searching them out, or both.

What is undeniable is that the repression was more intense. With the accession of the Tudors, the English Church seems to have adopted a policy of 'zero tolerance' towards dissent. This can be traced in the statistics for the burning of heretics. Some 25 Lollards are known to have been burned in the first century of Lollardy, but from 1485 to 1536 we know of about 50 victims. As with the figures for abjurations, which also increase markedly under the Tudors, it is hard to be sure whether we are looking at more Lollards, more repression, or simply better survival of records. However, an intensification of punishment would fit with the general intensification of penal policy by the Tudors.[62] It is difficult to assess the statistical frequency of burning compared with abjuration, for often we know of the burnings from anecdotal rather than archival sources. There may have been other burnings, and it is certain that behind at least some of the burnings lay more numerous abjurations of which no record has survived. The small numbers of martyrs and obvious deficiencies of the evidence regarding pre-Tudor Lollardy therefore preclude reliable comparisons. But the impression remains that punishment became more severe. We are probably looking at a mixture of better survival of records and more vigorous investigation.

Most of those prosecuted under the Tudors came from areas with a long established tradition of Lollardy. There is little sign of expansion into new areas. The solitary Lollard found in Yorkshire, whose new faith was derived from further south, can hardly be regarded as the harbinger of a popular dissident movement. The Lollards of Lincoln diocese were almost all in the familiar Chiltern heartland around Amersham. The startling numbers of Lollards found in the diocese of Salisbury were mostly from Berkshire, near to that Chiltern heartland and to the Thames-Severn artery which loosely linked so many known Lollard communities; and they were located on the margins of the diocese, where it bordered with Lincoln. Colchester and London provided most of those investigated in the London diocese. In other words, if Lollardy was reviving, it was doing so in a strange fashion, widening its appeal in those areas where it had always been established without winning new supporters in new fields. It was, moreover, reviving with virtually no academic or clerical leadership. The few priests found among them were not graduates. In particular, even under the Tudors there was still no sign of Lollard heresy among the friars, who were everywhere so crucial to the success of the Protestant Reformation. Nor do we know of any fresh Lollard literature produced after 1485; while none of the older literature found its way into print until after the Protestant Reformation had begun. Its appeal reached no further up the social ladder. A few burgesses, with one or two yeomen or minor gentry, were the summit of its ambition. Nor, finally, did it seem to enjoy any connections with religious dissidents abroad. In other words, apart from an apparent rise in numbers, early Tudor Lollardy displays none of the characteristics one would expect of an evangelical movement in the early modern era. There are no great missionary figures of the sort usually associated with the spread of a religious movement. There is no sign of political support or patronage.

Lollardy was certainly more of a concern for the bishops in the 1520s than in the 1470s. In addition to the intensification of repression for domestic reasons of Church reform and dynastic legitimation, further impetus was supplied by the arrival of new heresies from the Continent. The teachings of Martin Luther and his followers were soon known in England, condemned publicly as early as 1521, and finding sympathetic ears not long after. The English authorities in Church and State were swift to detect a connection between the old heresy and the new. 'Lollardy' remained a generic term for heretical deviation even when it began to take on distinctly Lutheran or evangelical characteristics, and there were enough common features between the old dissent and the new to disturb the most sanguine bishop or archdeacon. The nature, extent, and importance of the perceived connection between Lollardy and Protestantism, however, is the subject of the next chapter.

5

FROM LOLLARDY TO PROTESTANTISM

The relationship between Lollardy and Protestantism has long been the subject of intense debate. On the one side, Lollardy has been seen as at least preparing the soil if not sowing the seeds of Protestantism. On the other, it has been dismissed, in terms of the Reformation, as at worst an irrelevance and at best a sideshow. On both sides it can probably be agreed that the debate is longer on arguments than on evidence. There is little direct evidence that Lollardy paved the way for Protestantism. And by the nature of things there can be no direct evidence to the contrary. That leaves arguments, which on the one side rest chiefly on the massive doctrinal overlap between the two bodies of teaching, and on the other on the paucity of evidence for significant contact between adherents of the two movements.

John Foxe, of course, saw the contribution of Wyclif and Lollardy to the English Reformation in an essentially providential light, and his vision underpinned the view that held sway almost unchallenged until, early in this century, James Gairdner published his massive *Lollardy and the Reformation in England*. Gairdner, Anglo-Catholic by faith and conservative by temperament, was inclined to emphasise both the role of the State and the limitations of Protestant influence in his account. Nevertheless, his insistence on the numerical insignificance of Lollardy and the absence of direct evidence connecting it to the Reformation, as well as his dismissal of the argument from doctrinal resemblance, were all points well made. But his case, while difficult to contest, was far from universally

115

accepted. For the most part, later historians have either taken his word for it or, despite everything, upheld the traditional view on the grounds of doctrinal similarity. Recent views of the contribution of Lollardy have thus ranged from Scarisbrick's lofty dismissal of the movement as 'upland semi-paganism' to the unbridled enthusiasm of J. F. Davis, who sees the English Reformation as 'a process of religious change that gradually spread upwards from Lollard artisans and merchants to academic reformers of Evangelism and Erastianism, and then to the aristocracy'. Towards the middle ground one finds A. G. Dickens, who describes Lollardy as the 'springboard of critical dissent from which the Protestant Reformation could overleap the walls of orthodoxy'. Rather more cautious is Margaret Aston, who sees the traditional view as a 'plausible hypothesis', while acknowledging the difficulty of testing it.[1]

The contention that Lollardy contributed to the rise of Protestantism in England has always rested first and foremost on the undeniable fact that the two religious movements shared many common doctrines. Thus, early this century, an influential textbook of English history rejected Gairdner's case as 'hopeless' on the grounds that 'Wyclif was a Protestant, pure and simple, in nine out of ten theological positions that he took up.'[2] Wyclif and his followers unquestionably anticipated many of the most striking of the Reformers' doctrines, or to be more precise, of their denials of Roman Catholic doctrines: denial of transubstantiation and even of the real presence in the eucharist; of the veneration of relics and images of saints; of the intercession of the saints; of pilgrimage; of auricular confession; of an order of priesthood; of indulgences; and of papal authority. These similarities extended to two of the main principles of the Reformation: the equation of the papacy with Antichrist and the assertion of the sole and supreme authority of scripture in doctrinal matters. Moreover, the similarity in beliefs was such that the ecclesiastical authorities who found themselves interrogating suspects in the 1520s and 1530s were able to avail themselves of many of the same questions that had been in use for a hundred years or more. However, the argument from doctrinal resemblance is nothing more than *post hoc ergo propter hoc*. There were, after all, many resemblances between Luther's doctrines and those of the Bohemian Hussites. Yet Luther was not in the least degree influenced by the Hussites, to whom he was in his earliest years implacably opposed, and with whom he made contact only after the Leipzig Disputation, when they came to him. Similarities can also be found between Calvinism and Waldensianism, but nobody now maintains that Calvinist doctrines can be traced to Waldensian roots, still less that Waldensianism paved the way for Calvinism.[3]

Recent research has no longer been satisfied with an assertion of continuity based on the doctrinal similarities between Lollardy and Protestantism. Quentin Skinner has taught us to beware of deducing the intellectual 'influence' of one text or author on another in the absence of any plausible evidence that the parties influenced could have encountered the ideas, texts, or traditions alleged to have affected them.[4] Accordingly, the search for such evidence in this case has come to concentrate on identifying Lollards who became, or came into contact with, Protestants, on Protestant interest in Lollard texts and origins, and on the possibility that areas in which Lollardy struck root showed at a later date a greater propensity for Protestant, or even radical Protestant, teachings. A. G. Dickens's study of religious dissent in early Tudor Yorkshire was the first systematic attempt to trace historical links between the two movements. However, his ambitious project foundered on the shortage of evidence. The few Lollards who appear in early Tudor Yorkshire imbibed their doctrines while sojourning further south – and found little sympathy when they brought their new doctrines back home. Moreover, the statistical and methodological grounds on which Dickens sought to trace the spread of Protestant doctrines in Yorkshire from the evidence of wills have been subjected to such devastating criticism as to leave his conclusions on this matter unacceptable without a further reworking of the whole area.[5] With very few Lollards and not many Protestants, it is hardly surprising that this local study yields no evidence at all of connections between the two. Anne Hudson has made perhaps the most ambitious attempt in recent years to trace a significant Lollard contribution to the rise of early English Protestantism. In the final chapter of her *Premature Reformation*, she brings together most of the evidence for direct links between Lollardy and Protestantism. In addition, new evidence connecting Lollards with Protestants in the Thames Valley and the Chilterns has been unearthed by Derek Plumb.[6]

This evidence directly connecting Lollards with Protestants is scattered and can be quickly summed up. We know of one or two cases in which Lollards betook themselves to the sermons of newer-style Reformers, such as Thomas Bilney and Miles Coverdale, and liked what they heard. Some East Anglian Lollards were even inspired by the preaching of Thomas Rose, evangelical curate of Hadleigh, to burn down the Rood of Dovercourt. Almost every textbook tells how Robert Barnes sold copies of Tyndale's English New Testament to a pair of Essex Lollards around Michaelmas 1526. John Tewkesbury, a London Lollard in the 1510s, was eventually burned as a relapsed heretic in 1532, having been caught in possession of books by Luther and Tyndale.[7] Similar circumstances may lie behind the case of Thomas Harding of Amersham who, having been in trouble for his Lollard beliefs in 1506 and 1522, was subjected to close investigation in 1532, and was found to have acquired numerous works of William Tyndale as well as his New Testament.[8] And Richard Harman of Cranbrook, an associate of Tyndale at Antwerp in the 1520s, may represent another link between Lollardy and the printed New Testament.[9] The commitment of both Lollardy and Protestantism to vernacular scripture is well known. But the fact that a cheap, uniform, and readable printed translation of scripture should have replaced expensive and often closely written manuscript versions in an increasingly archaic dialect is hardly surprising, and hardly entails any theological relationship.

Other individual cases can be found. Nicholas Durdant of Iver Court, scion of an old Lollard family, made a will in 1538 which evinces contemporary evangelical phraseology, and appointed as supervisor Dr Simon Heynes, a prominent evangelical theologian from Cambridge who had attracted royal favour through his work for Henry VIII's divorce.[10] Alice Saunders of Amersham, wife of the fantastically wealthy Richard Saunders, was a notorious Lollard in 1521, who trusted in the preamble to her will (1543) to be saved by her faith (although she did leave 13s 4d to procure masses for her soul).[11] Thomas Lound, one of a number of men present at a Lollard gathering around 1530, was said to have spent time in Germany with Luther. And there are occasional hints of family connections between Lollardy and Protestantism. We know of a Kentish Lollard, John Browne, burned in 1511, whose son Robert was in prison for his beliefs when Mary Tudor died, and would otherwise certainly have been burned himself.[12] Likewise, the deranged Cowbridge, burned for heresy at Oxford in the later

1530s, was said by Foxe to have come 'of a good stock and family, whose ancestors, even from Wickliff's time ... had been always favourers of the gospel'. His mother, Margaret Cowbridge, excused herself from a charge of heresy by compurgation in 1528 – her compurgators may have been especially willing as her husband, Robert, was 'a wealthy man, and head baily of Colchester'.[13] However, Foxe's coyness about the precise charges against Cowbridge gives grounds for doubting whether Cowbridge was more Lollard, or perhaps radical, than mainstream evangelical. Another Colchester man, John Pykas, was noted as a Lollard in the 1520s, and by the 1570s had become one of the godly magistrates of the now reformed town.[14] Yet in terms of the plentiful data on both Lollards and Protestants in early Tudor England, these crumbs are statistically insignificant. Some Lollards seem to have been drawn towards leading evangelicals, their books, and their sermons, but there is little if any sign that the evangelical leaders made a special effort to contact their 'forerunners', nor that this contact was especially helpful to their mission.

It is certainly not possible to maintain that Lollardy had no connections at all with English Protestantism. However, it can be shown that the claim that Lollardy contributed to the rise of Protestantism remains implausible. The argument rests on the sociological differences between the phenomena of later Lollardy and early Protestantism, and on the undoubted fact that the vast majority of early English Protestants about whom anything is known (and this class is weighted disproportionately towards the more influential sectors of society) came not from Lollard, but from devout Catholic backgrounds. In other words, the explanatory task for historians of the English Reformation is not to explain why Lollards might have become Protestants, but why Catholics actually did so. Once it is appreciated that early Protestants for the most part came from devout Catholic backgrounds, the virtual irrelevance of Lollardy to the emergence of English Protestantism becomes apparent.

Comparative Geography of Lollardy and Protestantism

One of the commonest arguments advanced in recent times for the importance of Lollardy to the Reformation is that areas where

Lollardy had once been strong became areas where Protestantism, perhaps even Puritanism, was strong later. For example, it has been said that the relative strength of Lollardy in the diocese of Norwich early in the fifteenth century 'offsets East Anglia's reputation as an exceptionally "High Church" area in the late Middle Ages and helps to explain why it later became a Puritan stronghold'.[15] Such claims are problematic. For it is doubtful that Lollardy was strong anywhere other than around Amersham on the eve of the Reformation. Derek Plumb estimates Lollards at 10 or 15 per cent of the population in this region, and regards this as a useful foundation on which to build the Reformation.[16] But we can be sure that Lollardy was nowhere else as numerous and as socially significant as it was there. Generalising about Lollardy and the Reformation from south Buckinghamshire is as risky as generalising about Catholicism and the Reformation from north Lancashire. However, the case has been proposed with the greatest care and subtlety by Diarmaid MacCulloch, who maps the old Lollard centres (London, Kent, East Anglia, the Severn-Thames river-system, and Bristol) on to the heartlands of the English evangelical movement in the first generation. At the same time, he maps the large areas all but untouched by Lollardy on to the areas which proved slowest to receive the new gospel under the Tudors: the North and the South-West, which rose against aspects of the Reformation in 1536 and 1549 respectively; the conservative expanses of the Welsh Marches and west Midlands, long to be troubled by recusancy; and even southern counties such as those encompassed by the diocese of Winchester, where gentry resistance to Reformation persisted deep into the reign of Elizabeth.[17]

The geography of Lollardy and Protestantism is, if anything, unfavourable to the proposed genealogy of dissent. Lollardy was by this time a largely rural phenomenon, or at best a thing of small country towns. Protestantism was, in contrast, emphatically urban. Of course there were towns where a Lollard tradition gave place to zeal for Protestantism, places like London, Bristol, Colchester, Coventry, and perhaps Ipswich. Yet the Reformation could be equally successful in towns entirely innocent of Lollardy, such as Cambridge, Doncaster, Halifax, Norwich, Sandwich, and Warwick.[18] Nor can the Lollard tradition be invoked to explain variations in resistance to the Reformation. Colchester and Ipswich, like Doncaster and Sandwich, saw little opposition, while in London,

Bristol, Cambridge, and Coventry there was conflict and strife. Adherence and resistance to Protestantism, as to Wycliffism over a century before, varied with the quality and commitment of local preachers and patrons rather than on any supposedly long-term social predisposition. In many places where evangelical doctrines made an early impact, no Lollard tradition is known to historians.

Many examples of correlation between Lollardy and Protestantism which seem promising at first sight prove less convincing on closer examination. The strength of Lollardy in early Tudor, and of Protestantism in mid-Tudor, Kent provides a case in point. The Medway valley in Kent, where Protestantism later flourished, produced but a handful of Lollards in 1511–12. Arguments about concealment, poor records, or inefficient investigation will not do here. Much of the valley lay in the small diocese of Rochester, which under Bishop John Fisher (1504–35) was probably the most closely administered in England.[19] The records for Fisher's episcopate are among the best for any sixteenth-century diocese, and he took a close personal interest in heresy. There were only ten cases recorded during his entire episcopate – all in the register, which makes the possibility of a now lost act book for a serious prosecution seem very remote. Some of these were clearly early evangelicals, and most of the rest were prosecuted for the sort of alehouse scepticism with which a less vigilant bishop would hardly have bothered. Few cases reflect distinctively Lollard views, and none suggest that Lollard communities flourished in his diocese.[20] The sheer bulk of his voluminous Latin writings against Protestantism and the pained anguish of his English sermons against Luther show how anxious Fisher was over heresy. Yet his surviving writings show no concern at all over Lollardy. If he found so little, there was probably little to find. Moreover, Fisher attracted serious biographical attention in Mary Tudor's reign, within a generation of his execution. This attention was motivated by a strong vein of Catholic apologetic, which emphasised both his pastoral zeal and his polemical writings. Had his episcopal zeal included major campaigns against heresy within his diocese, then some approving recollection of this activity would certainly have been made by his many surviving friends, colleagues, and pupils. As a final argument, albeit also from silence, it is inconceivable that the thorough researches of John Foxe, who was so keen to damage Fisher's reputation by peddling flimsy allegations of cruelty against him, would have found no written or oral record of a large-scale prosecution in a diocese so close to London.

The rest of Kent, under Canterbury jurisdiction, adds no support to the case for continuity. Protestantism certainly spread more rapidly in Kent than in most other parts of England during the 1530s and 1540s. Yet the credit for this is not due to any preparation of the ground by Lollardy. The convulsion of enthusiasm for the entirely traditional religious style of the Holy Maid of Kent in the 1520s is a far better index of the county's devotional mentality on the eve of the Reformation than the dissident communities of the relatively isolated South Downs. And it is noteworthy that while this young nun prophesied at length against the dangers of the 'new learning' (as the evangelical teachings were often known), she is not known to have said anything about Lollardy. The rapid advance of the Reformation in Kent, which began with the discrediting of the Holy Maid herself, was, as Diarmaid MacCulloch himself has emphasised, due to the stirling labours of Archbishop Thomas Cranmer and his men.[21] The evidence compiled by Cranmer's enemies in the early 1540s shows how active (and in many respects how unpopular) his preachers were. With convinced and articulate evangelical preachers like Lancelot Ridley ensconced in Canterbury Cathedral, or like John Bland and Thomas Swynnerton in Adisham and Sandwich, one need look no further for the source of new doctrines. Canterbury itself, like most cathedral cities, had no Lollard tradition. The few Lollards turned up in the city during the purge of 1511–12 were but an offshoot from the main body at Tenterden.[22] The most detailed investigation of the Reformation in Kent so far attempted, by Peter Clark, found no evidence for Lollard roots beneath the emergence of religious dissent in Canterbury, though he did see significance in the tradition of tension between the civic elite and the religious houses of the city.[23] Cranbrook, despite producing some early evangelicals, proved slower than most of the county in adopting evangelical practices, which suggests that its strong pre-Reformation attachment to Catholicism was at least as significant for its future as its Lollard tradition.[24]

London is another test case for the thesis of continuity in dissent. The strength and persistence of the Lollard tradition in the capital is as uncontested as the early success and ultimate triumph there of the Protestant Reformation. Yet the researches of Susan Brigden into the early Reformation in London conclude that the evangelical message was finding, or rather creating, an essentially new dissident constituency: more numerous, more vigorous, more evangelical, perhaps linked to Lollardy, but scarcely indebted to it.[25] Moreover, the populous anonymity of what was Tudor England's only metropolis itself explains why both Lollardy and Protestantism might have flourished there without any particular dependence of one upon the other. London, like Cranmer's Kent, is too much an exception by character to prove the rule in question. The history of the Reformation in the rest of the London diocese (Surrey, Hertfordshire, and Middlesex – for Essex, see below) awaits detailed investigation, but while Protestantism certainly triumphed, there is no reason to believe that Lollardy – all but unknown in most of these counties – played any part in this victory.

East Anglia at first sight offers better support for the notion of geographical continuity between pre-Reformation dissent and Protestantism. There are signs of a continuous Lollard presence in several particular areas, such as Colchester and Thaxted (at opposite ends of Essex), perhaps Ipswich, and the valley of the Stour, around the borders of Norfolk and Suffolk. Although only a few cases turn up in the records of the last pre-Reformation bishop, Richard Nix (1500–35), the four burnings recorded by John Foxe as having taken place in the years 1510–12 may very well reflect a large-scale purge of the kind carried out in several English dioceses at that time.[26] Certainly Nix, then in his prime, and legendarily sensitive to the smell of heresy, was one of those bishops associated with the reform movement at the 1510 Convocation which inspired that purge. The pattern of prosecutions was, after all, to produce relatively large numbers of suspects and abjurations against mere handfuls of burnings, so that we might well conclude that dozens, perhaps more than a hundred, had to answer for their beliefs and practices at this time. Moreover, as we have seen, the Lollards of East Anglia certainly took an interest in the preaching of evangelicals such as Thomas Bilney in the 1520s and Thomas Rose in the 1530s.

Nevertheless, Norwich itself, which became a centre of fervent Puritanism, produced but a single case of Lollardy in the entire history of the movement: Thomas Myles, a Norwich capper, in 1535. Houlbrooke wonders whether his opinions reflect Continental influence, but his unsophisticated rejection of the real presence, the cult of the saints, and the sacrality of church buildings

are redolent of native Lollardy.[27] Yet the city's religion was quint-
essentially orthodox and relatively untroubled in the later Middle
Ages. Protestant convictions emerge only gradually in the city's
wills from the later 1530s onwards, under the impetus of evangelical preachers such as the former Carmelite John Barrett.[28] While
Colchester indeed became a centre of zealous Protestantism, and
probably concealed a Lollard community throughout the later
Middle Ages, Ipswich, another major Puritan centre, has rather
flimsier Lollard credentials. The only Lollard definitely connected with Ipswich, Nicholas Peke (a victim of the 1511–12
purge), is a shadowy figure, by no means certainly a native of
a town whose religious temperature is probably better taken by
considering the crowds of over a thousand who gathered in 1516
to witness the miraculous cure of the Maid of Ipswich at the town's
rapidly growing shrine, Our Lady of Grace. The spread of Protestant beliefs in and around Ipswich from the 1530s is to be attributed rather to the influence of Lord Thomas Wentworth, the local
magnate and early convert who himself won over John Bale to the
new doctrines.[29] Bale, an inveterate chronicler well acquainted
with both Norwich and Ipswich, nowhere suggests that either
borough nurtured a strong dissenting tradition. A recent study of
Hadleigh, the small town lauded by John Foxe for its openness
and fidelity to the gospel, which he traced to the preaching of
Bilney in the 1520s, found no evidence there of pre-Reformation
dissent. It showed instead that the evangelical movement there
was led by the rector, Rowland Taylor – who was presented to the
parish by none other than Cranmer, and met with stiff opposition
from a powerful Catholic clique.[30] The emergence of vigorous
Protestantism in Elizabethan Bury St Edmunds is hardly to be
traced to the borough's monastic past, which showed not even
a hint of Lollardy after a single case in 1428. All the signs are that
Protestantism in centres like Bury, Hadleigh, Ipswich, and Norwich
owed nothing to indigenous tradition, and everything to parsons
and preaching, to patronage and politics.

   The vast diocese of Lincoln, which swept down from the North
Sea coast (Lincolnshire) through the east Midlands (Bedfordshire,
Huntingdonshire, Leicestershire and Northamptonshire) to the
Thames Valley (Buckinghamshire and Oxfordshire), covered many
towns and regions which were to become famous for Puritanism.
Bedford, Huntingdon, Northampton, and Peterborough, however,

show no signs of Lollardy in the Tudor period, and only around Leicester, Northampton, Oxford, and Amersham had the heresy ever enjoyed much success. Study of the Puritans of Northamptonshire has made it clear that the Protestant development of this shire owed more to the evangelical efforts of dedicated Elizabethan clergymen than to any Lollard predisposition.[31] The success of Puritanism at Leicester is probably to be traced to the Earl of Huntingdon, who set up William Whittingham as preacher there in 1561. Lollardy had long ceased to trouble the city's peace. Lincoln diocese also contained the district around Lutterworth, where Wyclif himself had ended his days, but here, too, little memory remained of the master and his teaching. After a long struggle, Oxford itself had been purged of heresy by the 1430s, so that when dissent once more emerged in the 1520s, the university authorities found it a novel problem. The Lollards of the Chilterns, centred on Amersham, were of course a continual thorn in the Bishop's side. But South Buckinghamshire did not become the engine-room of Reformation that one might have expected had native dissent contributed heavily to religious change.

The west Midlands and the Welsh Marches (Warwickshire, Gloucestershire, Herefordshire, Worcestershire, Shropshire) make a useful counter-example to the thesis of Lollard influence on Protestantism. For this region had several centres of Lollardy in the late fourteenth and early fifteenth centuries, and there were probably continuous traditions of dissent in several places, for example Coventry and the Forest of Dean. Yet it is hard to see that the Lollards of Coventry made that city any more receptive to Protestant preaching than nearby Warwick, where no cases are known to have been found. The Puritanism of Coventry can be traced more plausibly to the long pastorate of Thomas Lever under Elizabeth, and that of Warwick to the patronage of Robert Dudley, Earl of Leicester, whose hospital foundation just inside the west gate housed a succession of talented preachers. It would, in any case, be tendentious to regard Coventry's slender Lollard tradition as more significant for the city's future than the rich tradition of civic pageantry and drama that had flourished there throughout the later Middle Ages – which perhaps helps explain the very real resistance which Protestantism met there. As centres of Lollardy went, Coventry was more significant than most, yet saw no early evangelical success.

Despite Latimer's vigorous evangelism, Protestantism made headway but slowly in the diocese of Worcester, and where it did, it owed little to Lollardy. The first Tudor heretic prosecuted in the diocese was William Levett of Newland, who abjured errors regarding the sacrament of the altar early in 1539. Although his error could have represented Lollardy, its formulation in the register is more redolent of Zwingli or Frith, defining the sacrament as figurative and maintaining that the real presence was inconsistent with the doctrine of Christ's ascension into heaven. Newland, was but a few miles from Worcester, where evangelical preachers had dominated the pulpit under Latimer. The prosecution of Levett under Latimer's successor, John Bell, may well have been undertaken in order to spell out the implications of the replacement of an evangelical bishop by a deeply conservative one. The county was distinctly slow to accept the Elizabethan Settlement, with a notable proportion of ungodly or recusant families among the gentry. And if Worcester itself was more prompt to embrace the Reformation, this is attributable to Latimer and his evangelical successors under Edward VI and Elizabeth.[32] If we are led to wonder why Cranmer made such a deep impact in Canterbury while Latimer was so much less successful in his diocese, the answer is not far to seek: lack of time. Latimer resigned in the wake of the Act of Six Articles, which made denial of the real presence a capital crime, and with less than five years in post, it is hardly surprising that he achieved little.

Gloucestershire had seen rather more of Lollardy, yet even here it had little obvious connection with the rise of Protestantism. For the county in general, K. G. Powell's anecdotal argument for the Lollard roots of Protestant ascendancy has been superseded by the more thorough researches of Caroline Litzenberger.[33] Bristol, of course, had a long tradition of heresy, yet it took the preaching of Hugh Latimer in the early 1530s to produce religious division in the city's elite and population. Gloucester itself became a Puritan stronghold, but without Lollard roots. In such cases, it is again to the preachers and patrons of the sixteenth century itself that we should look for an explanation of the success of Reformed doctrine. Hereford diocese saw no heresy trials, Lollard or Lutheran, during the vigilant episcopate of Charles Booth (1516–35), contributed nothing to the geography of Marian Protestantism, and was far from keen to accept the Elizabethan Settlement. While Lollardy probably survived in the seclusion of the Forest of Dean, this region was hardly a nursery of Reformation, so yet again the argument for geographical continuity of dissent breaks down.

Southern England tells us a similar story. The diocese of Chichester, pretty much coterminous with the county of Sussex, remained as free from Lollardy under the Tudors as it had been under the Lancastrians. As the bishops were usually theologians and resident, it is unlikely that the absence of prosecutions reflects managerial indolence. Although Mayhew suggests that the emergence of an evangelical minority in Rye during the 1530s 'built on older, residual Lollard views', he advances no evidence for this, and it is difficult to be sure how many, if any, came from the Lollard tradition. Conversely, it is plain that evangelical preachers active there in the mid-1530s, with the decisive support of Thomas Cromwell, were what gave the faction its impetus and made Rye easily the most fertile ground for the early Reformation in East Sussex.[34] Local studies have concurred in presenting post-Reformation Sussex as the most conservative of the southern counties, mainly because of the domination of the county by the Catholic peer Lord Montague.[35] Yet notwithstanding the early difficulties of the Reformation and the persistence of Catholic recusancy among the gentry, the Reformation was ultimately successful there, thanks to the tireless efforts of the post-Reformation bishops and their preachers, as a result of which towns like Lewes and Rye became bastions of Puritan zeal.

Winchester diocese, covering Hampshire and parts of Surrey, offers a broadly similar picture. The early Reformation made very little headway under the long episcopate of that staunch conservative, Stephen Gardiner (1531–55, briefly interrupted by the Protestant John Ponet, 1551–53). Earlier records, as we have seen, are defective, but the episcopal registers for the Tudor period are in good order and, with one exception (see above, p. 000), show no evidence of any major purges against Lollardy. It has to be said that Richard Fox, Thomas Wolsey, and Stephen Gardiner all spent more time out of their diocese than in it, so that there remains room for doubt. But all three were talented administrators, dedicated to upholding law and order (and the association between Lollardy and sedition was one of the main reasons for prosecuting it). Fox's last years were spent in redeeming a career in royal service by a close attention to his pastoral responsibilities, which was praised by no less a critic than John Fisher. His personal attachment to the

medieval doctrine of the eucharist was expressed in his founda-
tion of an Oxford College under the dedication of Corpus Christi.
He would not have allowed Lollardy to flourish unopposed.
Stephen Gardiner, like Fisher, manifested his detestation of
heresy by producing a small library of polemical theology, mostly
in defence of Catholic eucharistic doctrine – and always against
Protestant opponents: he apparently never saw old-fashioned
Lollardy as anything like the same kind of threat. Moreover, his
Chancellor and Vicar-General, Dr Edmund Steward, came to him
from the diocese of Norwich, where he had served for many years
in Nix's administration: he would have known what Lollardy was
and how to find it. If Wolsey and Gardiner, in particular, had
launched any spectacular crusade against Lollardy in their diocese,
the Protestant chroniclers would never have allowed us to forget
it. The chances are there was not much to find. Even as evangelical
ideas began to obtain some wider circulation from the 1530s,
exponents of the new learning, like those of Lollardy before them,
turned up mostly in Southwark – influenced far more by the nearby
metropolis than by its distant cathedral city.

Salisbury's Puritan tradition must be traced to something other
than the solitary Lollard denounced there in 1405. In fact, the city
manifested clear hostility to the early stages of the Reformation in
the 1530s, when the evangelical Bishop Nicholas Shaxton was
promoting new doctrines with some vigour. And, as with Latimer
at Worcester, if we seek a reason for the relative failure of Shaxton
compared to Cranmer, the reason is once more that of time: Shaxton, like Latimer, resigned in the wake of the Six Articles after
barely five years in his diocese. In his study of the diocese of
Salisbury, which covered Berkshire, Wiltshire, and Dorset, A. D.
Brown has granted as much as he can to the continuity thesis, and
has warned judiciously against facile conclusions about the insignificance of Lollardy drawn from the paucity of convicted heretics
in surviving records. He produces the interesting case of East
Hendred, which housed influential Lollards before the Reformation (the Lollard community included a wealthy yeoman and
a pair of churchwardens), and which had still not replaced
its rood by 1556. Yet the continuity thesis receives a heavy
blow from his observation that 'most of the places in the diocese
where Lollardy was found after Wyclif saw their parish
churches extensively rebuilt' before the Reformation.[36] The

exiguous Lollard traditions in these places look scant foundation for the powerful traditions of Puritanism which emerged in
the region under Elizabeth I and James I. Nor was the Newbury-
Reading area, where Lollardy maintained a persistent presence, noticeably more receptive to the Protestant Reformation
than the rest of the diocese. Certainly Miles Coverdale was
gloomy enough about evangelical success there in the later
1530s.[37]

The northern Midlands (Derbyshire, Nottinghamshire, Stafford-
shire, and Cheshire) seem to have remained almost as immune
from Lollardy as the six counties of the North (Yorkshire, Lancashire, Durham, Cumberland, Westmoreland, and Northumberland). The patchy Protestant advances in these regions later in
the sixteenth century cannot be ascribed to any established traditions of dissent. On the south-western peninsula, after the Oldcastle
Rising, no case of Lollardy was ever recorded west of Taunton,
and only one other case west of Bristol itself. The sturdy seagoing
Puritans of the Elizabethan era reflect the Protestant lead given by
the Russells, especially the second Earl of Bedford, who inherited
the strong position in the region which his father had built up under
Henry and Edward. Wales, too, was untouched by Lollardy. Two
heresy cases are recorded in the registers of St Davids, one
concerning an Irish mass-priest with an inflated sense of his own
importance, and the other a local layman who had seriously
misunderstood a sermon preached by his archdeacon. The priest
believed that his sacerdotal powers were such that, during the
consecration, he could make Christ really present for some
communicants but not for others, while the layman thought he
had been told that Christ was not omnipotent until after the
Ascension. Neither of them could by any stretch of the imagination be considered a Lollard. Yet the fact that these rather trivial
cases came to court at all suggests a sensitivity to orthodoxy and
heresy which would have led to prosecutions of Lollardy had
there been any to prosecute. Needless to say, there are no traces of
Lollard dissent in the bardic literature of Welsh Wales, which
continued to reflect traditional devotional values right up to the
Reformation. When the Reformation came to Wales, it faced an
uphill struggle.[38]

The geography of Lollardy and the geography of the English
'magisterial Reformation' do not coincide in such a way as to suggest

important connections between them. Not even Diarmaid MacCulloch's sophisticated presentation of the argument can be judged convincing. At the particular level where the history of the reception of the Reformation must ultimately be written, there are simply too many exceptions in both directions to bear out what, at a more general level, look alluringly like significant mappings from late Lollard to early evangelical movements. Broad arguments which talk in terms of counties or even dioceses may suggest correlations. But doubts have recently been cast on the significance of the county as an organising unit for historical study in the later Middle Ages, and these doubts must hold *a fortiori* for the diocese.[39] And the evidence for both later Lollardy and early Protestantism is far too thinly spread to support arguments advanced at such levels. Moreover, when there is a discernible geographical correlation, we must be careful about assessing its precise significance. Catholic recusants in Elizabethan Norfolk clustered in the same southern deaneries of the county as had the Lollards in Lancastrian Norfolk, and the Forest of Dean, once a den of Lollardy, subsequently became noted for recusancy. Nobody has ever stretched the 'continuity of dissent' thesis so far as to suggest that Lollards became recusants, and in these cases it is clear that we are observing consequences of the relative jurisdictional inaccessibility of these regions.[40] In general, arguments for continuity are plausible only at or near the parochial level. When we narrow the geographical scope sufficiently for the evidence to permit meaningful statements, dealing with such places as Amersham, Bristol, Cranbrook, Hadleigh, Ipswich, Newbury, Norwich, Rye, Salisbury, and Sandwich, we find that the decisive variables in the progress of Reformation are not local Lollard traditions, but evangelical preachers and the degree of support enlisted from local elites, diocesan authorities, or even central government.

The case might be summed up by recalling A. G. Dickens's famous description of the early German Reformation as 'an essentially urban phenomenon'. It is true as much in England as in Germany that the early impact of the Protestant Reformation was felt most obviously in towns, albeit often small towns still integrated into the rural hinterland. Later Lollardy, in contrast, was not strongly urban. It flourished mostly in jurisdictionally remote areas, off the beaten track. Few of the towns and cities of England showed any trace of Lollardy in the early Tudor period, whereas from the 1530s and 1540s town after town saw evangelical communities emerge. Cathedral cities, monastic centres, shire towns and many lesser market centres were touched by the preaching of the 'new learning'. Lollards, in contrast, were found in but a handful of major towns and cities (London, Bristol, Colchester, Coventry, Ipswich, Newbury, Reading), more often in minor market towns (Amersham, Chelmsford, Chesham, Cranbrook) and their surrounding villages. Nor were they numerous in any but one or two of these places. The 10–15 per cent of the population around Amersham and Chesham probably represent the greatest strength attained by Lollardy at any time or place in its history. And in this area there is precious little evidence for significant early evangelical advance. In most places, Lollards were a tiny minority, sometimes isolated individuals who had to travel to find fellow believers. The new ideas were for the most part brought first to the larger towns by educated men, mostly clergy from the universities or the religious orders, sometimes laymen like Thomas Wentworth. The evangelical movement which developed from the 1530s does not seem to have appealed more strongly to Lollards than to the conventionally devout.

The Moral Contrast between Lollardy and Protestantism

Despite the undeniable doctrinal overlap between Lollardy and Protestantism, there was a significant difference in ethos between later Lollardy and early Protestantism. The later Lollards were far from evangelical. They kept themselves to themselves, and were conformist to the verge of quietism. For the most part, it was only by accident or in a crisis that they betrayed themselves. At other times they lived as part of the community around them, attending church services and even (on occasion) holding office as churchwardens or vergers. They did not, however, throw themselves enthusiastically into such works of supererogation as pilgrimage. And it seems unlikely that many Lollards endowed obits or other forms of prayer for their souls.

If Lollardy had, in effect, no public face, it was equally quiescent internally. There is little evidence for the continued copying of Lollard manuscripts, and no evidence whatsoever that Lollards

were addressing the intellectual issues or social challenges of the
day in new writings. Nor had the Lollards anything new to say
against the preaching and teaching of the Catholic Church. Indeed,
many of the criticisms often levelled against the late medieval Church are far better fitted to late medieval Lollardy. It
was Lollardy, not Catholicism, that was morally bankrupt, intel-
lectually empty, and in a state of terminal decay on the eve of
the Reformation.

Early Protestantism, however, was different. It was new and
vigorous, evangelical in every sense of the word. Its converts might
show a degree of caution, but were nevertheless bursting to
spread the good news to friends, relatives, and colleagues. The
early masters, Luther and Zwingli on the Continent, Tyndale,
Bilney, and Frith in England, had plenty to say for themselves.
They offered a complete and coherent analysis of the problems of
both church and society in terms of the entrenchment of false
doctrine, and they presented a fresh alternative. They spoke not
only on matters of faith, but on social order and civil government,
poverty and mendicancy, education, marriage, and trade. They
backed their teaching with an attractive appeal to scripture, and
gave at least as good as they got in dispute with their Catholic
opponents. What they offered was not a reclusive quietism hidden
beneath outward conformity, but a new heaven and a new earth.
Their appeal in England spread far beyond the relatively humble
circles within which Lollardy was confined. They scorned hypocrisy.
Where Lollards had invariably recanted as often as was necessary
or possible rather than bear witness for their beliefs with the
ultimate sacrifice, the early Protestants soon showed that they
were made of sterner stuff. Although Thomas More was still able
to argue in 1528 that he had yet to meet a heretic who would not
swear himself blind to save his skin, his argument was soon
refuted. Those Protestants who did abjure against their con-
sciences, like Bilney and Bainham, experienced pangs of guilt
which they sought to allay by public reaffirmation of their beliefs
and consequent martyrdom. Early Protestantism was intellec-
tually vital, socially relevant, and utterly self-confident. The contrast
with later Lollardy could hardly have been greater. The conversion of a Lollard to this new and vibrant form of religious life
must have been as radical a change of heart as the conversion of
a Catholic.[41]

The Social Contrast between Lollards and the English Reformers

While much of the early support for Protestantism came from the same strata of society which had tended to harbour Lollardy – craftsmen and artisans, and even substantial merchants – the success of the Reformation was crucially promoted by the spread of evangelical doctrines among two social groups which had long been almost impervious to Lollardy: the clergy and the gentry. It was among these groups that the most influential early English Reformers were recruited. There was thus something of a social gulf between the Reformers and the traditional English dissidents. A similar gulf has been observed between the Waldensians of the Alps and the Protestant Reformers with whom they came into contact from around 1530.[42] When we can ascertain anything about the religious antecedents of the English Reformers, we find that they came from highly orthodox backgrounds. Some came gradually to Protestant reform through an Erasmian phase – and the ideas of Erasmus were highly respectable, enjoying the support of such pillars of the Church as Archbishop Warham, Cardinal Wolsey, Thomas More, John Fisher, and Cuthbert Tunstall, not to mention the King himself. Thomas Bilney, for example, explained to Bishop Tunstall that his conversion was initiated by reading Erasmus's edition of the New Testament. Although this was a somewhat disingenuous and not particularly skilful attempt to pull the wool over Tunstall's eyes (the tone of his letters to the bishop is unmistakably evangelical), there is certainly nothing in his words to indicate a Lollard background.[43] William Tyndale first comes to our attention as the translator of Erasmus's devotional work, the *Handbook of a Christian Soldier*. And when he first conceived the idea of translating the Bible into English, he attempted to enlist the support of Erasmus's friend Tunstall, the bishop of London. Miles Coverdale converted a fellow Augustinian friar by means of Erasmus's *Colloquies*.

Another road to Reformation began in the religious orders. Many of the early English Protestants were former friars or monks – strong evidence again of orthodox antecedents. This should come as no surprise, for it has often been noted how many of the Continental Reformers came from the ranks of the friars – Luther, first among them. In England this phenomenon was evident at the highest level. Of 24 Protestant bishops in the mid-Tudor period, 16 had once been members of religious orders. And it was not only the Protestant prelates, but many humbler clergy who came from the monasteries. William Roy, Tyndale's assistant, was a former Observant Franciscan. John Bale, one of the Reformation's most prolific pamphleteers, had been the Carmelite prior at Doncaster, and prayed 'God mercy a thousand times' that he had been a papist himself. Robert Barnes, the first Cambridge Lutheran, was the Augustinian prior there. He converted, among many others, Richard Bayfield, a Benedictine from Bury St Edmunds.[44] Simon Clerkson was the Carmelite prior at York until the dissolution in 1538, yet became a zealous adherent of the Henrician regime, and was eventually deprived under Queen Mary. John Barrett, the prior of the Cambridge Carmelites in the early 1530s, left his order in June 1535, and was soon preaching Sacramentarian eucharistic doctrine. John Cardmaker, warden of the Exeter Greyfriars, left his order before the dissolution, in 1537, and died for his faith at Smithfield on 30 May 1555. Thomas Chapman, warden of the Greyfriars of Ware and later of London, became a client of Thomas Cromwell and married under Edward VI. William Oliver, prior of the Dominicans of Cambridge and later of Bristol, began to preach against religious vows in the latter city in the later 1530s. The Dominican John Joseph became part of Latimer's 'team of preachers in Worcester diocese, was presented by Cranmer to the London benefice of St Mary-le-Bow, adopted the Swiss doctrine of the eucharist, and married under Edward VI.[45] The religious orders, in particular the mendicant orders, had been implacable enemies of Lollardy, providing most of the scholarly opponents of Wyclif. Their ethos was entirely opposed to the secular and anti-formalist ethos of Lollardy. Of course, there were one or two cases of renegade monks or friars receiving shelter from Lollards. But a man from a Lollard background would hardly become a monk, let alone a friar. And as a monk or a friar, a man was hardly likely to come into contact with Lollardy. The fact that friars found Protestant doctrines more appealing than Wycliffite doctrines is one of the most important differences between the 'premature Reformation' and the English Reformation.

Among these early reformers some had even begun as opponents of Protestantism. Before Hugh Latimer was converted by

Bilney to radical beliefs (which still fell far short of Protestantism),
he had been a keen opponent of Lutheranism and even of Erasmian humanism. Latimer's servant, Richard Webb, described his
own father Rowland Webb as a papist, and reported to John Foxe
how his father used to tell him of the burning of a Lollard which
he had witnessed, in order to deter him from heresy. John Hilsey,
the Lutheranising Bishop of Rochester in the later 1530s, had
previously been the Dominican prior of Bristol, in which capacity
he preached against Latimer in 1533. Richard Ingworth, another
Dominican theologian, had testified against Bilney in the 1520s,
yet went on to become a fervent supporter of Cromwell and Cranmer in the 1530s and 1540s. In the 1520s, Thomas Cranmer had
read and annotated with approval the anti-Lutheran writings of
John Fisher, before becoming more sympathetic to evangelical
teachings in the Augsburg household of Andreas Osiander.[46]
Doctor Gilbert Barclay, a Franciscan of York, had continued to
wear his religious habit even after the dissolution in 1538, abandoning it only when browbeaten by Thomas Cromwell. He went
on to become a convinced Protestant, an exile under Queen
Mary, and Bishop of Bath and Wells under Elizabeth. John Hun-
tington, a popular balladeer, was writing against Protestantism
around 1540, yet had converted to the new learning by 1545.
Bernard Gilpin, who from 1549 drifted towards Protestantism,
ending as the chief Anglican preacher in the North-East under
Elizabeth, had been a zealous Catholic at Oxford, disputing in
favour of transubstantiation against John Hooper and Peter Martyr.
Examples of men less sympathetic to Lollard doctrines can hardly
be imagined.

Many of the early Reformers were from Cambridge University.
Apart from those already mentioned, such names as Nicholas
Ridley, Matthew Parker, Simon Heynes, William Butts, George
Joye, Thomas Bennett, and Thomas Arthur are a roll of honour
for the English Reformation. Most had been fellows of Cambridge
colleges, yet no fellow or even member of a Cambridge college
had ever been accused of Lollardy. The university prided itself on
its doctrinal purity at a time when Oxford had begotten a heresi-
arch in John Wyclif.[47] Nor is family background likely to bring
Lollardy into play. In case after case we find that the early Reformers
came from decidedly or at least conventionally orthodox families.
Cranmer's father made a perfectly orthodox will. Ridley's uncle,

also a Cambridge fellow, was an active antilutheran. Thomas Arthur had been a chantry priest in Norfolk, and was converted by Bilney. Thomas Bennett seems likewise to have been converted by Bilney at Cambridge in the early 1520s. The story was much the same at Oxford. Anthony Dalaber, an associate of Thomas Garrett who was in trouble for his beliefs in 1528, recalled that his brother, an Oxford MA and a Dorset parson, 'was a rank papist... the most mortal enemy that ever I had for the gospel's sake', which would suggest they shared an orthodox upbringing.[48] Some early Reformers showed a touching concern for the eternal fate of their papist parents and forefathers. Others were more robust. When William Senes, the chaplain of the song school at Jesus College, Rotherham, was delated for his beliefs in 1537, among his reported comments was this: 'Thy father was a liar and is in Hell, and so is my father in Hell also; my father never knew scripture and now it is come forth'. Senes had been reading Frith, and he obviously did not come from a Lollard background.[49] The Windsor martyrs of the 1540s, Robert Testwood (who struck the nose off an image of the Virgin) and others, may have come from a town which had previously nurtured Lollards, but there is no discernible connection, for two of the suspects in this case were drawn from the singing men of the Chapel Royal, a most improbable occupation for putative Lollards.[50] Most English Reformers had not Lollard but Catholic roots. As Susan Brigden has remarked of the early Reformation in London: 'Everyone, or almost everyone, converted to a more radical view of the path to salvation had once been of the old faith.'[51]

The early clerical leaders of the English Reformation owed nothing to Lollardy. They were, on the contrary, from the best that the orthodox Church had to offer. The same is true of the laity. There is no evidence of Lollardy among the Boleyn family. Nor can Henry VIII's early devotion to Roman Catholicism be doubted. Even Thomas Cromwell, as late as 1529, was found by George Cavendish reciting Our Lady's Matins, a typically Catholic devotion. Edward Seymour and John Dudley, who presided over the introduction of Protestant worship in the reign of Edward VI, acquired their evangelical convictions at Henry VIII's court in the 1530s. Their ancestors show no signs of dissident sympathies. Anne Askew, recalled John Bale, 'in process of time, by oft reading the sacred bible... fell clearly from all old superstitions of papistry'.

Humphrey Monmouth, the London merchant who became the patron of Tyndale and many other Reforming clerics, had earlier been the patron of such stalwart Catholics as Dr John Watson and Dr John Reston (masters respectively of Christ's and Jesus Colleges, Cambridge). He had undertaken pilgrimages to Rome and Jerusalem, and can hardly be presented as a Lollard turned Protestant. James Bainham (who was William Tracy's nephew and Simon Fish's brother-in-law) appears in the pages of John Foxe as a man whose beliefs derive entirely from Protestant sources. He maintained that Latimer and Cromwell were the only true preachers he had ever heard, endorsed a whole series of doctrines in unequivocally Protestant terms, and referred to the works of Tyndale and Frith. Although it has been suggested that he may have been exposed to Lollard influence though his upbringing in Gloucestershire, no evidence has ever been produced to support this (other than the fact that there were a few Lollards in that county). And the most recent research into the Reformation in Gloucestershire has revealed that his parents both composed perfectly conventional wills, and concludes that they were conservative in religion. Duffy has an illuminating story of a Catholic father in Chelmsford who tried to wean his son off evangelical doctrine by reciting Latin Matins with him.[52] And, as late as the reign of Mary, it was still common for Catholic prosecutors to challenge recalcitrant heretics to judge the Catholic convictions of their parents and forefathers.[53] The eccentric evangelical Sir Francis Bigod of Yorkshire was the grandson of the man who gave John Fisher his first church benefice. William Cecil favourably endorsed a copy of Fisher's defence of the real presence in the eucharist as late as 1545. He may already have entertained evangelical doctrines by this time, as his father Richard seems to have done at Stamford in the 1530s. But his own attachment at this point to the real presence, along with his grandfather's years of membership in the fraternity of St Catherine at Stamford (and endowment of an obit in his will of 1535), rule out Lollard influence in his upbringing. In short, the secular leaders of the English Reformation, like such Continental counterparts as Lazarus Spengler, Johannes Sturm, and Luther's patron, the Elector Frederick of Saxony, came from perfectly orthodox Catholic backgrounds.

So, too, as far as we can tell, did the vast majority of adherents of the new learning. More telling still, all the evangelical leaders came from such backgrounds. There is no evidence to suggest that any Protestant evangelist was decisively, or even tangentially, influenced by Lollardy before or during his conversion. The important Protestants – those responsible for promulgating and promoting the doctrines and interests of the Reformation – were not former Lollards. They did not come from social groups in which Lollardy had exercised influence. The importance of Protestantism lies precisely in the fact that it managed to reach a constituency which Lollardy had for a century been unable to reach. When both the leaders and the led were from the Catholic majority, there is no need to invoke the tiny dissident minority in an explanatory role. In explaining the English Reformation, the Lollards are simply redundant.

This does not mean, however, that Lollardy was utterly insignificant in the English Reformation. Lollardy – rather than the Lollards – served an important function, but it was theoretical or theological rather than practical. In general, the encounters between sixteenth-century Protestantism and surviving medieval heresies were historiographical rather than historical. Protestant ecclesiology was anxious to distance itself from the Church of Rome, yet Protestants were as convinced as Catholics that Christ's promises regarding the indefectibility of the true Church required a visible witness to true belief between apostolic and modern times. Where Catholics saw this in the Church of Rome, Protestants, who could hardly see it in what was for them the house of Antichrist, saw it apocalyptically in the faithful remnant of the elect. The existence through the later Middle Ages, at least from Innocent III's pontificate, of a series of dissident movements and individuals whose beliefs could be plausibly presented as anticipations of the revival of the gospel was an essential element of the Tudor Protestant self-image. The danger for modern historians lies in confusing this providential interpretation of history with the reality of historical change. Protestant ecclesiology did not require that there should be any direct historical connection between the medieval dissidents and themselves. It was enough theologically that there should have been witnesses to the truth in every age, even if one group of witnesses had no contact with another. Apostolicity was not for Protestants a matter of a continuous tradition or succession, as it was for Catholics. It was enough that the doctrine of an individual or a group should match and conform to that of the apostles.

The position of the surviving dissidents with respect to the new Protestant movements must also be considered. Contacts were certainly established once the new movements had appeared. Just as English Lollards sought out Bilney and Barnes, so, too, Bohemian Hussites sought out Luther, and Waldensians sought out Farel, Bucer, and later Calvin. But there is no reason to suppose that these contacts had anything more to do with the success of Protestantism in England than with the success of Lutheranism in central and northern Europe, or of Calvinism in Switzerland and France. The medieval dissidents certainly recognised kindred spirits in the Reformers, but (as Euan Cameron has shown in the case of the Waldensians) the new Reformers tended to be somewhat imperialistic towards their forerunners,[54] and the relatively sophisticated Waldensians found the radically new doctrine of justification by faith alone as disturbing and challenging as did their Catholic contemporaries.[55] It was the same in England. John Foxe was quite happy to annex the Lollards to his apocalyptic vision of English and ecclesiastical history and to accommodate them in the divine plan. But that does not mean that they necessarily made any important contribution to the rise of Protestantism. In large parts of England, as in vast areas of France and Germany, Protestant evangelism was able to make considerable headway in the complete absence of any native dissident tradition.

Lollardy and Calvinism

The notion that Lollardy predisposed England to the Reformed rather than to the Lutheran tradition is really the last throw of the Lollard dice in the game of Reformation history.[56] But the explanation is redundant. Lutheranism made little impact anywhere outside the Germanic world.[57] Calvinism was the predominant variety of Reformation outside Germany, and it requires no special explanation to account for its appeal in England, when it was equally if not more appealing in Scotland, France, and the Netherlands. Putting this the other way round, Calvinism struck root easily enough in regions abroad which lacked the Lollard traditions of some parts of England, or anything like them. In England itself Calvinism proved arguably more popular in Cambridge, with no Lollard background, than in Oxford, the birthplace of Lollardy;

and as popular in Exeter and Hull, apparently untouched by Lollardy, as in such of its traditional centres as Bristol and Coventry. Lollardy, here, is an explanation which does not explain, an answer without a question.

The Fate of Lollardy

Lollardy disappeared in the course of the English Reformation. As Lollards are unlikely to have become Roman Catholics now that their former dissent seemed to have been vindicated by providence, they must either have become conforming members of the Reformed Church of England, like John Pykas of Colchester, or else, like Joan Bocher of Kent, have affiliated themselves to the new dissident movements which deviated from the Church by law established (the Anabaptists and the Family of Love in the sixteenth century, the Baptists and the Quakers in the seventeenth).[58] Both of these possibilities have something to be said for them. The Protestant Reformation eliminated most of the features of the Church of England against which Lollard protest had been directed: the mass, the cult of the saints, auricular confession, and the papacy. As the Church of England, whose services most Lollards doubtless attended, changed before their eyes, their sense of distance from it might have diminished to a vanishing point where the parallel lines of Lollardy and Protestantism converged. The distinctive features of Lollardy as dissent quite simply ceased to be distinctive. The Lollards had always been outwardly conformist, and conformity with an established Church with which Lollards had no doctrinal quarrel might gradually have replaced conformity with an established Church with which they had had serious quarrel. Convergence rather than causation would be the appropriate model for understanding such a relationship. And it would certainly fit what little data we can find regarding known Lollards after the Reformation. The stray links with evangelical preachers, the acquisition of evangelical texts, and the handful of evangelical wills which we can identify would all fit a model of convergence.

The alternative theory, that Lollard dissent transmuted into new varieties of dissent from the new establishment, has received some support from the work of a team assembled and led by Margaret Spufford. Their research suggests a high degree of continuity between the Lollards of the Chesham district in the early sixteenth century and the dissenters of the same district in the later seventeenth century. The names of families identifiable with varying degrees of probability as Lollard in Henry VIII's time show a remarkable stability in that region, far in excess of that for the names of the rest of the population, and show an equally remarkable overlap with the names of the Baptists. It is tragic that gaps in the historical record make it so hard to discern just what was going on in the interim, whether dissenting families were always set apart in some way from the rest, or whether they drifted into and then back out of the established church. Moreover, given that the Lollards did conform outwardly, and that the later Baptists and Quakers did not, it might be that the character of 'dissent' gradually changed across the period even as dissent itself passed down from generation to generation.[59] Whether these results can be replicated for other areas is, however, doubtful, because the much smaller numbers of known Lollards (in both absolute and relative terms) elsewhere make it not only less likely that such continuities existed, but also more difficult to detect them if they did. And although the theological resemblances between Lollardy and the Reformation have already been noted, the theological resemblances with the Radical Reformation are more striking, in, for example, the aversion to oaths, the anticlericalism, the antiformalism, and the avoidance of difficult dogmas such as predestination. If there were significant continuities between Lollardy and subsequent religious developments, these are likely to be found in the 'radical' rather than the 'magisterial' Reformation.

Irrespective of whether Lollardy dissolved forever into the English Reformation, or later precipitated out from it in the new guise of nonconformity, it had little to do with the success of the English Reformation. The Lollard protest against Catholicism had been strikingly unsuccessful throughout the later Middle Ages. Whatever the reasons for Protestant success in the early modern era, they can hardly have included its family resemblance to or its occasional connections with native dissent. Nor did surviving pockets of Lollardy prove any more receptive to the mainstream Reformation than many impeccably orthodox and conformist regions. Reformers were no doubt happy to recruit Lollards to their ranks. But we find no Lollards among the movers and shakers of the English Reformation. Catholic writers such as Thomas

More claimed to see Lutheranism as a descendant of Lollardy.
But this must be qualified by the fact that Catholic polemicists saw
all heresies from Simon Magus onwards as linked in a continuous
tradition of diabolically inspired conspiracy. Tarring Luther with
the Lollard brush was a crude polemical gambit. Reformers availed
themselves of the figleaf of historical continuity which the Lollard
tradition offered them, and published Lollard tracts as evidence
of an enduring witness against the papacy even in the darkest ages
of their past. But their teachings were not derived from that tradition, and the exploitation of the Lollard tradition for propaganda
purposes by John Bale or John Foxe is a very different thing from
evidence of a causal relationship. The English Reformation did
not come from Lollardy, owed nothing in practice to Lollardy,
and would probably have developed along much the same lines
without Lollardy. The key to the success of the English Reformation lies not in the conversion of Lollards, but in the conversion of
Catholics. And that is quite another story.

6

CONCLUSION

What, then, was the significance of Lollardy? It has certainly been easy for historians to exaggerate. This is partly because of the disproportionate survival of Lollard literature, preponderantly of the English Bible; partly because of the vigour with which Church and State responded to the threat of lay heresy; and partly because of the enduring impact of the English Reformation's quest for historical legitimation. However, none of this suffices to justify the significance which has been ascribed to the Lollards. The notion that they somehow paved the way for the Reformation has, as we have seen, little to be said for it. The harshness of the sanctions imposed says more about the readiness of the establishment to defend its values than about the numerical strength of the dissidents. Nor is the survival of the Wycliffite Bible any index of the strength of Lollardy, given the considerable evidence for its orthodox ownership and the fact that many of the copies must have been made before Arundel's censorship began to take effect. Subtracting the vernacular scriptures, one is left with a less impressive body of texts, often in unique exemplars. Their survival testifies more to the systematic preservation of the Lollard heritage after the Reformation than to the prevalence of heresy before it. Surviving heresy investigations, while showing that some Lollards did own books, do not suggest that their library was voluminous. Only a very restricted range of titles circulated. But add to the seductive abundance of manuscripts the status of the Lollards as an oppressed minority and, as with the Catholic recusants, there is a recipe for disproportionate historiographical attention.

Although Lollardy can hardly be compared with recusancy in scale, the comparison is not altogether inapposite. Few recent historians have shared the optimism or pessimism of those Catholic and Protestant zealots who, around 1600, took seriously the revolutionary potential of the English Catholic community. Yet the tens of thousands of publicly committed Catholic recusants (not to mention the wider, but uncountable penumbra of 'church papist' sympathisers) far outnumber the mostly secretive and conformist Lollards in both absolute and relative terms. Even the poorly supported Catholic rising of the Northern Earls in 1569 was a greater threat than the Oldcastle Rising of 1414. Recusancy, within strict limits, flourished: Lollardy barely survived. The difference lies in the attitudes of the gentry. If, as Anne Hudson has justly observed, it is the alliance between Lollard academics and the gentry that accounts for the early success of Lollardy, the collapse of support among the gentry accounts for its ultimate failure. It was the enduring alliance between the gentry and the friars which ensured that the friars' main competitors, the Wycliffite secular clergy, remained a marginal group.

If recent advances in the history of the Reformation and of the late medieval Church of England have made it harder to credit Lollardy with long-term social or political consequences, it is still possible for historians to exaggerate the place of the Lollards in the fifteenth century itself. An interpretation now finding favour in some quarters situates the relative wealth of manuscript evidence in the theoretical perspectives of modern social sciences to present the Lollards as essential to the 'construction' of late medieval English Catholic identity.[1] 'The Lollard', in other words, became a scapegoat whose exclusion and elimination enabled a divided society to experience reconciliation and unity. If one adopts a view of human communities or societies as primarily shaped by those they exclude, the Lollards are certainly the prime candidates for this role in late medieval England. Societies, however, can commune around positive as well as negative symbols, and the relative balance of the positive and the negative, of the inclusive and the exclusive, varies with time and place. Few historians would question, for example, that the late Tudor and early Stuart Church of England was crucially shaped by 'antipopery', which, as Peter Lake has shown, was a shared construction of an 'other' which enabled disparate tendencies within the established Church ('Puritans' and 'conformists') to bury their differences and experience unity.[2] With the return of demographic and economic growth in the early fifteenth century, the Lancastrian Church did not have the kind of internal tensions which made the magnification of an external threat crucial to the preservation of unity. One does not need to be a Catholic romantic or a Tory reactionary to conclude that late medieval England was less deeply divided than early modern England. The polemic against Lollardy around 1400 is of an entirely different order from the pervasive polemic against popery which fills religious (and often secular) literature around 1600. The apocalyptic thrill audible in the antipapal rhetoric of Elizabethan and Jacobean England is lacking in the complacent reproofs of dissent penned by friars in the generation after Wyclif. Although in its early stages the Lollard movement generated widespread fears at least in the hierarchy and the religious orders, these cannot be compared with the Protestant obsession with popery around 1600. The role of 'anti-Lollardy' in the fifteenth century simply will not stand comparison with the massive presence of antipopery in the politics of the seventeenth.[3]

This is not to deny that Lollardy was seen as a threat by the authorities in fifteenth-century England. The history of Lollardy shows that dissent was neither inconceivable nor impractical in late medieval England. While most English people were never directly, or even indirectly, exposed to heretical teaching, that teaching in itself constituted an uncompromising challenge to the doctrine and authority of the established Church. Whether one chooses to interpret the hierarchy's response as deriving from a sense of pastoral obligation or from a defence of vested interests (and the truth is probably, as usual in human affairs, a little bit of both), the bishops and theologians were behaving perfectly rationally in seeking to silence and discipline religious dissidence. And the traditional association of heresy with sedition, vindicated first by the Peasants' Revolt and then by the Oldcastle Rising, meant that the officers of the crown were keen to assist the hierarchy of the Church in suppressing it. We find few signs of sympathy for Lollards when they were prosecuted, not even when they were burned. 'Lollardy', like 'popery' two centuries later, was as much a political as a religious pejorative.

The point, however, is that Lollardy was far from uppermost in the minds of clergy or laity in the fifteenth century. Heresy

investigations were sporadic. Devotional literature only rarely
alludes to the threat of heresy, and with little passion. Lollards
wrote, and later talked, a great deal about their beliefs, but few
others did so. Polemics against Lollardy mostly date from the
same early period as Lollard literature itself, and do not survive in
the sort of quantities which suggest that they were much read. Only
one anti-Lollard work, Netter's *Doctrinale*, was of lasting importance, becoming in the age of the Reformation a handy arsenal of
arguments and proof-texts for a later generation of controversialists.
It already has something of the character of a retrospective view
of an argument to all intents and purposes won. When Reginald
Pecock subsequently attempted a comprehensive refutation of
Lollardy in the vernacular, his efforts were seen by his colleagues
as more of a threat than the doctrines he was rebutting. Anti-
Lollard literature may show that the contemporary Church of
England was confident in upholding its teachings and its authority,
but does not bespeak anxiety of the kind so evident in Catholic
polemics against Lutherans in the 1520s, Reformation polemics
against Anabaptists, or Tudor and Stuart polemics against Catholics. And while decisive public action against heresy certainly
helped Henry IV and Henry V bolster the legitimacy of their
somewhat shaky claim to the English throne, heresy was instru-
mental rather than indispensable. If the Lollards had not existed,
the Lancastrians would hardly have found it necessary to invent
them.[4]

If Lollardy really had played the symbolic role for Catholicism
which some scholars have latterly ascribed to it, other literary genres
would also have evinced more pressing concern with the problem
of heresy. In search of evidence for such concern, there have been
attempts to read various fifteenth-century compositions as 'implicit'
critiques of Lollardy.[5] Yet it is to be doubted whether the readers
of an age as yet largely innocent even of the sophistication of
Renaissance humanism would have been aware of subtleties
hidden from all but the most alert of twentieth-century critics. Why
should opponents of Lollardy make their criticisms so obliquely
when the Lollards themselves made their criticisms so bluntly? In
fact, early fifteenth-century polemic is as obvious as its early
modern or modern equivalents when it is found, as in the exchange
between 'Jack Upland' and 'Friar Daw', or Hoccleve's rhymed
remonstrance against Oldcastle.[6] Even the religious drama which

flourished in the later Middle Ages was largely oblivious to Lollardy. Although some critics have claimed to detect subtle polemics against heresy in one or two of the plays, the vast bulk of the surviving texts are bluntly didactic and catechetical rather than subtly polemical. There is nothing to compare with the explicit polemic of the Jesuit drama or the Spanish *autos sacramentales* of the seventeenth century, not to mention the Protestant morality plays of John Bale.

The distinctive features of late medieval English Catholicism were not shaped to any great extent by Lollard pressures. The cult of the saints, that backbone of traditional piety, had long been in place when Wyclif launched his assault upon it, and neither devotional practices nor the development of new cults were significantly redirected by Lollardy, except in the expansion of the usual canon with conversion or chastisement miracles by which Lollards were either brought back to the fold or providentially punished for their blasphemous obstinacy. Even the devotion to Corpus Christi, which might at first sight look a likely candidate for a reaction to heresy (the devotion had originated in such a reaction in the thirteenth century), was deeply rooted in English religious life before Wyclif developed his own eucharistic theology. It would be far more realistic to see in Lollardy a reaction against Corpus Christi. As for the two most visible changes in the outward life of the Church, the proliferation of chantries and fraternities, these were both under way by the mid-fourteenth century and were neither impeded nor impelled by the Lollard polemic against saints and the Mass. Fraternity statutes after the 1380s reveal no special concern to resist heresy, such as can be seen in many French confraternities from the 1560s onwards.[7]

International comparisons of this kind can be illuminating. It is very difficult to argue that late medieval English Catholicism was substantially different from the Catholicism of late medieval France, Spain, Portugal, or Germany (though that has not stopped people doing so). Local variations there certainly were in cult and rite, yet the structures of belief and worship show indisputable continuities across national boundaries: a fact most strikingly established by the international pilgrimage trade. Margery Kempe and Richard Guildford may have reaped all sorts of spiritual rewards from their travels to shrines throughout Europe. But their accounts show no sign of awareness of religious boundaries until they come across the Orthodox Christians of the East. A Scandinavian would know how to behave at Walsingham as readily as an Englishman at Santiago da Compostela. Medieval visitors to Rome may have been perennially shocked by the immorality of the Holy City, but they were not surprised (as their early modern English successors were) by its religiosity. The features of late medieval English Catholicism – obsession with purgatory, masses for the dead, confraternities, Our Lady, the saints, Corpus Christi, holy water, indulgences – were found to a greater or lesser extent all over western Europe. Even the devotional literature was shared. The writings of Catherine of Siena, Bridget of Sweden, Thomas à Kempis, and Jean Gerson could be read anywhere in Catholic Europe, and were translated into many languages. There were differences, of course. The penitential confraternities of flagellants so popular in the cities of Italy and Spain never really caught on north of the Alps. The Corpus Christi festivities of Seville were very different from those of York. Catholicism was by no means as devotionally and liturgically, or for that matter theologically, homogenous in the fifteenth century as it was to be in the seventeenth. Yet the postmodern obsession with difference must not be allowed to exaggerate the varieties of Catholicism, which was recognisable as a single system of belief and practice (not least because it conceived itself as such) the length and breadth of western Europe. To invoke Lollardy in an attempt to account for the general character of late medieval English Catholicism is to invoke a redundant cause.

This is not to say that Lollardy was without impact on the English Church. The threat of heresy stimulated catechetical efforts. It provoked the system of preaching licences and censorship. More importantly, it engendered a culture of suspicion about vernacular scripture which endured until the sixteenth century. It even gave the State a more prominent role in religious affairs than it had hitherto enjoyed.[8] The suppression of heresy had long been regarded as an obligation of the State towards the Church in Europe, but only now did the English Church feel the need to call upon the Crown in this capacity. But the changes of direction or emphasis in mainstream English religious life which can be attributed to reaction against Lollardy are few enough and relatively superficial. The scattered and sporadic burning of heretics was hardly a reign of terror: it never even approached the scale of the

1530s or the 1550s, let alone that of the Spanish Inquisition under Ferdinand and Isabella. There is no reason to suppose that the English people adhered to the Church out of fear. Catholic hegemony was maintained not through tyranny and systematic repression, but through the less formal pressures of pre-modern communities, stiflingly conformist as they could be. Affection, loyalty, and conformity are more than adequate to account for the phenomenon.

Although the study of Lollardy is far from explaining the character of late medieval English Catholicism, it can nevertheless illuminate it. The passionate defence of those things and practices which Wyclif and his followers impugned shows us just what late medieval Englishmen held most sacred. The weakness of Lollardy is testimony to the general popularity of Catholicism, just as the growing effectiveness of episcopal action against Lollardy under the Tudors is testimony to the rising tide of clerical reformism within the Church. However, it is equally interesting to note that there were parts of England, such as Essex, the Kentish Weald, and the Chilterns, where Lollard minorities seem to have been tolerated to some extent by their conformist neighbours. The possibility of heresy was real, and in practice heresy could be assimilated.

The chief reason for studying Lollardy, then, is neither to explain the Reformation nor to explain the character of late medieval English Catholicism. The reason must be to appreciate what Lollardy was and what it meant to its adherents and its opponents. The Lollards were a small, scattered minority of dissidents united by their sense of being the few true Christians on earth, the 'known men', almost overwhelmed by the boundless seas of mainstream church practice by which they were surrounded. After the early years, there was no earthly hope for them, only the hope of heaven. Sustained only by the apocalyptic sense of living in the last days, they faced general disapproval which could turn at any moment into ostracism and prosecution. Life as a Lollard was hard and dangerous. Although the vast majority of Lollards were not executed for their dissent from the norms of Church and Realm, that final sanction was always a very real threat. Not surprisingly, therefore, most Lollards conformed to the external requirements of parish religion. At times, they are even found serving as churchwardens, parish clerks, or the wardens of guilds – presumably out of a sense of communal obligation rather than of personal devotion. Never, though, do we have clear evidence of Lollards participating in the voluntary aspects of late medieval devotion. They did not go on pilgrimage – a practice which enjoyed their special contempt – and there is no reason to suppose that they engaged in any of the multifarious aspects of the cult of the saints and the 'cult of the dead' which bulked so large in late medieval Catholic practice. Their 'voluntary religion' consisted not in those practices, but in their readings and conversations, based on a few books of the Bible and a handful of Wycliffite pamphlets.

So ineluctably has the Reformation shaped our view of Lollardy that even this final summary reminds us inescapably that the Lollards anticipated the Protestant reformers of a later era in countless ways. And while this must not lure us back into an unhistorical assumption of a causal relationship between them, we can still learn something important from it. Such is the proper lesson to be drawn from the title of the most sympathetic account of Lollardy to appear in recent years, Anne Hudson's *The Premature Reformation*. Hudson's title alerts us to the historical value of examining Lollardy in the light of the Reformation. As J. A. F. Thomson observes, medieval heretical movements fell mostly into two classes: the popular and the academic. Against that background, Lollardy stands out as both popular and academic. So, too, as Thomson also observes, does the related Hussite movement of Bohemia.[9] Early modern heretical movements, such as Lutheranism, Calvinism, and Zwinglianism, also tended to combine the academic and popular. Viewed against this background, both Lollardy and Hussitism, with their strongly nationalistic aspects, fall into place. They both look much more like sixteenth-century heresies than thirteenth-century heresies. In that sense, it is far from anachronistic to see Lollardy and its Bohemian cousin as instances of a 'Premature Reformation'; and to that extent, Wyclif was indeed the 'morning star of the Reformation'. He was not the dawn, but he was a sign of things to come.

NOTES

Introduction

1. K. B. McFarlane, *John Wycliffe and the Beginnings of English Noncon-formity* (London, 1952). I have used the Penguin edition, entitled *Wycliffe and English Nonconformity* (London, 1972).
2. J. A. F. Thomson, *The Later Lollards, 1414–1520* (Oxford, 1965). M. Aston's essays are mostly now available in her two collections, *Lollards and Reformers* (London, 1984) and *Faith and Fire* (London, 1993). Anne Hudson, *The Premature Reformation: Wycliffite Texts and Lollard History* (Oxford, 1988). See also her collection, *Lollards and their Books* (London, 1985).
3. R. G. Davies, 'Lollardy and locality', *Transactions of the Royal Historical Society*, 6th series 1 (1991), pp. 191–212, at p. 212.
4. Edward Powell, *Kingship, Law, and Society* (Oxford, 1989), ch. 6, pp. 141–67. Maureen Jurkowski, 'Lawyers and Lollardy in the early fifteenth century', in *Lollardy and the Gentry in the Later Middle Ages*, ed. Margaret Aston and Colin Richmond (Stroud, 1997), pp. 155–82.

1 The Church of England in the Later Middle Ages

1. For Boston, see Roger Dymmok, *Liber contra XII Errores et Hereses Lol-lardorum*, ed. H. S. Cronin (London, 1922), p. xiv.
2. Dorothy M. Owen, *Church and Society in Medieval Lincolnshire* (Lincoln, 1971; History of Lincolnshire 5), pp. 140–1.
3. W. A. Pantin, *The English Church in the Fourteenth Century* (Oxford, 1955), p. 4.
4. W. M. Ormrod, *The Reign of Edward III* (New Haven, CT, and London, 1990), pp. 136–7.
5. Pantin, *English Church*, pp. 14–16. R. G. Davies notes the continuation of this trend throughout the early fifteenth century, with Carlisle, Chichester, and Rochester the usual sees for the token scholars on the bench. R. G. Davies, 'The episcopate', in *Profession, Vocation, and Culture in Later Medieval England*, ed. C. H. Clough (Liverpool, 1982), pp. 51–89, at p. 58.

6. Davies, however, notes the reversal of this rule in the adult years of
    Henry VI ('The episcopate', p. 57).
7. A. B. Cobban, *The King's Hall within the University of Cambridge in the
    Later Middle Ages* (Cambridge, 1969), pp. 251–8.
8. Jeremy Catto brings out the significance of the regime's profound
    hostility to Pecock in his article 'The king's government and the fall
    of Pecock', in *Rulers and Ruled in Late Medieval England*, ed. R. E.
    Archer and S. Walker (London, 1995), pp. 200–22.
9. E. W. Ives, 'The reputation of the common lawyer in English society,
    1450–1550', *University of Birmingham Historical Journal* 7 (1959–60),
    pp. 130–61, esp. pp. 131–5.
10. W. T. Waugh, 'The Great Statute of Praemunire', *English Historical
    Review* 37 (1922), pp. 173–205, esp. pp. 200–4. See also G. L. Harriss,
    Cardinal Beaufort (Oxford, 1988), pp. 214–18.
11. David Knowles, *The Religious Orders in England* (3 vols, Cambridge,
    1948–59), II, p. 258.
12. J. I. Catto, 'Religion and the English nobility in the later fourteenth
    century', in *History and Imagination*, ed. H. Lloyd-Jones et al. (London,
    1981), pp. 43–55, at p. 50.
13. Christine Carpenter, 'The religion of the gentry in fifteenth-century
    England', in *England in the Fifteenth Century: Proceedings of the 1986
    Harlaxton Symposium*, ed. D. Williams (Woodbridge, 1987), pp. 53–74,
    at p. 63; Nigel Saul, 'The religious sympathies of the gentry in
    Gloucestershire, 1200–1500', *Transactions of the Bristol and Gloucestershire
    Archaeological Society* 98 (1980), pp. 99–112.
14. C. L. Kingsford, *The Greyfriars of London* (Aberdeen, 1915), pp. 70–133.
15. Knowles, *Religious Orders*, II, pp. 64–7.
16. Knowles, *Religious Orders*, II, 129–38. See also Catto, 'Religion and
    nobility', pp. 43 and 52; and A. Tuck, 'Carthusian monks and
    Lollard knights: religious attitudes at the Court of Richard II', in
    *Studies in the Age of Chaucer. Proceedings, No. 1, 1984. Reconstructing
    Chaucer*, ed. P. Strohm and T. J. Heffernan (Knoxville, TN, 1985),
    pp. 149–61, at pp. 154–7.
17. C. H. Lawrence, *The Friars* (London, 1994), pp. 2–4, 8–10, and 102–8.
18. For a useful contrast with the English experience, see Richard
    Kieckhefer, *Repression of Heresy in Medieval Germany* (Liverpool,
    1979), esp. pp. 29–31 for the specific point.
19. Pantin, *English Church*, ch. 10; Catto, 'Religion and nobility', pp. 44–5,
    and 51–2; Eamon Duffy, *The Stripping of the Altars* (New Haven, CT,
    and London, 1992), pp. 68–77.
20. Duffy, *Stripping of the Altars*, pp. 53–5.
21. Although the difference between the dramatic traditions of the two
    regions has recently been pointed out by P. J. P. Goldberg, who sees
    cycle plays prevailing in the north and non-cycle plays in the east.
    See his 'Performing the word of God: Corpus Christi drama in
    the northern province', in *Life and Thought in the Northern Church,
    c.1100–c.1700*, ed. D. Wood (Woodbridge, 1999), pp. 145–70, at
    pp. 147–8.

22. This is one of the general themes of Duffy, *Stripping of the Altars*, but see esp. pp. 2–4, and pp. 275–98.

23. See the documents on pilgrimage in England compiled by Diana Webb, *Pilgrims and Pilgrimage in the Medieval West* (London, 1999), pp. 163–212.

24. Jennifer R. Bray, 'Concepts of sainthood in fourteenth-century England', *Bulletin of the John Rylands Library of Manchester* 66 (1983–84), pp. 40–77. For Grosseteste and Dalderby, see Owen, *Church and Society in Medieval Lincolnshire*, p. 126. See also S. Walker, 'Political saints in later medieval England', in *The McFarlane Legacy*, ed. R. H. Britnell and A. J. Pollard (Stroud, 1995), pp. 77–106, esp. pp. 78–9.

25. F. R. Johnston, 'The English cult of St Bridget of Sweden', *Analecta Bollandiana* 103 (1985), pp. 75–93.

26. M. Rubin, 'Corpus Christi fraternities and late medieval piety', *Studies in Church History* 23 (1986), pp. 97–109, at p. 103. See also her 'Small groups: Identity and solidarity in the late Middle Ages', in *Enterprise and Individuals in Fifteenth-Century England*, ed. J. Kermode (Stroud, 1991), pp. 132–50; and of course her *Corpus Christi* (Cambridge, 1991).

27. For an introduction to this vast subject, see Duffy, *Stripping of the Altars*, ch. 3. See also Rubin, *Corpus Christi*; and J. I. Catto, 'John Wyclif and the cult of the eucharist', in *The Bible in the Medieval World*, ed. Katherine Walsh and Diana Wood (Oxford, 1985), pp. 269–86.

28. R. W. Pfaff, *New Liturgical Feasts in Late Medieval England* (Oxford, 1970), pp. 62–83; Duffy, *Stripping of the Altars*, pp. 45, 115, and 238–48; and Rob Lutton, 'Connections between Lollards and gentry in Tenterden in the late fifteenth and early sixteenth centuries', in Aston and Richmond (eds), *Lollardy and the Gentry*, pp. 199–228, at pp. 212–16.

29. See the fundamental article by John Bossy, 'The Mass as a social institution, 1200–1700', *Past & Present* 100 (1983), pp. 29–61.

30. For a refreshing challenge to cosy notions of medieval community, see R. M. Smith, 'Modernization and the corporate medieval village community in England: Some sceptical reflections', in *Explorations in Historical Geography*, ed. A. R. H. Baker and D. Gregory (Cambridge, 1984), pp. 140–79.

31. G. J. C. Snoek, *Medieval Piety from Relics to the Eucharist* (Leiden, 1995).

32. Duffy, *Stripping of the Altars*, pp. 94–5.

33. *The Episcopal Registers of the Diocese of St David's, 1397 to 1518. Vol. 2. 1407–1518*, ed. R. F. Isaacson (London, 1917), pp. 478–83.

34. An observation for which he found himself suspect of heresy, though his ideas had nothing to do with Wyclif or Lollardy. See *Heresy Trials in the Diocese of Norwich, 1428–31*, ed. N. P. Tanner (London, 1977; henceforth cited as *Norwich Heresy Trials*), pp. 89–92, at p. 90.

35. Michael Hicks, 'Chantries, obits, and almshouses: The Hungerford foundations, 1325–1478', in *The Church in Pre-Reformation Society*,

ed. C. M. Barron and C. Harper-Bill (Woodbridge, 1985), pp. 123–42, at pp. 141–2.

36.   Owen, *Church and Society in Medieval Lincolnshire*, p. 94.

37.   The words are Caroline Barron's, from her 'The parish fraternities of medieval London', in Barron and Harper-Bill (eds), *The Church in Pre-Reformation Society*, pp. 13–37, p. 36. For a brief introduction to the nature and scope of these bodies, see Duffy, *Stripping of the Altars*, pp. 141–54. The classic English account is H. F. Westlake, *The Parish Gilds of Mediaeval England* (London, 1919). See more recently Virginia Bainbridge, *Gilds in the Medieval Countryside* (Woodbridge, 1996); and David J. F. Crouch, *Piety, Fraternity and Power* (York, 2000).

38.   Barron, 'Parish fraternities', p. 23. Barron cites evidence from wills to confirm that the records reflect a real change, as testamentary bequests to confraternities appear only in the decade 1340–50. See also Bainbridge, *Gilds in the Medieval Countryside*, pp. 33–41.

39.   Owen, *Church and Society in Medieval Lincolnshire*, p. 127. Crouch, *Piety, Fraternity and Power*, pp. 40–1.

40.   Westlake, *Parish Gilds*, p. 41. Bainbridge notes that some more have been identified since he wrote (*Gilds in the Medieval Countryside*, p. 27). See also Rubin, 'Corpus Christi fraternities', p. 103, and 'Small groups', p. 137; and Crouch, *Piety, Fraternity and Power*, p. 39.

41.   For the case of York, see Crouch, *Piety, Fraternity and Power*, pp. 160–95.

42.   Statistics compiled from *The Register of the Gild of the Holy Cross ... Stratford-upon-Avon*, ed. J. Harvey Bloom (London, 1907).

43.   Rubin, 'Corpus Christi fraternities', p. 109. Goldberg, 'Performing the word of God', pp. 145, and 149.

44.   Richard Beadle, 'The York cycle', in *The Cambridge Companion to Medieval English Theatre*, ed. R. Beadle (Cambridge, 1994), pp. 85–108, at p. 90.

45.   John C. Coldewey, 'The non-cycle plays and the East Anglian tradition', pp. 189–210, in Beadle (ed.), *Cambridge Companion to Medieval English Theatre*, esp. pp. 189–94 for its cultural primacy.

46.   Beat Kumin, *The Shaping of a Community* (Aldershot, 1996). See pp. 148–9, and 152–9 for the points about lights and guilds.

47.   See, in particular, G. Rosser, 'Communities of parish and guild in the late Middle Ages', in *Parish Church and People*, ed. S. J. Wright (London, 1988), pp. 29–55. See also Duffy, *Stripping of the Altars*, ch. 4, esp. pp. 144–50; and Crouch, *Piety, Fraternity and Power*, pp. 32, and 93–7.

48.   Colin Richmond, 'Religion and the fifteenth-century English gentleman', in *The Church, Politics and Patronage*, ed. B. Dobson (Gloucester, 1984), pp. 193–208.

49.   For Roger Martin's recollections of pre-Reformation religious practice in Long Melford, see *The Spoil of Melford Church*, ed. D. Dymond and C. Paine (Ipswich, 1992). For further critique of Richmond's thesis, see Carpenter, 'Gentry religion', pp. 65–6.

2 John Wyclif and His Theology

1. George Holmes, *The Good Parliament* (Oxford, 1975), p. 175.
2. Davies, 'The episcopate', p. 56.
3. For Easton's role see Margaret Harvey, 'Adam Easton and the condemnation of John Wyclif, 1377', *English Historical Review* 113 (1998), 321–34.
4. H. B. Workman, *John Wyclif* (2 vols, Oxford, 1926), I. pp. 275–324, discussing the 'summit of his influence'. Some versions of the story had Wyclif attending Parliament as a sort of clerical observer in the king's interest as early as 1371, but this is no longer accepted.
5. Joseph Dahmus, *The Prosecution of John Wyclyf* (New Haven, CT, 1952). See also his 'John Wyclif and the English government', *Speculum* 35 (1960), pp. 51–68.
6. Holmes, *Good Parliament*, pp. 166–98.
7. M. Wilks, 'Royal priesthood: The origins of Lollardy', in *The Church in a Changing Society* (Uppsala, 1978), pp. 63–70, at p. 65. Although this article contains some useful insights, it is predicated upon assumptions about the massive spread of Lollard teachings for which there is no evidence beyond the hyperbole of a couple of over-anxious monastic chroniclers.
8. See, e.g. Chris Given-Wilson, *The Royal Household and the King's Affinity* (New Haven, CT, and London, 1986), p. 52. The exception is Anthony Goodman, *John of Gaunt* (Harlow, 1992), which mentions Wyclif or the Lollards half a dozen times (pp. 12, 37, 60–1, 93, and 241–3), but proves the rule by producing no evidence that Gaunt sympathised with Wyclif's teachings, and noting the lack of evidence that Gaunt ever rewarded him (p. 37).
9. Thomas Walsingham, *Chronicon Angliae*, ed. E. M. Thompson (London, 1874), pp. 115–20. Walsingham states (p. 115) that Gaunt summoned Wyclif to join his own council, but this seems to be retrospective conjecture. If Wyclif had been a Lancastrian retainer, he would surely have received some reward from Gaunt – which he did not.
10. PRO E 403/460, Exchequer Roll, Annunciation to Michaelmas 50 Edward III (1376), membrane 26. The entry is transcribed in *Issues of the Exchequer*, ed. F. Devon (London, 1836), p. 200. For its interpretation, see e.g. Workman, I. pp. 278–9; McFarlane, *Wycliffe*, p. 57; Dahmus, 'John Wyclif and the English government', pp. 53–4; Holmes, *Good Parliament*, p. 166.
11. Wyclif, *Opera minora*, p. 422 ('cum sim peculiaris regis clericus'). No public record ever attaches this relatively common title to his name. In this case, it may tell us nothing more than that Wyclif had received ecclesiastical preferment from the Crown.
12. *Calendar of Patent Rolls. Edward III. Vol. XVI. A. D. 1374–1377* (London, 1916), pp. 195 (grant to Robert de Faryngton, 18 Nov. 1375), and 393 (revocation of that grant, 22 Dec. 1376). The possible connection between Wyclif's summons and this dispute has not previously been drawn.

13. McFarlane, *Wyclif*, p. 62.
14. Walsingham, *Chronicon Angliae*, pp. 115–20. See the critique in Dahmus, *Prosecution of Wyclyf*, pp. 16–18, and 21.
15. Dahmus, *Prosecution of Wyclyf*, pp. 18–22.
16. McFarlane, *Wyclif*, p. 62, observes that the bishops had just scored off Gaunt by winning permission for Bishop William Wykeham to attend Convocation in London despite having been prohibited from coming within 20 miles of the King. But note that I am reading events differently from McFarlane.
17. Harvey, 'Adam Easton', p. 327. On p. 331 she concludes that Easton was the Pope's main source of information on Wyclif's teachings. See also P. J. Horner, 'The King taught us the lesson: Benedictine support for Henry V's suppression of the Lollards', *Mediaeval Studies* 52 (1990), pp. 190–220, at pp. 193, and 202–5.
18. Wyclif recalled this outburst in his *De ecclesia*, p. 354. He refers to the occasion as 'in publico parliamento', but Brinton's comments do not seem appropriate to the time of the parliament later in 1377. For Brinton spoke of having received information about Wyclif's condemnation (perhaps from Easton along their Benedictine order's lines of communication), whereas by the time of parliament the bulls had almost certainly arrived. Also, Wyclif might well have attended a great council, whereas it is difficult to see how he could have attended the 1377 parliament. As for 'in publico parliamento', Wyclif might have been referring primarily to the place (the great council probably met in the parliament house); and might, in any case, have confused the great council with the parliament at least in his recollection.
19. See his *Libellus* (a response to the papal bull) and *Responsio* (on withholding payments to Rome), in *Fasciculi Zizaniorum*, ed. W. W. Shirley (London, 1858), pp. 245–57, and 258–71. On these documents, see the acute discussion by Dahmus, *Prosecution of Wyclyf*, pp. 56–61.
20. J. I. Catto, 'Wyclif and Wycliffism at Oxford, 1356–1430', in *The History of the University of Oxford. Volume II. Late Medieval Oxford*, ed. J. I. Catto and R. Evans (Oxford, 1992), pp. 175–261, pp. 207–8.
21. *The Anonimalle Chronicle*, ed. V. H. Galbraith (Manchester, 1927), p. 213.
22. Catto, 'Wyclif and Wycliffism', pp. 213–14.
23. My understanding of Wyclif's apocalyptic response in 1378 was crucially advanced by Curtis Bostick's insightful study of Lollard apocalypticism, *The Antichrist and the Lollards* (Leiden, 1998).
24. *De ecclesia*, p. 358.
25. *De potestate pape*, p. 248 (also cited by Kenny, *Wyclif*, p. 76).
26. *Opus evangelicum*, IV, pp. 325–6.
27. For a succinct account of Wyclif's 'metaphysical realism', see Anthony Kenny's typically incisive study, *Wyclif* (Oxford, 1985), pp. 9–17; and for a more extensive treatment, J. A. Robson, *Wyclif and the Oxford Schools* (Cambridge, 1961), pp. 141–70. See also the helpful introduction by P. V. Spade, in Wyclif, *On Universals* (1985), at pp. xii–xx.

28. Maurice Keen, 'Wyclif, the Bible, and transubstantiation', in *Wyclif in his Times*, ed. A. Kenny (Oxford, 1986), pp. 1–16, contrasts Wyclif's 'realist metaphysic' with the 'logic of holy scripture' (pp. 12–13). But in my view, he makes a contrast where Wyclif made an identification. For an explicit contrast drawn by Wyclif between nominalist logic and the 'logic of holy scripture', see G. A. Benrath, *Wyclifs Bibelkommentar* (Berlin, 1966), p. 220, esp. note 543.

29. Robson, *Wyclif and the Oxford Schools*, pp. 163–5. Beryl Smalley, 'The Bible and eternity: John Wyclif's dilemma', in her *Studies in Medieval Thought and Learning from Abelard to Wyclif* (London, 1981), pp. 399–415, esp. pp. 403–7 for Wyclif's conversion. For the citation (from Wyclif, *De dominio divino*, p. 65), see p. 406.

30. Beryl Smalley, 'John Wyclif's *Postilla super totam Bibliam*', *Bodleian Library Record* 4 (1952–53), pp. 186–205. Benrath, *Wyclifs Bibelkommentar*, p. 8, notes that Wyclif cannot have taken the books in their biblical order.

31. Smalley, 'Bible and eternity', p. 412.

32. This paragraph takes its departure from the argument advanced in M. T. Clanchy, *From Memory to Written Record* (2nd edn Oxford, 1993).

33. *De mandatis divinis*, pp. 21–2: 'Omne igitur iudicium, opus, vel documentum quod illa [i.e., scripture] non regulat est iniquum.'

34. W. Farr, *John Wyclif as Legal Reformer* (Leiden, 1974), esp. pp. 122–38, and 163–7.

35. *Opus evangelicum*, I, p. 34.

36. *De mandatis*, ca. 3, p. 20; see also p. 18 for equation of a right to a thing with God's will that the thing belong.

37. *De mandatis*, ca. 21, p. 279, 'Sic ergo resistitur voluntati Domini, quandocumque contempnitur eius consilium vel preceptum'.

38. *De mandatis*, p. 366: 'omnis peccans mortaliter facit furtum'.

39. *De civili dominio*, I, p. xxvii; Catto, 'Wyclif and Wycliffism', p. 202.

40. *De ecclesia*, pp. 284–5, citing principally Ezechiel 44.28–30; Deuteronomy 18.1; and Numbers 18.20.

41. *De ecclesia*, pp. 290, and 292.

42. *Trialogus*, ed. G. Lechler (Oxford, 1869), pp. 299–314.

43. Keen, 'Wyclif, the Bible, and transubstantiation', p. 3.

44. Kenny, *Wyclif*, pp. 39–41.

45. The link between the eternity of the things as ideas in the divine mind and the absolute necessity of future events is spelled out in *De ecclesia*, pp. 106–07.

46. See *Opus evangelicum*, II, ch. 55, p. 451 for free will and sin; and *De veritate sacrae scripturae* II.222 for compatibility of free will and predestination. See also *De ecclesia*, p. 281, for free will.

47. Kenny, *Wyclif*, pp. 70–1.

48. *De ecclesia*, pp. 2–4, and 78–80. Kenny, *Wyclif*, pp. 68–70.

49. Michael Hurley, 'Scriptura sola: Wyclif and his critics', *Traditio* 16 (1960), pp. 275–352, esp. pp. 294–301, and 344–45.

50. *De potestate pape*, p. 328. Bostick, *The Antichrist and the Lollards*, pp. 69–73.

51. *De mandatis*, p. 381.
52. *De ecclesia*, p. 325, in ch. 14.
53. *Trialogus*, p. 301.
54. See, e.g., *Speculum ecclesiae militantis*, pp. 24, and 45.
55. *De nova praevaricantia mandatorum*, in Wyclif's *Polemical Works in Latin*, ed. R. Buddensieg (2 vols, 1883), p. 124.
56. *Opus evangelicum*, III, pp. 75–6.
57. Paul Strohm, *England's Empty Throne* (New Haven, CT, and London, 1998), pp. 45–9, has suggested that Wyclif was here the victim of the shrewd tactics of his opponents, who obliged him to fight on this ground not because of its intrinsic importance but because it was possible to trap anybody on it. In fact, Wyclif himself affirmed that this was a central question (*Opus evangelicum*, III, p. 142, 'videtur quod heresis de hostia consecrata teneat gradum summum', see also p. 169; *pace* Strohm, who claims on p. 48 that Wyclif and his followers were surprised at the attention devoted to this topic). For Wyclif's assessment of his opponents' motives, see *De blasphemia*, pp. 286–7.
58. *De benedicta incarnacione*, pp. 190–1.
59. *Tractatus De trinitate*, ed. A. W. Breck (Boulder, CO, 1962), p. 111. See also Catto, 'Wyclif and Wycliffism', p. 213. See also Wyclif's *De mandatis* (1375), pp. 465–6, for discussion of the eucharist with none of his later polemics against transubstantiation.
60. Strohm, *England's Empty Throne*, pp. 47, and 49. I would add, if they were guilty.
61. Keen, 'Wyclif, the Bible, and transubstantiation', argues that Wyclif's eucharistic heresy arose from his reading of the Bible rather than from his metaphysics, dissenting from the consensus that Wyclif's critique of transubstantiation was primarily a response to its intellectual problems. In my view, he has slightly misunderstood the significance of the 'logic of holy scripture' (see above, note 28).
62. Keen, 'Wyclif, the Bible, and transubstantiation', p. 11.
63. *Sermones*, III, p. 507.
64. *De eucharistia*, pp. 78, and (for the 'Questio ad fratres de sacramento altaris') pp. 347–8.
65. Workman, II, pp. 36–8. Kenny, *Wyclif*, pp. 81–2; Keen, 'Wyclif, the Bible, and transubstantiation', p. 15; J. A. F. Thomson, 'Orthodox religion and the origins of Lollardy', *History* 74 (1989), pp. 39–55, at p. 54. Gordon Leff somewhat confusingly asserts first that Wyclif postulated a 'figurative' presence of Christ in the eucharist, and then that he nevertheless upheld a 'real presence'. See his 'Ockham and Wyclif on the eucharist', *Reading Medieval Studies* 2 (1976), pp. 1–11, at pp. 7–8.
66. *De eucharistia*, pp. 205–6, and 211–12. Duffy, *Stripping of the Altars*, p. 98.
67. Wyclif himself comes close to making the connection in *De apostasia*, p. 148.

68. *De ecclesia*, pp. 457, and 459.
69. *De ecclesia*, pp. 467–8.
70. *Trialogus*, p. 317.
71. This summary is based on *De blasphemia*, chs 8–11; *Trialogus*, IV, chs 23–4; and *De eucharistia et penitentia* (*De eucharistia*, pp. 329–43).
72. *De ecclesia*, p. 515.
73. *De potestate pape*, pp. 169, 306,
74. *De potestate pape*, p. 312.
75. *De potestate pape*, p. 309.
76. *De officio pastorali*, in *English Wyclif Tracts*, ed. C. Lindberg (Oslo, 1991), p. 31.
77. See Catto, *Wyclif and Wycliffism at Oxford, 1356–1430*, pp. 212–13. *De ecclesia*, pp. 429–30.
78. *Sermones*, II, pp. 145–6; *De officio regis*, p. 206.
79. See e.g. *De triplici vinculo amoris*, pp. 173–6; and the *De quattuor sectis novellis*. Virtually every pamphlet in the *Polemical Works in Latin* is a rant against the 'four sects', esp. the friars.
80. *De ecclesia*, ch. 22, pp. 524–48
81. *De ecclesia*, p. 547.
82. *Opus evangelicum*, I, p. 37. For blasphemy, see *De potestate pape*, pp. 208, and 391. See also *De ecclesia*, pp. 549–87; and *Speculum ecclesie militantis*, p. 50 ('fantasmata non fundata').
83. *De ecclesia*, p. 8. *De nova praevaricantia mandatorum*, in *Polemical Works in Latin*, pp. 147–8. His tripartite division of the Church into milit-ant (on earth), triumphant (in heaven), and dormant (in between) requires purgatory to house the third element.
84. *Sermones*, II, p. 1. See also *De ecclesia*, p. 44–5; and *Trialogus*, p. 237.
85. *Sermones*, II, pp. 8–9.
86. See, e.g., *De ecclesia*, p. 465; *Speculum ecclesie militantis*, p. 32; *Sermones*, II, pp. 164–5, and 341; *De potestate pape*, pp. 329, and 337; and *Trialogus*, p. 238.
87. *Trialogus*, p. 235.
88. Farr, *Wyclif as Legal Reformer*, pp. 34–6.
89. *De officio regis*, pp. 31, 48, 51, 72, 125, 176–77, and 245. Farr, *Wyclif as Legal Reformer*, pp. 66–70.
90. Wilks, 'Royal priesthood', pp. 65–6. Where Wilks errs, as we shall see, is in assuming that this appeal was successful.
91. John Hatcher, 'England in the aftermath of the Black Death', *Past & Present* 144 (1994), pp. 3–35.
92. Goodman, *John of Gaunt*, p. 243.
93. See Walsingham, *Chronicon Angliae*, pp. 285–312, for his earlier account of the revolt. On pp. 311–12 he offers an explanation in terms of providential chastisement. So far is he from blaming the Lollards as such that, on p. 312, he attaches particular blame to the sins of the friars. In his later *Historia Anglicana*, ed. H. T. Riley (2 vols London, 1863–64), I., pp. 453–84, and II, pp. 1–34, he offers no general explanation, but states that John Ball preached Wycliffite doctrines (p. 32). His claim is hardly borne out by the account of his

message of human equality, nor by the 'letters of John Ball' which he transcribes (pp. 33–4).

3   The Early Diffusion of Lollardy

1. Thomson, *Later Lollards*, generally; and also 'Orthodox religion', pp. 48–50. S. Justice, 'Lollardy', in *The Cambridge History of Medieval English Literature*, ed. D. Wallace (Cambridge, 1999), pp. 662–89, at p. 662 questions the coherence of Lollardy, as does R. N. Swanson, *Church and Society in Late Medieval England* (Oxford, 1989), pp. 329–47. Davies, 'Lollardy and locality', pp. 191, and 211–12.
2. Hudson, *Premature Reformation*. C. Kightly, 'The early Lollards: A survey of popular Lollard activity in England, 1382–1428', York University PhD, 1975. McHardy, 'The dissemination of Wyclif's ideas', in *From Ockham to Wyclif*, ed. Anne Hudson and Michael Wilks (Oxford, 1987), pp. 361–8; and 'Bishop Buckingham and the Lollards of Lincoln diocese', in *Schism, Heresy and Religious Protest*, ed. Derek Baker (Cambridge, 1972), pp. 131–45. McFarlane, *Wycliffe*.
3. See Aston, 'Wyclif and the vernacular', in her *Faith and Fire*, pp. 27–72 (esp. p. 30 for the difficulty of certainly ascribing English texts to Wyclif).
4. Wyclif, *Sermones*, I, p. 110, values preaching above the power of consecration.
5. This judgement is shared by almost all scholars of Wyclif. The only dissident view comes from H. Kaminsky, who finds Wyclif's language a perfect vehicle for his thought. See his 'Wyclifism as ideology of revolution', *Church History* 32 (1963), 57–74, at p. 71, note 7. One can only agree in so far as Wyclif's thought is often as convoluted and tortuous as his prose.
6. *Knighton's Chronicle, 1337–1396*, ed. and trans. G. H. Martin (Oxford, 1995), pp. xlii–xlvi, and 283–99.
7. McHardy, 'Dissemination of Wyclif's ideas', pp. 361–2. Aston, 'Wycliffe and the vernacular', p. 38.
8. McHardy, 'Bishop Buckingham and the Lollards', pp. 131–2.
9. Kightly, 'The early Lollards', p. 267. Martin argues that Aston may have preached at Gloucester in 1382 (*Knighton's Chronicle*, p. 289, note 5).
10. *Knighton's Chronicle*, pp. 283–5, and 291–3.
11. Geoffrey Martin, 'Knighton's Lollards', in Aston and Richmond (eds), *Lollardy and the Gentry*, pp. 28–40, at pp. 32–6. See his edition of *Knighton's Chronicle*, pp. xliii and 283 for the decent concealment of Repingdon's name by Knighton; and pp. 307–23 for Swinderby.
12. *Two Wycliffite Texts*, ed. A. Hudson (Oxford, 1993), p. 38.
13. McHardy, 'Dissemination of Wyclif's ideas', pp. 362–3, and 368.
14. Kightly, 'The early Lollards', pp. 231–2.

15. McHardy, 'Dissemination of Wyclif's ideas', pp. 363–4.
16. *English Wycliffite Sermons*, ed. Anne Hudson and Pamela Gradon (5 vols, Oxford, 1983–96), III, p. 162: 'for do a man that in him is, and God is ready to his deeds', which reads very much like a didactic jingle.
17. *English Wycliffite Sermons*, III, pp. 183–4.
18. Andrew Brown, *Popular Piety in Late Medieval England* (Oxford, 1995), p. 222.
19. Hudson, *Premature Reformation*, p. 117.
20. *Knighton's Chronicle*, pp. 294–5 (Latimer, Clifford, Sturry, John Trussel, John Peachey, and Reginald Hilton). Walsingham, *Historia Anglicana*, II. p. 159, names Latimer, Clifford, Sturry, Sir William Neville, Sir John Clanvowe, and Sir John Montagu. See K. B. McFarlane, *Lancastrian Kings and Lollard Knights* (Oxford, 1972), pp. 148–76.
21. *Annales Ricardi Secundi et Henrici Quarti*, in *Johannis de Trokelowe et Henrici de Blaneforde . . . Chronica et Annales*, ed. H. T. Riley (London, 1866), pp. 153–420, at p. 183. See also Nigel Saul, *Richard II* (New Haven, CT, and London, 1997), p. 301.
22. *Annales Ricardi Secundi et Henrici Quarti*, pp. 347–8. The chronicle describes Clifford as 'Lollardis fautor', that is, as a patron of the heresy.
23. McFarlane, *Wycliffe*, p. 159; J. I. Catto, 'Religious change under Henry V', in *Henry V*, ed. G. L. Harriss (Oxford, 1985), pp. 97–115, at p. 113.
24. Tuck, 'Carthusian monks and Lollard knights', pp. 150–2, and 159–60.
25. W. J. Dohar, *The Black Death and Pastoral Leadership* (Philadelphia, PA, 1995), p. 144.
26. *Register of Thomas Spofford*, pp. 152–3.
27. McFarlane, *Wycliffe*, pp. 145–6.
28. Kightly, 'The early Lollards', pp. 180–5.
29. M. Jurkowski, 'Lancastrian royal service, Lollardy and forgery: The career of Thomas Tykhill', in *Crown, Government and People in the Fifteenth Century*, ed. R. A. Archer (Stroud, 1995), pp. 33–52, at p. 38.
30. J. I. Catto, 'Sir William Beauchamp between chivalry and Lollardy', in *The Ideals and Practice of Medieval Knighthood III: Papers from the Fourth Strawberry Hill Conference, 1988*, ed. C. Harper-Bill and R. Harvey (Woodbridge, 1990), pp. 39–48, at pp. 42–3. See also Catto, 'Wycliffism at Oxford', pp. 226, and 233.
31. Stormesworth's petition is transcribed in R. M. Serjeantson, *A History of the Church of All Saints, Northampton* (Northampton, 1901), pp. 34–6. See also *Historia Vitae et Regni Richardi Secundi*, ed. G. B. Stow (Philadelphia, PA, 1977), p. 93; McFarlane, *Wycliffe*, pp. 126–9; and McHardy, 'Bishop Buckingham and the Lollards', pp. 137–40. It may be mere coincidence, but the name of Braybrooke is of course the name of Sir Thomas Latimer's home village.
32. McHardy, 'Bishop Buckingham and the Lollards', pp. 138–9. Buckingham clearly needed to be pushed, and McFarlane has pointed to doubts expressed at the time as to his competence.

33. For the towns, see Maurice Keen, *English Society in the Later Middle Ages, 1348–1500* (London, 1990), p. 87.

34. Peter McNiven, *Heresy and Politics in the Reign of Henry IV* (Woodbridge, 1987), p. 117.

35. For the rebels, see *Register of Philip Repingdon*, III, p. 73, note 4. For Comberworth, see above, note 27.

36. *The Register of Robert Hallum, Bishop of Salisbury, 1407–17*, ed. J. M. Horn (Torquay, 1972; Canterbury and York Society, 72), nos 1133 and 1142.

37. Kightly, 'The early Lollards', p. 390.

38. McFarlane questions whether Lollardy had anything to do with this anticlerical outburst (*Wycliffe*, p. 124). Walsingham was inclined to see reds under the bed. Yet he does not attach the charge of Lollardy to many specific incidents, and a strongly anti-fraternal display in the midst of the Wycliffite polemic against the friars would be very difficult to distinguish convincingly from Lollardy. And of all the friars, the Augustinians seem to have been the most attracted to Wyclif's teachings, perhaps because of the affinities between his teaching on lordship in grace and that of their order's greatest theologian, Giles of Rome.

39. Kightly, 'The early Lollards', p. 372.

40. *The Brut*, ed. F. W. D. Brie (2 vols, London, 1906–08), II, p. 448. *Fasciculi zizaniorum*, p. 418. Kightly, 'The early Lollards', pp. 406–8.

41. L. R. Poos, *A Rural Society after the Black Death: Essex, 1350–1525* (Cambridge, 1991), pp. 264–5.

42. E. J. B. Reid, 'Lollards at Colchester in 1414', *English Historical Review* 29 (1914), pp. 101–4.

43. Kightly, 'The early Lollards', p. 115.

44. For Dereham, see Davies, 'The episcopate', p. 86, note 52.

45. Hudson, *Premature Reformation*, pp. 92–4. Margaret Aston cites Lydgate on Cambridge's vaunted immunity in her 'Bishops and heresy: The defence of the faith', in *Faith and Fire*, pp. 73–93, at p. 85.

46. *Knighton's Chronicle*, pp. 293–7.

47. See *Knighton's Chronicle*, p. 309, for the Duke's grant of the hermitage, clearly some time before Swynderby was tainted with heresy; and p. 313 for the Duke's intervention at his trial.

48. McFarlane, *Wycliffe*, p. 109.

49. M. Aston, *Thomas Arundel* (Oxford, 1967), pp. 330–1.

50. *Register of Philip Repingdon*, I, pp. xxxiv–xxxv.

51. Kightly, 'The early Lollards', p. 148.

52. *Register of Philip Repingdon*, III, pp. 196–8. His case is undated, but it is transcribed among documents from 1417–18.

53. Kightly, 'The early Lollards', p. 200. *Two Wycliffite Texts*, pp. 42–3.

54. *Knighton's Chronicle*, pp. 290–3. *Register of Nicholas Bubwith*, I pp. lxv, 35, 142–3, 283–90.

55. *Two Wycliffite Texts*, p. 29. In 1407 Archbishop Arundel accused Thorpe of having preached in the North and elsewhere 'this twenti wyntir and more'.

56. R. L. Storey, *Thomas Langley and the Bishopric of Durham, 1406–1437* (London, 1961), p. 206.
57. Kightly, 'The early Lollards', pp. 335–6.
58. *The Register of Edmund Lacy*, esp. comment in V, p. xvii.
59. Carpenter, 'Gentry religion', in general.
60. Powell, *Kingship, Law, and Society*, pp. 159–61.
61. Poos, *Rural Society*, pp. 269–71. R. A. Griffiths, *The Reign of Henry VI* (London, 1981), p. 643, voices reservations about the Lollard component of indictments of Cade's followers.
62. Michael Wilks, 'Wyclif and the great persecution', in *Prophecy and Eschatology*, ed. M. Wilks (Oxford 1994), pp. 39–63, at pp. 62–3. Bostick, *Antichrist and the Lollard*, p. 174, notes the lack of millennial themes in Lollard apocalyptic. Although now and again he ascribes revolutionary potential to it, this is only tenable for the first generation of Lollardy, and even then only with major reservations.
63. M. Aston, *England's Iconoclasts. Vol.1. Laws against Images* (Oxford, 1988), p. 133.
64. J. I. Catto, 'Wyclif and the cult of the eucharist', pp. 269–70, and 274–9. Paul Strohm, in contrast, sees the eucharistic question as immaterial, 'arbitrary and empty, except as the means to an altogether different end'. See his *England's Empty Throne*, p. 51. But his heavily reductive reading reflects a twentieth-century rather than a medieval sense as to the importance of theological and sacramental things.
65. Poos, *Rural Society*, pp. 286–8.
66. Kightly, 'The early Lollards', p. 237.
67. Hudson, *Premature Reformation*, pp. 23, and 238.
68. Hudson, *Premature Reformation*, p. 205. Hudson states that most known owners of surviving copies were 'not certain members of the sect'. I would go further and say that most were certainly not members of the sect.
69. Hudson, *Premature Reformation*, p. 22. Of course, as a bishop, he was empowered under Arundel's Constitutions to license others to have and read the English Bible, so there was no question of his actually breaking canon law. Nevertheless, use of the Lollard Bible could still have been used as a smear if it had been thought worthwhile.
70. Margaret Deanesley's *The Lollard Bible and Other Medieval Biblical Versions* (Cambridge, 1920) was an investigation into More's error, for which see in particular pp. 1–17, and 370–3. Cranmer used the same idea for different purposes in his prologue to the Great Bible of 1539.
71. Anne Hudson suggests that this treatise, which is first mentioned in surviving records in the later fifteenth century, may have been of late compilation (*Premature Reformation*, p. 18). However, the author refers to his own work on translating the Book of Genesis, from which it can be inferred that he was one of Wyclif's Oxford disciples who produced the Lollard Bible. The text as printed has almost certainly been slightly emended by its Protestant editors.

72. Powell, *Kingship, Law, and Society*, p. 149.
73. Maureen Jurkowski, 'New light on John Purvey', *English Historical Review* 110 (1995), pp. 1180–90, at p. 1182.
74. Griffiths, *Henry VI*, p. 139.
75. I owe this insight to the generosity of Professor James Carley, who has shared with me the fruits of his wide knowledge of late medieval and Tudor manuscripts and libraries.
76. I owe the first figure to Professor Nigel Morgan, who has kindly made available to me the results of his census of manuscript Books of Hours. Books of Hours tended to be in private hands, and to be passed down in families. For the second, see Duffy, *Stripping of the Altars*, p. 212.
77. M. T. Brady, '*The Pore Caitif*: An introductory study', *Traditio* 10 (1954), pp. 529–48; and 'Lollard sources of *The Pore Caitif*', *Traditio* 44 (1988), pp. 389–418. See also Hudson, *Premature Reformation*, pp. 422–9.
78. McFarlane, *Lancastrian Kings and Lollard Knights*, pp. 207–20 on the wills.
79. On the commitment of the Lollard knights, I am not convinced that the extra information amassed by McFarlane in *Lancastrian Kings and Lollard Knights* is enough to justify his departure (at e.g. pp. 139 and 143) from the scepticism of his earlier *Wycliffe*, pp. 129–31.
80. McFarlane, *Lancastrian Kings and Lollard Knights*, pp. 224–5, although I would not entirely accept the sweeping characterisation of the 'contemporary spirit in religion' which he offers here.
81. Sandra Raban, *Mortmain Legislation and the English Church, 1279–1500* (Cambridge, 1982), p. 139.
82. For some fruitful reflections on the noble milieu in which both Lollard and Carthusian spirituality could gain a hearing, see Catto, 'Religion and the English nobility', pp. 43–55.
83. Griffiths, *Henry VI*, pp. 139–40.
84. See Derek Plumb, 'The social and economic status of the later Lollards', in *The World of Rural Dissenters, 1520–1725*, ed. Margaret Spufford (Cambridge, 1995), pp. 103–31, at p. 121, note 50, for an elaboration of Tanner's conclusions. See also his 'A gathered church? Lollards and their society', pp. 132–63 of the same work, at pp. 154–6.
85. Davies, 'Lollardy and locality', pp. 195–7. See also Shannon McSheffrey, *Gender and Heresy* (Philadelphia, PA, 1995), esp. p. 137.
86. Anne Hudson, 'Springing cockel in our clene corn: Lollard preaching in England around 1400', in *Christendom and its Discontents*, ed. Scott L. Waugh and Peter D. Diehl (Cambridge, 1996), pp. 132–47, at p. 139.
87. Hudson, *Premature Reformation*, p. 139.
88. Walsingham, *Historia Anglicana*, II. p. 307.
89. *Norwich Heresy Trials*, p. 33. For White, see *Fasciculi zizaniorum*, pp. 423–4.
90. Saul, *Richard II*, esp. pp. 304–26. Saul argues that in his early years Richard was to some extent influenced by the anticlerical and even perhaps unorthodox ideas of the Lollard knights and others

(pp. 297–9). However, his own evidence for Richard's enthusiastic-ally orthodox piety from as early as 1381 (p. 304) points in another direction: Richard may have been complacent or unconcerned about heresy in the 1380s, but he was in no sense favourable to it. Nevertheless, Saul's conclusion that it was the influence of Arch-bishop Arundel which induced Richard to take vigorous action against the Lollards in the 1390s (p. 300) is compelling.

91. See e.g., Michael Wilks, 'Thomas Arundel of York: The appellant Archbishop', in *Life and Thought in the Northern Church, c.1100–c.1700*, ed. Diana Wood (Woodbridge, 1999), pp. 87–103. See Tuck, 'Carthusian monks and Lollard knights', for an earlier, but still convincing refutation of the thesis.

92. McNiven, *Heresy and Politics*, pp. 95–8. McNiven ascribes rather more political importance to Lollardy than I do.

93. A record of the proceedings against Oldcastle was circulated to all dioceses on the orders of Arundel. See *The Episcopal Register of Robert Rede*, I, pp. 151–6.

94. See Powell, *Kingship, Law, and Society*, pp. 154–6 for the numbers involved; and ch. 6, 'The Lollard revolt' (pp. 141–67) for the best analysis of the whole episode.

95. Jurkowski, 'New light on John Purvey', pp. 1180–2, and 1190.

96. Strohm, *England's Empty Throne*, pp. 67–71.

97. *The Episcopal Register of Robert Rede*, I, pp. 158–60.

98. Powell, *Kingship, Law, and Society*, p. 157, comments on the fact that most of those indicted came from areas where Lollard preachers had enjoyed support from members of local elites.

99. Strohm, *England's Empty Throne*, pp. 85–6.

100. Harriss, *Cardinal Beaufort*, pp. 71, 151, and 179.

101. Powell, *Kingship, Law, and Society*, p. 162.

102. See e.g. the *Register of Philip Repingdon*, III, pp. 69–74, 117–18, 128–31, and elsewhere.

103. Griffiths, *Henry VI*, p. 643.

104. J. A. F. Thomson, 'Knightly piety and the margins of Lollardy', in Aston and Richmond (eds), *Lollardy and the Gentry*, pp. 95–111, at p. 109.

105. Catto, 'Religious change under Henry V', pp. 101–11. See also his 'Religion and the English nobility', and Carpenter, 'Religion of the gentry'.

4 Survival and Revival

1. Thomson, *Later Lollards*, in general, esp. pp. 192–201 for the North. Hudson, *Premature Reformation*, pp. 126–7.

2. See Eric Acheson, *A Gentry Community: Leicestershire in the Fifteenth Century, c. 1422–c.1485* (Cambridge, 1992), pp. 186–98, esp. p. 194, for an assessment of the overwhelmingly orthodox character of

Leicestershire gentry religion; James Crompton, 'Leicestershire Lollards', *Transactions of the Leicestershire Archaeological and Historical Society* 44 (1968–69), pp. 11–43, at pp. 30–3.

3. *Visitations of Religious Houses in the Diocese of Lincoln*, pp. xxix–xxx.

4. Hudson, *Premature Reformation*, p. 466 notes that 16 suspects were found at Amersham in 1464. For the Tudor era, see Plumb, 'Social and economic status of Lollards', pp. 110–11; and 'Gathered church?', pp. 149–50.

5. C. J. Drees, *Authority & Dissent in the English Church* (Lewiston, 1997), pp. 80–6. See pp. 63, 80, and 86 for some links between Lollards in the dioceses of Winchester, Salisbury, and Lincoln.

6. *Kent Heresy Proceedings, 1511–12*, ed. N. Tanner (Maidstone, 1997), pp. xvii, xxi, and 11.

7. *Norwich Heresy Trials*, p. 29.

8. Thomson, *Later Lollards*, p. 215.

9. Brown, *Popular Piety*, p. 217. Drees, *Authority & Dissent*, pp. 64–6.

10. Drees, *Authority & Dissent*, pp. 79–83.

11. See *The Register of Edmund Lacy*.

12. For the strays, see *Norwich Heresy Trials*, pp. 89–92, 102–5, 173–4, and 200–1.

13. Andrew Hope traces fascinating connections among the Colchester Lollards of this era in his 'The lady and the bailiff: Lollardy among the gentry in Yorkist and early Tudor England', in Aston and Richmond (eds), *Lollardy and the Gentry*, pp. 250–77, at pp. 260–3.

14. See e.g., *Register of Nicholas Bubwith*, I, p. 35; *Register of Thomas Bekynton*, I, pp. 120–7; *Registers of Robert Stillington and Richard Fox*, p. 109; and *Registers of Oliver King and Hadrian de Castello*, pp. 38 and 50.

15. J. Fines, 'Heresy trials in the diocese of Coventry and Lichfield, 1511–1512', *Journal of Ecclesiastical History* 14 (1963), pp. 160–74.

16. Thomson, *Later Lollards*, p. 102. *William Gregory's Chronicle of London*, in *The Historical Collections of a Citizen of London*, ed. J. Gairdner (London, 1876), pp. 55–239, at p. 172.

17. Poos, *Rural Society*, pp. 263, and 262. For Coventry, see C. Phythian-Adams, *Desolation of a City* (Cambridge, 1979), pp. 33–9, 182–3, and 252–7.

18. A. G. Dickens, *Lollards and Protestants in the Diocese of York, 1509–1558* (Oxford, 1959), p. 17. See also Crouch, *Piety, Fraternity and Power*, p. 223 for the lack of Yorkshire Lollardy.

19. Dickens, *Lollards and Protestants*, pp. 30–1.

20. *Register of Richard Mayew*, pp. 109–11.

21. Plumb, 'Gathered church?', p. 133.

22. Plumb, 'Gathered church?', p. 159.

23. McFarlane, *Wycliffe*, p. 112. For similar comments, see Brown, *Popular Piety*, p. 219.

24. *Register of John Stanbury*, pp. 125–31.

25. See Martha C. Skeeters, *Community and Clergy* (Oxford, 1993), pp. 34–5 for the jurisdictional problems of Bristol.

26. For Lichfield, see Ann J. Kettle, 'City and close: Lichfield in the century before the Reformation', in Barron and Harper-Bill (eds), *The Church in Pre-Reformation Society*, pp. 158–69.

27. Walsingham, *Chronicon Angliae*, pp. 146, and 299–301.

28. John Foxe, *Actes and Monuments* (London, 1583), p. '799' (i.e., 803). See also Foxe, *Acts and Monuments*, ed. G. Townsend (8 vols, London, 1843–49), IV, p. 177. These works are henceforth cited as AM 1563 and AM 1843–49.

29. Foxe, AM 1583, pp. '798–9' (i.e., 802–3), notes 40 names from the period 1510–27 (AM 1843–9, IV, p. 174).

30. Susan Brigden, *London and the Reformation* (Oxford, 1989), pp. 82–106.

31. Poos, *Rural Society*, pp. 269–72; Brown, *Popular piety*, pp. 217–18. Fines, 'Heresy trials', p. 162. See also Hudson, *Premature Reformation*, pp. 128–30.

32. Plumb, 'Social and economic status of Lollards', pp. 111–29.

33. Imogen Luxton, 'The Lichfield court book: A postscript', *Bulletin of the Institute of Historical Research* 44 (1971), pp. 120–5. But see McSheffrey, *Gender and Heresy*, pp. 37–45.

34. Margaret Aston and Colin Richmond (eds), 'Introduction' in their *Lollardy and the Gentry*, pp. 1–27, at p. 20. The collection attempts a revision of received wisdom by investigating possible gentry involvement in Lollardy, but, in fact, finds little evidence for it, although it is valuable in many other ways.

35. R. W. Hoyle, 'The Earl, the Archbishop and the Council: The affray at Fulford, May 1504', in *Rulers and Ruled in Late Medieval England*, ed. R. E. Archer and S. Walker (London, 1995), pp. 239–56.

36. Jurkowski, 'Lancastrian royal service', pp. 49–50.

37. *Norwich Heresy Trials*, pp. 41–51, and 138–44.

38. See J. F. Davis, 'Joan of Kent, Lollardy and the English Reformation', *Journal of Ecclesiastical History* 33 (1982), pp. 225–33, for her career.

39. C. Cross, 'Great reasoners in scripture: The activities of women Lollards, 1380–1530', in *Medieval Women*, ed. Derek Baker (Oxford, 1978), pp. 359–80, at p. 359 (and also p. 378).

40. Plumb, 'Gathered church?', pp. 146, 149, and 155. M. Aston, 'Lollard women priests?', in her *Lollards and Reformers* (London, 1984), pp. 49–70.

41. McSheffrey, *Gender and Heresy*, pp. 151–66.

42. The term used by Cross, 'Great reasoners', p. 360.

43. See *Fasciculi zizaniorum*, pp. 420 and 423 for White's wife; and Foxe, AM 1583, pp. 815–18 (AM 1843–9, IV, pp. 208–14). See McSheffrey, *Gender and Heresy*, p. 56 for further discussion.

44. McSheffrey, *Gender and Heresy*, pp. 87–107 for relationships, and pp. 54 and 79 for the question of honour.

45. William Tyndale, *An Answer to Sir Thomas More's Dialogue*, ed. H. Walter (Cambridge, 1850), p. 72.

46. See P. J. P. Goldberg, 'Women', in *Fifteenth-Century Attitudes*, ed. Rosemary Horrox (Cambridge, 1994), pp. 112–31, at p. 122, with

a caveat about the danger of taking contemporary iconography too literally. The other points I owe to conversations with Dr Duffy.

47. For some general remarks on this subject, see *Medieval London Widows, 1300–1500*, ed. Caroline M. Barron and Anne F. Sutton (London, 1994), esp. Barron's introduction, pp. xiii–xxxiv, at pp. xiv and xvii.

48. Barron, introduction, *Medieval London Widows*, p. xxvii.

49. Brown, *Popular Piety*, pp. 214, and 258.

50. For some useful remarks on the place of women in late medieval religion, see McSheffrey, *Gender and Heresy*, pp. 138–42. For women and guilds, see most recently, Crouch, *Piety, Fraternity and Power*, pp. 91–2.

51. See e.g., Alan Macfarlane, *The Origins of English Individualism* (Oxford, 1978), pp. 147–51; and Poos, *Rural Society*, pp. 159–79.

52. *Kent Heresy Proceedings*, pp. 1, 5, and 52.

53. Fines, 'Heresy trials', p. 164.

54. Foxe, AM 1583, p. 818 (AM 1843–9, p. 214).

55. *Norwich Heresy Trials*, pp. 47–8.

56. Claire Cross, *Church and People, 1450–1660* (London, 1976), p. 41. See John Strype, *Ecclesiastical Memorials* (3 vols in 6 parts, Oxford, 1822), vol. 1, pt 2, pp. 52–3, and 60–1.

57. Brigden, *London and the Reformation*, pp. 87–8. *Kent Heresy Proceedings*, pp. 65, and 75.

58. Plumb, 'Social and economic status of Lollards', p. 120.

59. *Norwich Heresy Trials*, p. 30. See also Hudson, *Premature Reformation*, pp. 175–86; Brown, *Popular Piety*, p. 219; Bostick, *The Antichrist and the Lollards*, p. 182; and Rita Copeland, 'Childhood, pedagogy, and the literal sense: From late antiquity to the Lollard heretical classroom', in *New Medieval Literatures I*, ed. W. Scase, R. Copeland and D. Lawton (Oxford, 1997), pp. 125–56, esp. p. 146.

60. *The Book of Margery Kempe*, ed. Barry Windeatt (London, 2000), pp. 95, 110, 224–5, 229, 248, 258, and 269–70. The specific accusation of heresy is not made in every case, but her troubles in these places are all of a piece.

61. Brown, *Popular Piety*, p. 217, with the map on pp. 220–1. For these years in particular see the *Register of Thomas Langton*.

62. J. A. Sharpe, *Judicial Punishment in England* (London, 1990), pp. 27–9.

5   From Lollardy to Protestantism

1. J. Gairdner, *Lollardy and the Reformation in England* (4 vols, London, 1908–13). J. J. Scarisbrick, *The Reformation and the English People* (Oxford, 1984), p. 6. J. F. Davis, 'Lollardy and the Reformation in England', *Archiv für Reformationsgeschichte* 73 (1982), pp. 217–36, at p. 219. See also his *Heresy and Reformation in the South East of England, 1520–1559* (London, 1983). A. G. Dickens, *The English Reformation* (2nd edn London, 1989), pp 46–60, esp. p. 59. Margaret Aston,

'Lollardy and the Reformation: Survival or revival?', *Journal of Ecclesiastical History* 49 (1964), pp. 149–70. Even Thomson, sceptical about the extent and coherence of Lollardy in the fifteenth and sixteenth centuries, concludes that Lollardy may well have prepared the ground for Lutheranism (which he sees as having spread speedily). See his *Later Lollards*, pp. 51, and 138.

2. C. R. L. Fletcher, *An Introductory History of England* (5 vols, London, 1904), I, p. 301. This reached its 10th printing in 1929.

3. Not since Euan Cameron's *The Reformation of the Heretics* (Oxford, 1984).

4. Q. Skinner, 'The limits of historical explanations', *Philosophy* 41 (1966), pp. 199–215. D. D. Smeeton, *Lollard Themes in the Reformation Theology of William Tyndale* (Kirksville, MO, 1986), is a study which (as I hope to show on another occasion) is entirely innocent of Skinner's critique and is in consequence massively flawed in its methods and its conclusions.

5. Dickens, *Lollards and Protestants*. For gentle criticisms of his methods and conclusions, see D. A. Palliser, *Tudor York* (Oxford, 1979), 249–53; and Duffy, *Stripping of the Altars*, ch. 15, esp. pp. 514–18.

6. Hudson, *Premature Reformation*, ch. 10. Plumb, 'Social and economic status of Lollards'; 'Gathered church?'; and 'The social and economic spread of rural Lollardy: A reappraisal', in *Voluntary Religion*, ed. W. J. Sheils and D. Wood (Oxford, 1986), pp. 111–29.

7. M. Aston, 'Iconoclasm in England: Official and clandestine', in *Faith and Fire* (London, 1993), pp. 261–89, at pp. 264–5. Brigden, *London and the Reformation*, p. 192.

8. Hudson, *Premature Reformation*, pp. 505–7.

9. P. Collinson, 'Cranbrook and the Fletchers', in his *Godly People* (London, 1983), pp. 399–428, at p. 402.

10. Plumb, 'Social and economic status of Lollards', p. 122.

11. It is not clear that her husband Richard, assessed at £200 in the subsidy returns of 1524–25, was also a Lollard. He is not mentioned in the Lincoln records abstracted by Foxe, and the masses and devotional images which he ordered in his will of 1524 smack of more than outward conformity (Plumb, 'Social and economic spread of rural Lollardy', pp. 121–2). It is inconceivable, though, that he could have been unaware of his wife's beliefs.

12. Foxe, AM 1583, p. 805 (AM 1843–9, IV, pp. 181–2). Browne had originally recanted *c.*1506, and was therefore burned as a relapsed heretic. For his son Robert, see P. Clark, *English Provincial Society from the Reformation to the Revolution* (Hassocks, 1977), p. 101.

13. Andrew Hope, 'Lollardy: The stone the builders rejected?', in *Protestantism and the National Church in the Sixteenth Century*, ed. Peter Lake and Maria Dowling (London, 1987), pp. 1–35, at p. 5. Foxe, *Actes and Monuments* (London, 1563; henceforth cited as AM 1563), pp. 570–1 (AM 1843–9, V, pp. 251–3).

14. Mark Byford, 'The birth of a Protestant Town: The process of Reformation in Tudor Colchester, 1530–80', in Collinson and Craig (eds), *The Reformation in English Towns*, pp. 23–47, at p. 40.

15. *Norwich Heresy Trials*, p. 1.
16. Plumb, 'Gathered church?', p. 150 (Chesham); 'Social and economic status of Lollards', p. 122 (Amersham).
17. Diarmaid MacCulloch, *Tudor Church Militant* (London, 1999), pp. 109–14.
18. For revealing insights into several of these urban reformations, see P. Collinson and J. Craig (eds), *The Reformation in English Towns, 1500–1640* (Basingstoke, 1998).
19. For Fisher's pastoral work, see Stephen Thompson, 'The bishop in his diocese', in *Humanism, Reform and Reformation*, ed. B. Bradshaw and E. Duffy (Cambridge, 1989), pp. 67–80.
20. See Maria Dowling, *Fisher of Men: A Life of John Fisher, 1469–1535* (Basingstoke, 1999), pp. 63–6.
21. It is important to note that MacCulloch, to whose work this stage of my argument is deeply indebted, himself points out that, because of the role of Cranmer and his aides, Kent in itself cannot serve as compelling evidence for a significant connection between Lollardy and Protestantism (*Tudor Church Militant*, p. 112).
22. The leaders at Canterbury seem to have been John Ive and Robert Harryson, both originally of Tenterden. Harryson had moved to Canterbury in his old age to live in an almshouse there. The fact that he could gain admittance to a religious foundation is further evidence of the discretion, or virtual anonymity, of Lollards. Agnes Ive was John Ive's widow. She and Elizabeth White both frequented Harryson's almshouse to hear him expound his beliefs. Agnes Chetynden was probably related to Laurence Chetynden, a witness against Harryson. See *Kent Heresy Proceedings*, pp. xviii, 1–5, 33, 35, and 73.
23. Clark, *English Provincial Society*, pp. 30 (Lollards), and 38–44 (Canterbury).
24. Duffy, *Stripping of the Altars*, p. 479. Collinson, 'Cranbrook and the Fletchers', pp. 406–7.
25. Brigden, *London and the Reformation*, p. 108.
26. R. A. Houlbrooke, 'Persecution of heresy and Protestantism in the diocese of Norwich under Henry VIII', *Norfolk Archaeology* 35 (1970–73), pp. 308–26, esp. pp. 311 and 322–23. These four cases left no trace in the diocesan records, unlike the other known burnings, in which case they may have been recorded in separate documentation now lost.
27. N. P. Tanner, *The Church in Late Medieval Norwich, 1370–1532* (Toronto, 1984), p. 162, for the absence of recorded Lollardy to 1532; see Houlbrooke, 'Persecution of heresy', p. 312, and p. 323 (appendix, no. 46), for Myles.
28. M. C. McClendon, *The Quiet Reformation* (Stanford, 1999), pp. 68, 75, and 142.
29. For Colchester, see Byford, 'The birth of a Protestant town'. D. MacCulloch, *Suffolk and the Tudors* (Oxford, 1986), p. 160. Wentworth came of an impeccably orthodox family, as did his wife Margaret Fortescue, so there is no likelihood of Lollard influence there.

30. J. Craig, 'Reformers, conflict, and revisionism: The Reformation in sixteenth-century Hadleigh', *Historical Journal* 42 (1999), pp. 1–23.

31. W. J. Sheils, *The Puritans in the Diocese of Peterborough, 1558–1610* (Northampton, 1979), pp. 13–14.

32. On the city, see D. MacCulloch, 'Worcester: A cathedral city in the Reformation', in Collinson and Craig (eds), *The Reformation in English Towns*, pp. 94–112.

33. K. G. Powell, 'The beginnings of Protestantism in Gloucestershire', *Transactions of the Bristol and Gloucestershire Archaeological Society* 90 (1971), pp. 141–57. Caroline Litzenberger, *The English Reformation and the Laity* (Cambridge, 1997).

34. G. J. Mayhew, 'Religion, faction and politics in Reformation Rye', *Sussex Archaeological Collections* 120 (1982), pp. 139–60, at pp. 142–3.

35. R. B. Manning, *Religion and Society in Elizabethan Sussex* (Leicester, 1969), pp. 151–4, 159–64, and 221–37. M. J. Kitch, 'The Reformation in Sussex', in *Studies in Sussex Church History*, ed. M. J. Kitch (London, 1981), pp. 77–98. Sussex would seem to fit MacCulloch's pattern of a southern county without a Lollard tradition (*Tudor Church Militant*, pp. 112, and 199), yet the Montague influence seems in itself quite enough to explain its protracted resistance to the Reformation.

36. Brown, *Popular Piety*, pp. 217–22. It is of course even more dangerous to draw from such exiguous evidence conclusions as to the significance of Lollardy.

37. Duffy, *Stripping of the Altars*, p. 418.

38. Glanmor Williams, *Wales and the Reformation* (Cardiff, 1997), p. 32.

39. C. Carpenter, 'Gentry and community in medieval England', *Journal of British Studies* 33 (1994), pp. 340–80, esp. pp. 341–52. By the end of the Tudor era the county had become a far more significant unit.

40. Andrew Sulston, 'Catholic recusancy in Elizabethan Norfolk', *Norfolk Archaeology* 43 (1998), pp. 98–110, at p. 100. Litzenberger, *English Reformation and the Laity*, p. 28.

41. Brigden makes a similar point in *London and the Reformation*, p. 276.

42. Cameron, *Reformation of the Heretics*, pp. 167–71.

43. Hudson's suggestion that Bilney's views in 1527 were 'genuinely only Lollard' (*Premature Reformation*, p. 500) is hardly tenable given his key role in the evangelical movement in Cambridge in the 1520s. For a restatement of Bilney's evangelical credentials, see Richard Rex, 'The early impact of Reformation theology at Cambridge', *Reformation & Renaissance Review* 2 (1999), pp. 38–71, esp. pp. 50–1.

44. Foxe, AM 1583, pp. 1621–4 (AM 1843–9, IV, p. 681).

45. Brigden, *London and the Reformation*, pp. 450–1; for Joseph, see S. Wabuda, 'Fruitful preaching in the diocese of Worcester: Bishop Hugh Latimer and his influence, 1535–1539', in *Religion and the English People, 1500–1640*, ed. E. J. Carlson (Kirksville, MO, 1998), pp. 49–74, esp. pp. 60 and 73.

46. D. MacCulloch, *Thomas Cranmer* (New Haven, CT, and London, 1996), pp. 26–9.

47. M. Aston, 'Bishops and heresy: The defence of the faith', in her *Faith and Fire*, pp. 73–93, at p. 85.
48. Foxe, AM 1563, p. 604 (AM 1843–9, V, p. 421).
49. Dickens, *Lollards and Protestants*, pp. 40 and 43.
50. Foxe, AM 1583, pp. 1210–12 (AM 1843–9, V, pp. 467–8).
51. Brigden, *London and the Reformation*, p. 108.
52. Duffy, *Stripping of the Altars*, p. 222.
53. See e.g. Dr Alban Langdale reminding the Protestant Richard Woodman of his father's Catholicism. Foxe, AM 1563, p. 1588 (AM 1843–9, VIII, p. 353).
54. See Cameron, *Reformation of the Heretics*, pp. 176–85 for the mixed feelings of the Waldensians about the Reformers; pp. 243–52 for the uses of the Waldensians to Protestant history and theology; and pp. 262–3 for the Protestant revision of the Waldensian past.
55. Gabriel Audisio, *The Waldensian Dissent* (Cambridge, 1999), pp. 162–9, esp. 168. See also Cameron, *Reformation of the Heretics*, pp. 216–29 for the limits of the Reformation among the Waldensian communities.
56. For this thesis, see Basil Hall, 'The early rise and gradual decline of Lutheranism in England, 1520–1600', in his *Humanists and Protestants, 1500–1900* (Edinburgh, 1990), pp. 208–36, at pp. 214–15.
57. Bernd Moeller, 'Luther in Europe: His works in translation, 1517–46', in *Politics and Society in Reformation Europe*, ed. E. I. Kouri and Tom Scott (Liverpool, 1987), pp. 235–51.
58. For Joan Bocher, see J. F. Davis, 'Joan of Kent'; and also C. J. Clement, *Religious Radicalism in England, 1535–1635* (Edinburgh, 1997), pp. 35–67, who investigates links between Lollardy and radical religion.
59. For this thesis, see the excellent contributions in *The World of Rural Dissenters, 1520–1725*, ed. M. Spufford (Cambridge, 1995).

7   Conclusion

1. See, e.g., David Aers, 'Altars of power: Reflections on Eamon Duffy's *The Stripping of the Altars*', *Literature & History*, 3rd series, 3, no. 2 (1994), pp. 90–105.
2. Peter Lake, 'Anti-popery: The structure of a prejudice', in *Conflict in Early Stuart England*, ed. R. Cust and A. Hughes (London, 1989), pp. 72–106. See also his 'The significance of the Elizabethan identification of the Pope as Anti-Christ', *Journal of Ecclesiastical History* 31 (1980), pp. 161–78; and Robin Clifton, 'Fear of popery', in *The Origins of the English Civil War*, ed. C. Russell (London, 1973), pp. 144–67.
3. For a penetrating account of this, see Jonathan Scott, *England's Troubles* (Cambridge, 2000), esp. at pp. 29–31, 56–7, 94–7, 1170–3 and 184–7.
4. For an alternative view attaching greater importance to the role of the Lollards in Lancastrian legitimation, see Strohm, *England's Empty Throne*.

5. C. Cutts, 'The Croxton play: An anti-Lollard piece', *Modern Language Quarterly* 5 (1944), pp. 45–60. Lauren Lepow, *Enacting the Sacramental* (London, 1990).

6. *Selections from Hoccleve*, ed. M. C. Seymour (Oxford, 1981), pp. 61–74. The recent editor spreads the three pieces of the Upland exchange over 30 years, ending around 1450, but his arguments are not compelling. On the contrary, the remarkable fidelity of the Upland texts to Wyclif's idiosyncratic eucharistic doctrine suggests an early and educated author for both pieces, and weighs heavily against composition in a later period, when Wyclif's complex eucharistic theology had been reduced to a plain denial of the real presence. The three tracts are *prima facie* more likely to represent a quickfire exchange of handbills in the early years of the century, in accordance with the traditional view. See *Jack Upland*, ed. P. L. Heyworth (London, 1968), pp. 9–19.

7. See John Bossy, 'Leagues and associations in sixteenth-century French Catholicism', in *Voluntary Religion*, ed. W. J. Sheils and D. Wood (Oxford, 1986), pp. 171–89; and J. Lecler, 'Aux origines de la Ligue: Premiers projets et premiers essais (1561–1570), *Études* 227 (1936), pp. 188–208.

8. Catto, 'Religious change under Henry V', esp. pp. 97 and 115, though his talk of a royal supremacy *avant la lettre* is a forgivable exaggeration that must not be allowed to obscure the very real difference in the royal hold over the Church of England before and after the break with Rome.

9. Thomson, 'Orthodox religion', p. 39.

BIBLIOGRAPHY

An excellent online bibliography on the Lollards is maintained by Derrick Pitard, and can be consulted via the Lollard Society Homepage at: http://home.att.net/~ lollard/home.html

Printed Sources

The Anonimalle Chronicle, 1333 to 1381, ed. V. H. Galbraith (Manchester, 1927)

The Brut, or, The Chronicles of England, ed. F. W. D. Brie (2 vols, London, 1906–08. Early English Text Society, original series 131 and 136)

Calendar of Patent Rolls. Edward III. Vol. XVI. A.D. 1374–1377 (London, 1916)

Roger Dymmok, *Liber contra XII Errores et Hereses Lollardorum*, ed. H. S. Cronin (London, 1922)

English Wycliffite Sermons, ed. Anne Hudson and Pamela Gradon (5 vols, Oxford, 1983–96)

The Episcopal Registers of the Diocese of St David's, 1397 to 1518. Vol. 2. 1407–1518, ed. R. F. Isaacson (London, 1917; Cymmrodion Record Series, 6)

The Episcopal Register of Robert Rede, Ordinis Predicatorum, Lord Bishop of Chichester, 1397–1415, ed. Cecil Deedes (2 vols, London, 1908–10. Sussex Record Society, 8 and 11)

Fasciculi Zizaniorum, ed. W. W. Shirley (London, 1858; Rolls Series)

John Foxe, *Actes and Monuments* (London, 1563). Cited as AM 1563

John Foxe, *Actes and Monuments* (London, 1583). Cited as AM 1583

John Foxe, *Acts and Monuments*, ed. G. Townsend (8 vols, London, 1843–49). Cited as AM 1843–49

William Gregory, *William Gregory's Chronicle of London*, pp. 55–239 of *The Historical Collections of a Citizen of London*, ed. James Gairdner (London, 1876; Camden Society)

Heresy Trials in the Diocese of Norwich, 1428–31, ed. Norman P. Tanner (London, 1977; Camden Society, 4th series 20)

Historia Vitae et Regni Richardi Secundi, ed. G. B. Stow (Philadelphia, PA, 1977)

Thomas Hoccleve, *Selections from Hoccleve*, ed. M. C. Seymour (Oxford, 1981)

Issues of the Exchequer, ed. F. Devon (London, 1836)

Jack Upland, Friar Daw's Reply, and Upland's Rejoinder, ed. P. L. Heyworth (London, 1968)

Margery Kempe, *The Book of Margery Kempe*, ed. Barry Windeatt (London, 2000)

Kent Heresy Proceedings, 1511–12, ed. Norman Tanner (Maidstone, 1997; Kent Records, 26)

C. L. Kingsford, *The Greyfriars of London* (Aberdeen, 1915; British Society of Franciscan Studies, 6)

Knighton's Chronicle, 1337–1396, ed. and trans. G. H. Martin (Oxford, 1995)

Roger Martin, in *The Spoil of Melford Church: The Reformation in a Suffolk Parish*, ed. David Dymond and Clive Paine (Ipswich, 1992)

The Register of Edmund Lacy, Bishop of Exeter, 1420–1455, ed. G. R. Dunstan (5 vols, Torquay, 1963–72; Canterbury and York Society, 60–5)

The Register of John Stanbury, Bishop of Hereford (1453–1474), ed. A. T. Bannister (Hereford, 1918)

The Register of Nicholas Bubwith, Bishop of Bath and Wells, 1407–1424, ed. T. S. Holmes (2 vols, London, 1914; Somerset Record Society, 29–30)

The Register of Philip Repingdon, 1405–1419, ed. Margaret Archer (3 vols, 1963–82; Publications of the Lincoln Record Society, 57–8 and 74)

The Register of Richard Mayew, Bishop of Hereford (1504–1516), ed. A. T. Bannister (Hereford, 1919)

The Register of Robert Hallum, Bishop of Salisbury, 1407–17, ed. J. M. Horn (Torquay, 1972; Canterbury and York Society, 72)

The Register of the Gild of the Holy Cross ... Stratford-upon-Avon, ed. J. Harvey Bloom (London, 1907)

The Register of Thomas Bekynton, Bishop of Bath and Wells, 1443–1465, ed. H. C. Maxwell-Lyte and M. C. B. Davies (2 vols, London, 1934–35; Somerset Record Society, 49–50)

The Register of Thomas Langton, Bishop of Salisbury (1485–93), ed. D. P. Wright (Oxford, 1985; Canterbury and York Society, 74)

The Register of Thomas Spofford, Bishop of Hereford (1422–1448), ed. A. T. Bannister (Hereford, 1917)

The Registers of Oliver King, Bishop of Bath and Wells, 1496–1503 and Hadrian de Castello, Bishop of Bath and Wells, 1503–1518, ed. H. C. Maxwell-Lyte (London, 1939; Somerset Record Society, 54)

The Registers of Robert Stillington, Bishop of Bath and Wells, 1466–1491 and Richard Fox, Bishop of Bath and Wells, 1492–1494, ed. H. C. Maxwell-Lyte (London, 1937; Somerset Record Society, 52)

John Strype, *Ecclesiastical Memorials Relating Chiefly to Religion and the Reformation ... under King Henry VIII, King Edward VI, and Queen Mary I* (3 vols in 6 parts, Oxford, 1822)

Johannis de Trokelowe et Henrici de Blaneforde ... Chronica et Annales, ed. H. T. Riley (London, 1866; Rolls Series)

Two Wycliffite Texts: The Sermon of William Taylor, 1406; The Testimony of William Thorpe, 1407, ed. Anne Hudson (Oxford, 1993. Early English Text Society, original series 301)

William Tyndale, *An Answer to Sir Thomas More's Dialogue*, ed. H. Walter (Cambridge, 1850; Parker Society)

Visitations of Religious Houses in the Diocese of Lincoln. Volume 1. Injunctions and Other Documents from the Registers of Richard Flemyng and William Gray, ed. A. Hamilton Thompson (London, 1915; Canterbury and York Society, 17)

Thomas Walsingham, *Chronicon Angliae ab anno domini 1328 usque ad annum 1388*, ed. E. M. Thompson (London, 1874; Rolls Series)

Thomas Walsingham, *Historia Anglicana*, ed. H. T. Riley (2 vols, London, 1863–64; Rolls Series)

John Wyclif, *Wyclif's Latin Works* (35 vols, London, 1883–1922). I have made specific use of the following:

    Tractatus De apostasia, ed. M. H. Dziewicki (1889)
    Tractatus De benedicta incarnacione, ed. E. Harris (1886)
    Tractatus De blasphemia, ed. M. H. Dziewicki (1893)
    Tractatus De civili dominio, ed. R. L. Poole (4 vols, 1885–1904)
    Tractatus De dominio divino, ed. R. L. Poole (1890)
    Tractatus De ecclesia, ed. J. Loserth and F. D. Matthew (1886)
    De eucharistia tractatus maior, ed. J. Loserth (London, 1892)
    Tractatus De mandatis divinis, ed. J. Loserth and F. D. Matthew (1922)
    Tractatus De officio regis, ed. A. W. Pollard and C. S. Sayle (1887)
    Opera minora, ed. J. Loserth and F. D. Matthew (1913)
    Opus evangelicum, ed. J. Loserth (2 vols, 1895–96)
    Polemical Works in Latin, ed. R. Buddensieg (2 vols, 1883)
    Tractatus De potestate papae, ed. J. Loserth and F. D. Matthew (1907)
    Sermones, ed. J. Loserth and F. D. Matthew (4 vols, 1887–90)
    Dialogus sive Speculum ecclesie militantis, ed. A. W. Pollard (1886)
    De veritate sacrae scripturae, ed. R. Buddensieg (3 vols, 1905–06)

John Wyclif, *On Universals (Tractatus de Universalibus)*, trans. A. Kenny, introd. P. V. Spade (Oxford, 1985)

John Wyclif, *Tractatus De trinitate*, ed. A. W. Breck (Boulder, CO, 1962)

John Wyclif, *Trialogus*, ed. G. Lechler (Oxford, 1869)

John Wyclif, *English Wyclif Tracts*, ed. C. Lindberg (Oslo, 1991. Studia Anglistica Norvegica, 4)

Wycklyffes Wycket (Oxford, 1828)

Secondary Literature

Eric Acheson, *A Gentry Community: Leicestershire in the Fifteenth Century, c.1422–c.1485* (Cambridge, 1992)

David Aers, 'Altars of power: Reflections on Eamon Duffy's *The Stripping of the Altars*', *Literature & History*, 3rd series 3, no. 2 (1994), pp. 90–105

Margaret Aston, 'Bishops and heresy: The defence of the faith', in *Faith and Fire*, pp. 73–93

M. Aston, *England's Iconoclasts. Vol. 1. Laws against Images* (Oxford, 1988)

M. Aston, *Faith and Fire: Popular and Unpopular Religion, 1350–1600* (London, 1993)

M. Aston, 'Lollard women priests?', in her *Lollards and Reformers*, pp. 49–70

M. Aston, *Lollards and Reformers: Images and Literacy in Late Medieval Religion* (London, 1984)

M. Aston, 'Lollardy and the Reformation: Survival or revival?', *Journal of Ecclesiastical History* 49 (1964), pp. 149–70

M. Aston, *Thomas Arundel: A Study of Church Life in the Reign of Richard II* (Oxford, 1967)

Margaret Aston and Colin Richmond (eds), *Lollardy and the Gentry in the Later Middle Ages* (Stroud, 1997)

Gabriel Audisio, *The Waldensian Dissent: Persecution and Survival, c.1170–c.1570*, trans. C. Davison (Cambridge, 1999)

Virginia Bainbridge, *Gilds in the Medieval Countryside: Social and Religious Change in Cambridgeshire, c.1350–c.1558* (Woodbridge, 1996; Studies in the History of Medieval Religion, 10)

Caroline M. Barron, 'The parish fraternities of medieval London', in *The Church in Pre-Reformation Society: Essays in Honour of F. R. H. Du Boulay*, ed. Caroline M. Barron and Christopher Harper-Bill (Woodbridge, 1985), pp. 13–37

Caroline M. Barron and Anne F. Sutton (eds), *Medieval London Widows, 1300–1500* (London, 1994)

Richard Beadle, 'The York cycle', in *The Cambridge Companion to Medieval English Theatre*, ed. R. Beadle (Cambridge, 1994), pp. 85–108

Gustav A. Benrath, *Wyclifs Bibelkommentar* (Berlin, 1966; Arbeiten zur Kirchengeschichte, 36)

John Bossy, 'Leagues and associations in sixteenth-century French Catholicism', in *Voluntary Religion*, ed. W. J. Sheils and D. Wood (Oxford, 1986; Studies in Church History, 23), pp. 171–89

John Bossy, 'The Mass as a social institution, 1200–1700', *Past & Present* 100 (1983), pp. 29–61

Curtis V. Bostick, *The Antichrist and the Lollards: Apocalypticism in Late Medieval and Reformation England* (Leiden, 1998; Studies in Medieval and Reformation Thought, 70)

M. T. Brady, '*The Pore Caitif*: An introductory study', *Traditio* 10 (1954), pp. 529–48

M. T. Brady, 'Lollard sources of *The Pore Caitif*', *Traditio* 44 (1988), pp. 389–418

Jennifer R. Bray, 'Concepts of sainthood in fourteenth-century England', *Bulletin of the John Rylands Library of Manchester* 66 (1983–84), pp. 40–77

Susan Brigden, *London and the Reformation* (Oxford, 1989)

Andrew Brown, *Popular Piety in Late Medieval England: The Diocese of Salisbury, 1250–1550* (Oxford, 1995)

Mark Byford, 'The birth of a Protestant town: The process of Reformation in Tudor Colchester, 1530–80', in Collinson and Craig (eds), *The Reformation in English Towns*, pp. 23–47

Euan Cameron, *The Reformation of the Heretics: The Waldenses of the Alps, 1480–1580* (Oxford, 1984)

Christine Carpenter, 'The religion of the gentry in fifteenth-century England', in *England in the Fifteenth Century: Proceedings of the 1986 Harlaxton Symposium*, ed. D. Williams (Woodbridge, 1987), pp. 53–74, at p. 63

Christine Carpenter, 'Gentry and community in medieval England', *Journal of British Studies* 33 (1994), pp. 340–80

J. I. Catto, 'John Wyclif and the cult of the eucharist', in *The Bible in the Medieval World: Essays in Memory of Beryl Smalley*, ed. K. Walsh and D. Wood (Oxford, 1985), pp. 269–86

J. I. Catto, 'The king's government and the fall of Pecock', in *Rulers and Ruled in Late Medieval England: Essays Presented to Gerald Harriss*, ed. R. E. Archer and S. Walker (London, 1995), pp. 200–22

J. I. Catto, 'Religion and the English nobility in the later fourteenth century', in *History and Imagination: Essays in Honour of H. R. Trevor-Roper*, ed. H. Lloyd-Jones et al. (London, 1981), pp. 43–55

J. I. Catto, 'Religious change under Henry V', in *Henry V: The Practice of Kingship*, ed. G. L. Harriss (Oxford, 1985), pp. 97–115

J. I. Catto, 'Sir William Beauchamp between chivalry and Lollardy', in *The Ideals and Practice of Medieval Knighthood III: Papers from the Fourth Strawberry Hill Conference, 1988*, ed. C. Harper-Bill and R. Harvey (Woodbridge, 1990), pp. 39–48

J. I. Catto, 'Wyclif and Wycliffism at Oxford, 1356–1430', in *The History of the University of Oxford. Volume II. Late Medieval Oxford*, ed. J. I. Catto and R. Evans (Oxford, 1992), pp. 175–261

M. T. Clanchy, *From Memory to Written Record: England, 1066–1307* (2nd edn Oxford, 1993)

P. Clark, *English Provincial Society from the Reformation to the Revolution: Religion, Politics and Society in Kent, 1500–1640* (Hassocks, 1977)

C. J. Clement, *Religious Radicalism in England, 1535–1635* (Edinburgh, 1997)

Robin Clifton, 'Fear of popery', in *The Origins of the English Civil War*, ed. C. Russell (London, 1973), pp. 144–67

A. B. Cobban, *The King's Hall within the University of Cambridge in the Later Middle Ages* (Cambridge, 1969; Cambridge Studies in Medieval Life and Thought, 3rd series)

John C. Coldewey, 'The non-cycle plays and the East Anglian tradition', in Beadle (ed.), *Cambridge Companion to Medieval English Theatre*, pp. 189–210

P. Collinson, 'Cranbrook and the Fletchers', in his *Godly People* (London, 1983), pp. 399–428

P. Collinson and J. Craig (eds), *The Reformation in English Towns, 1500–1640* (Basingstoke, 1998)

Rita Copeland, 'Childhood, pedagogy, and the literal sense: From late antiquity to the Lollard heretical classroom, in *New Medieval Literatures I*, ed. W. Scase, R. Copeland and D. Lawton (Oxford, 1997), pp. 125–56

J. Craig, 'Reformers, conflict, and revisionism: The Reformation in sixteenth-century Hadleigh', *Historical Journal* 42 (1999), pp. 1–23

James Crompton, 'Leicestershire Lollards', *Transactions of the Leicestershire Archaeological and Historical Society* 44 (1968–69), pp. 11–43, at pp. 30–3

Claire Cross, *Church and People, 1450–1660* (London, 1976)

Claire Cross, 'Great reasoners in scripture: The activities of women Lollards, 1380–1530', in *Medieval Women*, ed. Derek Baker (Oxford, 1978. Studies in Church History. Subsidia, 1), pp. 359–80

David J. F. Crouch, *Piety, Fraternity and Power: Religious Gilds in Late Medieval Yorkshire, 1389–1547* (York, 2000)

C. Cutts, 'The Croxton play: An anti-Lollard piece', *Modern Language Quarterly* 5 (1944), pp. 45–60

Joseph Dahmus, 'John Wyclif and the English government', *Speculum* 35 (1960), pp. 51–68

Joseph Dahmus, *The Prosecution of John Wyclyf* (New Haven, CT, 1952)

R. G. Davies, 'The episcopate', in *Profession, Vocation, and Culture in Later Medieval England*, ed. C. H. Clough (Liverpool, 1982), pp. 51–89

R. G. Davies, 'Lollardy and locality', *Transactions of the Royal Historical Society*, 6th series 1 (1991), pp. 191–212

J. F. Davis, *Heresy and Reformation in the South East of England, 1520–1559* (London, 1983)

J. F. Davis, 'Joan of Kent, Lollardy and the English Reformation', *Journal of Ecclesiastical History* 33 (1982), pp. 225–33

J. F. Davis, 'Lollardy and the Reformation in England', *Archiv für Reformationsgeschichte* 73 (1982), pp. 217–36

Margaret Deanesley, *The Lollard Bible and Other Medieval Biblical Versions* (Cambridge, 1920)

A. G. Dickens, *The English Reformation* (2nd edn London, 1989)

A. G. Dickens, *Lollards and Protestants in the Diocese of York, 1509–1558* (Oxford, 1959)

W. J. Dohar, *The Black Death and Pastoral Leadership: The Diocese of Hereford in the Fifteenth Century* (Philadelphia, PA, 1995)

Maria Dowling, *Fisher of Men: A Life of John Fisher, 1469–1535* (Basingstoke, 1999)

Clayton J. Drees, *Authority & Dissent in the English Church: The Prosecution of Heresy and Religious Non-Conformity in the Diocese of Winchester, 1380–1547* (Lewiston, NY, 1997; Texts and Studies in Religion, 73)

Eamon Duffy, *The Stripping of the Altars* (New Haven, CT, and London, 1992)

William Farr, *John Wyclif as Legal Reformer* (Leiden, 1974. Studies in the History of Christian Thought, 10)

J. Fines, 'Heresy trials in the diocese of Coventry and Lichfield, 1511–1512', *Journal of Ecclesiastical History* 14 (1963), pp. 160–74

C. R. L. Fletcher, *An Introductory History of England* (5 vols, London, 1904)

J. Gairdner, *Lollardy and the Reformation in England* (4 vols, London, 1908–13)

Chris Given-Wilson, *The Royal Household and the King's Affinity: Service, Politics and Finance in England, 1360–1413* (New Haven, CT, and London, 1986)

P. J. P. Goldberg, 'Performing the word of God: Corpus Christi drama in the northern Province', in *Life and Thought in the Northern*

Church, c.1100–c.1700: Essays in Honour of Claire Cross, ed. D. Wood (Woodbridge, 1999; Studies in Church History. Subsidia, 12), pp. 145–70

P. J. P. Goldberg, 'Women', in *Fifteenth-Century Attitudes: Perceptions of Society in Late Medieval England*, ed. Rosemary Horrox (Cambridge, 1994), pp. 112–31

Anthony Goodman, *John of Gaunt: The Exercise of Princely Power in Fourteenth-Century England* (Harlow, 1992)

Ralph A. Griffiths, *The Reign of King Henry VI: The Exercise of Royal Authority, 1422–1461* (London, 1981)

Basil Hall, 'The early rise and gradual decline of Lutheranism in England, 1520–1600', in his *Humanists and Protestants, 1500–1900* (Edinburgh, 1990), pp. 208–36

G. L. Harriss, *Cardinal Beaufort: A Study of Lancastrian Ascendancy and Decline* (Oxford, 1988)

Margaret Harvey, 'Adam Easton and the condemnation of John Wyclif, 1377', *English Historical Review* 113 (1998), pp. 321–34

John Hatcher, 'England in the aftermath of the Black Death', *Past & Present* 144 (1994), pp. 3–35

Michael Hicks, 'Chantries, obits, and almshouses: The Hungerford foundations, 1325–1478', in *The Church in Pre-Reformation Society: Essays in Honour of F. R. H. Du Boulay*, ed. Caroline M. Barron and Christopher Harper-Bill (Woodbridge, 1985), pp. 123–42

George Holmes, *The Good Parliament* (Oxford, 1975)

Andrew Hope, 'Lollardy: The stone the builders rejected?', in *Protestantism and the National Church in the Sixteenth Century*, ed. Peter Lake and Maria Dowling (London, 1987), pp. 1–35

Andrew Hope, 'The lady and the bailiff: Lollardy among the gentry in Yorkist and early Tudor England', in *Lollardy and the Gentry in the Later Middle Ages*, ed. Margaret Aston and Colin Richmond (Stroud, 1997), pp. 250–77

P. J. Horner, 'The King taught us the lesson: Benedictine support for Henry V's suppression of the Lollards', *Mediaeval Studies* 52 (1990), pp. 190–220

R. A. Houlbrooke, 'Persecution of heresy and Protestantism in the diocese of Norwich under Henry VIII', *Norfolk Archaeology* 35 (1970–73), pp. 308–26

R. W. Hoyle, 'The Earl, the Archbishop and the Council: The affray at Fulford, May 1504', in *Rulers and Ruled in Late Medieval England: Essays Presented to Gerald Harriss*, ed. R. E. Archer and S. Walker (London, 1995), pp. 239–56

Anne Hudson, *Lollards and their Books* (London, 1985)

Anne Hudson, *The Premature Reformation* (Oxford, 1988)

Anne Hudson, 'Springing cockel in our clene corn: Lollard preaching in England around 1400', in *Christendom and its Discontents: Exclusion, Persecution, and Rebellion, 1000–1500*, ed. Scott L. Waugh and Peter D. Diehl (Cambridge, 1996), pp. 132–47

Anne Hudson. See Primary Sources, above, *English Wycliffite Sermons*

Michael Hurley, 'Scriptura sola: Wyclif and his critics', *Traditio* 16 (1960), pp. 275–352

E. W. Ives, 'The reputation of the common lawyer in English society, 1450–1550', *University of Birmingham Historical Journal* 7 (1959–60), pp. 130–61

F. R. Johnston, 'The English cult of St Bridget of Sweden', *Analecta Bollandiana* 103 (1985), pp. 75–93

Maureen Jurkowski, 'Lawyers and Lollardy in the early fifteenth century', in Aston and Richmond (eds), *Lollardy and the Gentry in the Later Middle Ages*, pp. 155–82

Maureen Jurkowski, 'Lancastrian royal service, Lollardy and forgery: The career of Thomas Tykhill', ed. R. A. Archer, in *Crown, Government and People in the Fifteenth Century* (Stroud, 1995), pp. 33–52

Maureen Jurkowski, 'New light on John Purvey', *English Historical Review* 110 (1995), pp. 1180–90

Steven Justice, 'Lollardy', in *The Cambridge History of Medieval English Literature*, ed. David Wallace (Cambridge, 1999), pp. 662–89

H. Kaminsky, 'Wyclifism as ideology of revolution', *Church History* 32 (1963), 57–74

Maurice Keen, *English Society in the Later Middle Ages, 1348–1500* (London, 1990)

Maurice Keen, 'Wyclif, the Bible, and transubstantiation', in Kenny (ed.), *Wyclif in his Times*, pp. 1–16

Anthony Kenny, *Wyclif* (Oxford, 1985)

Anthony Kenny (ed.), *Wyclif in his Times* (Oxford, 1986)

Ann J. Kettle, 'City and close: Lichfield in the century before the Reformation', in *The Church in Pre-Reformation Society: Essays in Honour of F. R. H. Du Boulay*, ed. Caroline M. Barron and Christopher Harper-Bill (Woodbridge, 1985), pp. 158–69

Richard Kieckhefer, *Repression of Heresy in Medieval Germany* (Liverpool, 1979)

Charles Kightly, 'The early Lollards: A survey of popular Lollard activity in England, 1382–1428'. York University PhD dissertation, 1975 (DX197636)

M. J. Kitch, 'The Reformation in Sussex', in *Studies in Sussex Church History*, ed. M. J. Kitch (London, 1981), pp. 77–98

David Knowles, *The Religious Orders in England* (3 vols, Cambridge, 1948–59)

Beat Kumin, *The Shaping of a Community: The Rise and Reformation of the English Parish, c.1400–c.1560* (Aldershot, 1996)

Peter Lake, 'Anti-popery: The structure of a prejudice', in *Conflict in Early Stuart England: Studies in Religion and Politics, 1603–1642*, ed. R. Cust and A. Hughes (London, 1989), pp. 72–106

Peter Lake, 'The significance of the Elizabethan identification of the Pope as Anti-Christ', *Journal of Ecclesiastical History* 31 (1980), pp. 161–78

C. H. Lawrence, *The Friars: The Impact of the Early Mendicant Movement on Western Society* (London, 1994)

J. Lecler, 'Aux origines de la Ligue: Premiers projets et premiers essais (1561–1570), *Études* 227 (1936), pp. 188–208

Gordon Leff, 'Ockham and Wyclif on the Eucharist', *Reading Medieval Studies* 2 (1976), pp. 1–11

Lauren Lepow, *Enacting the Sacramental: Counter-Lollardy in the Towneley Cycle* (London, 1990)

Caroline Litzenberger, *The English Reformation and the Laity: Gloucestershire, 1540–1580* (Cambridge, 1997)

Rob Lutton, 'Connections between Lollards and gentry in Tenterden in the late fifteenth and early sixteenth centuries', in Aston and Richmond (eds), *Lollardy and the Gentry in the Later Middle Ages*, pp. 199–228

Imogen Luxton, 'The Lichfield court book: A postscript', *Bulletin of the Institute of Historical Research* 44 (1971), pp. 120–5

Muriel C. McClendon, *The Quiet Reformation: Magistrates and the Emergence of Protestantism in Tudor Norwich* (Stanford, 1999)

Diarmaid MacCulloch, *Suffolk and the Tudors: Politics and Religion in an English County, 1500–1600* (Oxford, 1986)

Diarmaid MacCulloch, *Thomas Cranmer: A Life* (New Haven, CT, and London, 1996)

Diarmaid MacCulloch, *Tudor Church Militant: Edward VI and the Protestant Reformation* (London, 1999)

Diarmaid MacCulloch, 'Worcester: A cathedral city in the Reformation', in Collinson and Craig (eds), *The Reformation in English Towns*, pp. 94–112

Alan Macfarlane, *The Origins of English Individualism* (Oxford, 1978)

K. B. McFarlane, *Wycliffe and the Beginnings of English Nonconformity* (London, 1952)

K. B. McFarlane, *Wycliffe and English Nonconformity* (Penguin edn London, 1972)

K. B. McFarlane, *Lancastrian Kings and Lollard Knights* (Oxford, 1972)

A. K. McHardy, 'Bishop Buckingham and the Lollards of Lincoln diocese', in *Schism, Heresy and Religious Protest*, ed. Derek Baker (Cambridge, 1972; Studies in Church History, 9), pp. 131–45

A. K. McHardy, 'The dissemination of Wyclif's ideas', in *From Ockham to Wyclif*, ed. Anne Hudson and Michael Wilks (Oxford, 1987; Studies in Church History. Subsidia, 5), pp. 361–8

Peter McNiven, *Heresy and Politics in the Reign of Henry IV: The Burning of John Badby* (Woodbridge, 1987)

Shannon McSheffrey, *Gender and Heresy: Women and Men in Lollard Communities, 1420–1530* (Philadelphia, PA, 1995)

R. B. Manning, *Religion and Society in Elizabethan Sussex: A Study of the Enforcement of the Religious Settlement, 1558–1603* (Leicester, 1969)

Geoffrey Martin, 'Knighton's Lollards', in Aston and Richmond (eds), *Lollardy and the Gentry in the Later Middle Ages*, pp. 28–40

G. J. Mayhew, 'Religion, faction and politics in Reformation Rye', *Sussex Archaeological Collections* 120 (1982), pp. 139–60

Bernd Moeller, 'Luther in Europe: His works in translation, 1517–46', in *Politics and Society in Reformation Europe*, ed. E. I. Kouri and Tom Scott (Liverpool, 1987), pp. 235–51

W. A. Ormrod, *The Reign of Edward III: Crown and Political Society in England, 1327–1377* (New Haven, CT, and London, 1990)

Dorothy M. Owen, *Church and Society in Medieval Lincolnshire* (Lincoln, 1971; History of Lincolnshire, 5)

D. A. Palliser, *Tudor York* (Oxford, 1979)

W. A. Pantin, *The English Church in the Fourteenth Century* (Oxford, 1955)

R. W. Pfaff, *New Liturgical Feasts in Late Medieval England* (Oxford, 1970)

C. Phythian-Adams, *Desolation of a City: Coventry and the Urban Crisis of the Late Middle Ages* (Cambridge, 1979)

Derek Plumb, 'The social and economic spread of rural Lollardy: A reappraisal', in *Voluntary Religion*, ed. W. J. Sheils and D. Wood (Oxford, 1986; Studies in Church History, 23), pp. 111–29

Derek Plumb, 'The social and economic status of the later Lollards', in *The World of Rural Dissenters, 1520–1725* ed. Margaret Spufford (Cambridge, 1995), pp. 103–31

Derek Plumb, 'A gathered church? Lollards and their society', in Spufford (ed.), *The World of Rural Dissenters, 1520–1725*, pp. 132–63

L. R. Poos, *A Rural Society after the Black Death: Essex, 1350–1525* (Cambridge, 1991)

Edward Powell, *Kingship, Law, and Society: Criminal Justice in the Reign of Henry V* (Oxford, 1989)

K. G. Powell, 'The beginnings of Protestantism in Gloucestershire', *Transactions of the Bristol and Gloucestershire Archaeological Society* 90 (1971)

Sandra Raban, *Mortmain Legislation and the English Church, 1279–1500* (Cambridge, 1982)

E. J. B. Reid, 'Lollards at Colchester in 1414', *English Historical Review* 29 (1914), pp. 101–4

Richard Rex, 'The early impact of Reformation theology at Cambridge', *Reformation & Renaissance Review* 2 (1999), pp. 38–71

Colin Richmond, 'Religion and the fifteenth-century English gentleman', in *The Church, Politics and Patronage*, ed. B. Dobson (Gloucester, 1984), pp. 193–208

J. A. Robson, *Wyclif and the Oxford Schools: The Relation of the Summa de Ente to Scholastic Debates at Oxford in the Later Fourteenth Century* (Cambridge, 1961; Cambridge Studies in Medieval Life and Thought, new series 8)

G. Rosser, 'Communities of parish and guild in the late Middle Ages', in *Parish Church and People: Local Studies in Lay Religion, 1350–1750*, ed. S. J. Wright (London, 1988), pp. 29–55

Miri Rubin, *Corpus Christi* (Cambridge, 1991)

M. Rubin, 'Corpus Christi fraternities and late medieval piety', *Studies in Church History* 23 (1986), pp. 97–109

M. Rubin, 'Small groups: Identity and solidarity in the late Middle Ages', in *Enterprise and Individuals in Fifteenth-Century England*, ed. J. Kermode (Stroud, 1991), pp. 132–50

Nigel Saul, 'The religious sympathies of the gentry in Gloucestershire, 1200–1500', *Transactions of the Bristol and Gloucestershire Archaeological Society* 98 (1980), pp. 99–112

Nigel Saul, *Richard II* (New Haven, CT, and London, 1997)

Jonathan Scott, *England's Troubles: Seventeenth-Century English Political Instability in European Context* (Cambridge, 2000)

R. M. Serjeantson, *A History of the Church of All Saints, Northampton* (Northampton, 1901)

J. A. Sharpe, *Judicial Punishment in England* (London, 1990)

W. J. Sheils, *The Puritans in the Diocese of Peterborough, 1558–1610* (Northampton, 1979; Publications of the Northamptonshire Record Society, 30),

Martha C. Skeeters, *Community and Clergy: Bristol and the Reformation c.1530–c.1570* (Oxford, 1993)

Q. Skinner, 'The limits of historical explanations', *Philosophy* 41 (1966), pp. 199–215

Beryl Smalley, 'The Bible and eternity: John Wyclif's dilemma', in her *Studies in Medieval Thought and Learning from Abelard to Wyclif* (London, 1981), pp. 399–415

Beryl Smalley, 'John Wyclif's *Postilla super totam Bibliam*', *Bodleian Library Record* 4 (1952–53), pp. 186–205

D. D. Smeeton, *Lollard Themes in the Reformation Theology of William Tyndale* (Kirksville, MO, 1986; Sixteenth Century Essays & Studies, 6)

R. M. Smith, 'Modernization and the corporate medieval village community in England: Some sceptical reflections', in *Explorations in Historical Geography*, ed. A. R. H. Baker and D. Gregory (Cambridge, 1984), pp. 140–79.

G. J. C. Snoek, *Medieval Piety from Relics to the Eucharist: A Process of Mutual Interaction* (Leiden, 1995; Studies in the History of Christian Thought, 63)

Margaret Spufford (ed.), *The World of Rural Dissenters, 1520–1725* (Cambridge, 1995)

R. L. Storey, *Thomas Langley and the Bishopric of Durham, 1406–1437* (London, 1961)

Paul Strohm, *England's Empty Throne: Usurpation and the Language of Legitimation, 1399–1422* (New Haven, CT, and London, 1998)

Andrew Sulston, 'Catholic Recusancy in Elizabethan Norfolk', *Norfolk Archaeology* 43 (1998), pp. 98–110

R. N. Swanson, *Church and Society in Late Medieval England* (Oxford, 1989)

Norman P. Tanner, *The Church in Late Medieval Norwich, 1370–1532* (Toronto, 1984)

Stephen Thompson, 'The bishop in his diocese', in *Humanism, Reform and Reformation: The career of Bishop John Fisher*, ed. B. Bradshaw and E. Duffy (Cambridge, 1989)

J. A. F. Thomson, *The Later Lollards, 1414–1520* (Oxford, 1965)

J. A. F. Thomson, 'Knightly piety and the margins of Lollardy', in Aston and Richmond (eds), *Lollardy and the Gentry in the Later Middle Ages*, pp. 95–111

J. A. F. Thomson, 'Orthodox religion and the origins of Lollardy', *History* 74 (1989), pp. 39–55

W. R. Thomson, *The Latin Writings of John Wyclyf: An Annotated Catalog* (Toronto, 1983; Subsidia Mediaevalia, 14)

Anthony Tuck, 'Carthusian monks and Lollard knights: Religious attitudes at the Court of Richard II', in *Studies in the Age of Chaucer. Proceedings, No. 1, 1984. Reconstructing Chaucer*, ed. Paul Strohm and Thomas J. Heffernan (Knoxville, TN, 1985), pp. 149–61

S. Wabuda, 'Fruitful preaching in the diocese of Worcester: Bishop Hugh Latimer and his influence, 1535–1539', in *Religion and the English People, 1500–1640: New Voices, New Perspectives*, ed. E. J. Carlson (Kirksville, MO, 1998; Sixteenth Century Essays & Studies, 45), pp. 49–74

S. Walker, 'Political saints in later medieval England', in *The McFarlane Legacy: Studies in Late Medieval Politics and Society*, ed. R. H. Britnell and A. J. Pollard (Stroud, 1995), pp. 77–106

David Wallace (ed), *The Cambridge History of Medieval English Literature* (Cambridge 1999)

W. T. Waugh, 'The great statute of praemunire', *English Historical Review* 37 (1922), pp. 173–205

Diana Webb, *Pilgrims and Pilgrimage in the Medieval West* (London, 1999; The International Library of Historical Studies, 12)

H. F. Westlake, *The Parish Gilds of Mediaeval England* (London, 1919)

Michael Wilks, 'Royal priesthood: The origins of Lollardy', in *The Church in a Changing Society* (Uppsala, 1978; Publications of the Swedish Society of Church History, new series 30), pp. 63–70

Michael Wilks, 'Thomas Arundel of York: The appellant Archbishop', in *Life and Thought in the Northern Church, c.1100–c.1700: Essays in Honour of Claire Cross*, ed. Diana Wood (Woodbridge, 1999. Studies in Church History. Subsidia, 12), pp. 87–103

Michael Wilks, 'Wyclif and the great persecution', in *Prophecy and Eschatology*, ed. M. Wilks (Oxford 1994. Studies in Church History. Subsidia, 10), pp. 39–63

Glanmor Williams, *Wales and the Reformation* (Cardiff, 1997)

H. B. Workman, *John Wyclif* (2 vols, Oxford, 1926),

INDEX

Amersham, 65, 90, 110, 113, 118, 120, 125, 131
Antichrist, 43, 138
Artisans, 21, 72–3, 101–2, 103–4
Arundel, Thomas, Archbishop of Canterbury, 62, 68, 75, 79, 83, 84–5, 87
Aston, John, 57, 65

Bale, John, 78, 134, 136, 142, 147
Ball, John, 3, 52
Bath and Wells diocese, 70, 98
Barnes, Robert, 118, 134
Beaufort, Henry, 4, 6, 87, 92
Beverley, 22, 98
Bible, 75–6, 79, 102, 143, 148
Bilney, Thomas, 133, 135, 136
Bishops, 4, 8, 134
Black Death, 20–1, 56
Books of Hours, 13, 78
Brinton, Thomas, Bishop of Rochester, 30
Bristol, 57–9, 64, 69–70, 75, 95, 98, 106, 120
Buckingham, John, Bishop of Lincoln, 57, 64
Buckinghamshire, 59, 101, 104, 120
burning alive as penalty for heresy, 63, 66, 84, 87, 89, 90, 93, 94, 95, 100, 113, 118, 123, 132, 134, 135, 148
Bury St Edmunds, 2, 77, 99, 124, 134

Cambridge, 9, 13, 67, 94, 120, 134, 135–6
Canterbury, 91, 98, 109, 122
Carthusians, 9–10, 12–13, 76, 80
Chantries, 19–20
Chaucer, Geoffrey, 12, 22, 80
Chesham, 65, 90, 131, 141
Clifford, Lewis, 30, 61–2
Colchester, 66, 94, 110, 113, 119, 120, 123, 140
Comberworth, Thomas, 64, 65
Confraternities, 10, 15–16, 20–3, 103–4, 147
Corpus Christi, 15–17, 21, 22, 42, 61, 147, 148
Coventry, 59, 64, 80, 95–6, 99, 101–2, 104, 106, 110, 120, 125
Court (royal court), 29, 61, 79–80, 83
Cranmer, Thomas, Archbishop of Canterbury, 122, 124, 134, 135
crown and church, 3–6, 50–1

drama, 21–2

East Anglia, 12–13, 22, 64, 66, 94, 123
Easton, Adam, 27, 29
ecclesiastical property, 27, 36–7, 45
Essex, 66, 72, 74–5, 101

Eucharist, 17, 42–5, 73, 158
Exeter diocese, 70, 93

Fisher, John, Bishop of Rochester, 121, 127–8, 133, 137
Forest of Dean, 97, 98, 125, 126, 130
Foxe, John, 78, 90, 95, 101, 105, 115, 119, 121, 123, 139, 142
Friars, 7–9, 46, 47, 48, 49, 60, 70, 72, 75, 78, 83, 84, 112, 133–4

Gentry, 7, 21, 23, 61–3, 71, 87, 101–2, 144, 167
Gloucestershire, 126, 137
Great Schism, 5, 30
Gregory XI, 29, 30, 32, 37, 43

Henry IV, 83
Henry V, 10, 15, 83–7
Hereford, Nicholas, 57, 62, 65, 68, 80
Hereford diocese, 95, 126
heresy (other than Lollardy), 11, 15, 139, 150
hermits, 12

iconoclasm, 68, 73, 118, 136
indulgences, 49
Ipswich, 94, 120, 123–4

John of Gaunt, Duke of Lancaster, 27, 28, 29, 31, 48, 52, 68, 71, 72, 155, 156

Kempe, Margery, 12, 13, 16, 18, 69, 80, 97–8, 105, 111–12, 147
Kenningham, John, 34, 43
Kent, 63, 66, 90–1, 103, 109, 118, 121–2, 140

Latimer, Hugh, Bishop of Worcester, 126, 134
Latimer, Thomas, knight, 61–2, 71
Leicester, 57, 59, 67–8, 87, 89, 98, 125
Lichfield, 99
Lincoln, 98
Lincoln diocese, 67, 90, 112, 124–5
Lincolnshire, 2, 19, 20, 77, 90
Lollard Knights, 61–3, 71, 79
London, 20, 28–9, 31, 59, 64, 65, 77, 84, 85, 87, 91, 93, 100–1, 110, 111, 120, 122–3, 136

Maidstone, 66, 109
Man, Thomas, 105, 110
Mass, 18–19
Monks, 8–9, 99, 133
More, Christina, 70, 106, 107
More, Thomas, 76, 107, 132, 141–2

Netter, Thomas, 88
Newbury, 92, 110, 112, 129
Norfolk, 18, 67, 72, 77, 94, 110, 130
Norwich diocese, 66–7, 123–4, 128
Northampton, 63–4, 65, 89, 110, 125
Nottingham, 68, 77

Oldcastle, Sir John, Lord Cobham, 62–3, 66, 71, 77, 81, 83–7, 102
Oldcastle Revolt, 58, 65, 70, 71, 72, 77, 83–7, 92, 93, 106, 129, 144
Oxford, 25–6, 30, 31, 57–8, 59, 65, 69, 76, 79, 89, 118, 125

Parish, 23–4
Parliament, 27, 84, 87, 156
Peasants' Revolt, 3, 31, 52–3, 56, 159

Pecock, Reginald, Bishop of
    Chichester, 5, 76, 88, 91,
    102–3
Pilgrimage, 14, 16, 79, 99, 137,
    147–8
prayer for the dead, 19–20, 49
preaching, 8, 55–9, 64, 91,
    125, 130
Purvey, John, 57, 70, 77, 85

Ramsbury, William, not a 'Lollard
    priest', 82
Reading, 65, 92, 93, 100, 129
Realism, 33–4
Repingdon, Philip, Bishop of
    Lincoln, 57, 65, 67, 68–9
Richard II, 15, 62, 63, 65, 80,
    83, 164–5
Rose, Thomas, 73, 118, 123
Rowley, Alice, 104, 106, 107

Saints, 14–15, 50
St Alban's, 3, 77, 99
Salisbury, 82, 92, 98, 128
Salisbury diocese, 91–3, 112, 113
Shrewsbury, 15, 69
Sussex, 91, 127
Swynderby, William, 57, 62–3, 68

Taylor, William, 65, 70, 89
Tenterden, 66, 90–1, 93, 109, 111,
    122, 170
Thorpe, William, 15, 57–9, 65, 66,
    69, 70

Tyckhill, Thomas, 63, 102
towns, 64, 98–9, 120, 130–1
Transubstantiation, 15, 18, 42–5,
    60, 158

Urban VI, 32

vernacular religious literature, 12,
    74–9, 148

Wales, 70, 129
Walsingham, Thomas, 27–8,
    52–3, 61, 82, 99
Welsh Marches, 62, 69, 125
White, William, 66, 81, 82, 91,
    94, 105
Widows, 107
Wills, 7, 13–14, 79
Winchester diocese, 93, 120, 127
Woodford, William, 25, 36, 48, 72
Wyche, Richard, 59, 63, 70
Wyclif, John, 7, 13, 25–53, 54–5,
    59–60, 72, 116, 125, 150
    disappointed of promotion, 26
    not a royal councillor, 28
    papal censure in 1377, 30
    radical moves in 1378, 31
    condemnation in 1382, 31, 53
    death in 1384, 32
    theological principles, 33

York, 15, 97, 98, 134, 135
Yorkshire, 12–13, 20, 96, 113,
    117, 129